LIFE IN AN OLDER AMERICA

A Century Foundation Book

Life in an Older America

Robert N. Butler, M.D.,
Lawrence K. Grossman,
and Mia R. Oberlink
Editors

1999 ◆ THE CENTURY FOUNDATION PRESS ◆ NEW YORK

The Century Foundation, formerly the Twentieth Century Fund, sponsors and supervises timely analyses of economic policy, foreign affairs, and domestic political issues. Not-for-profit and nonpartisan, it was founded in 1919 and endowed by Edward A. Filene.

Cataloging in Publication Data

Life in an older America / Robert N. Butler, Lawrence K. Grossman, and Mia R. Oberlink, editors.
       p.   cm.
    Includes bibliographical references and index.
    ISBN 0–87078–424–2 (cloth: alk. paper). ISBN 0–87078–438–2 (paper: alk. paper).
    1. Aging--Government policy--United States.   2. Aged--United States--Social conditions.   3. Aged--United States--Economic conditions.   4. Retirement income--United States.   5. United States--Social policy.   6. United States--Economic policy.   I. Butler, Robert N., 1927– . II. Grossman, Lawrence K.   III. Oberlink, Mia R.
HQ1064.U504186   1998
305.26'0973--dc21   98–33344
                                                         CIP

FOREWORD

Until recently, increased longevity was viewed as a worthy goal for humankind. But with the retirement of the baby boom generation in sight, thinking about longevity has become more complex. Predictions abound that an older nation will be a poorer one. This dire version of life in the new century has moved to center stage in political and policy debates, providing the central justification for extreme proposals to reduce national pension and health programs for the aged. Unless we act now, some argue, the rising cost of these programs will lead to economic chaos in the next century. While some changes are inevitable, there is compelling evidence that only moderate adjustments in burdens and benefits are needed to solve those problems we can foresee.

The truth is that no one has a magic formula to resolve all the issues raised by an aging population. For all but a few fortunate individuals, as well as for the nation as a whole, many problems (like life's risks in general) cannot be wished or legislated away. Given the long-term nature of demographic shifts and the difficulty of seeing far into the future, uncertainty is unavoidable. Birthrates and medical advances are surprisingly unpredictable, securities markets are sure to remain immensely volatile, and even the most stable democracies may well experience sweeping transformations in politics and policy. As the past teaches us, the United States will continue to develop in ways that are always complex and frequently unprecedented. That national reality and the inevitability of personal risk are the fundamental reasons that more information about aging is essential for policymakers.

This book was designed with that need in mind. A joint product of The Century Foundation and the International Longevity Center, this volume assembles insights from many of the nation's leading analysts on population aging. They explore a wide range of issues, including Social Security, Medicare, pensions, family savings, and productivity. Significantly, the authors generally reject the widely repeated, alarmist views of the future. Their approach is more balanced and, in some cases, optimistic, making this a healthy antidote for the fearmongering that results in headlines. The authors are not, however, Pollyannas about the future. None dispute that population aging presents significant challenges and that a variety of steps could be taken in the near term to increase the probability that the nation will age gracefully. Rather than relying on hyperbole to make their case, these authors carefully parse facts from uncertainties and reasonable guesses from stabs in the dark. By doing so, they demonstrate that the United States may well be able to handle the retirement of the baby boomers as successfully as it handled their birth.

This is the second major cooperative venture that The Century Foundation has undertaken with the International Longevity Center, an organization that is becoming one of the world's most important sources of information about aging. Previously, we cosponsored weekend seminars for journalists around the country to inform them about the many issues examined in this book. Dr. Robert N. Butler, the director of the center, is an inspirational thinker and, along with his staff, a great partner.

The Century Foundation is deeply committed to informing the public about issues connected to population aging—issues that seem certain to be at the center of political debate in America for years to come. We have devoted special attention to the future of Social Security, publishing numerous books, reports, white papers, and issue briefs on this particularly valuable program. These materials can be located on our Social Security website (www.socsec.org). We are also sponsoring a task force on Medicare's future, as well as a variety of other publications related to aging issues.

We believe that this volume is an important addition to the ongoing discussion about demographic change in America. We thank Dr. Butler, his colleagues at the center, and the authors of the essays in this volume for their work.

RICHARD C. LEONE, *President*
The Century Foundation
May 1999

CONTENTS

ACKNOWLEDGMENTS

Our heartfelt gratitude to Richard C. Leone and The Century Foundation for their support in making this book possible. We are deeply indebted to Kenneth Emerson for his superb editorial direction. We are especially appreciative of the editorial contributions made by Judith Estrine.

INTRODUCTION

LIFE IN AN OLDER AMERICA:
THE REVOLUTION IN LONGEVITY

Robert N. Butler, M.D.,
Lawrence K. Grossman, and Mia R. Oberlink

A complete and adequate notion of life can never be attained by anyone who does not reach old age.
—Arthur Schopenhauer

Society is experiencing an extraordinary and unprecedented revolution in longevity. In less than a century, the industrial world has gained more than twenty-five years of life expectancy, accomplishing what had previously taken five thousand years of human history to attain. Between 1940 and 1980, the likelihood that people who reached age sixty-five would live to be ninety tripled. The Census Bureau predicts that from 1989 to the year 2000 the number of people over one hundred years of age will increase by 64 percent. We are more likely to live longer than our parents, and to see our children mature and grow older.

Baby boomers, who now comprise one-third of the nation's population, will reach their sixties starting in 2006. In the decade 2020 to 2030, one of five Americans will be over sixty-five. From the outset, society was ill-prepared to deal with the consequences of having unexpectedly produced the largest generation in U.S. history. Initially, there were not enough diapers for the large numbers of babies born after the Second World War. Then there were not enough public schools. As baby boomers matured, there were not enough colleges, jobs, or housing. Without planning, our society will again be unprepared as this generation enters the final phase of their lives.

The revolution in longevity is not limited to the United States or the developed world; it is worldwide. Indeed, already 60 percent of persons over sixty reside in the developing world, and in the twenty-first century the percentage will rise to 80 percent. China alone will soon have 20 percent of all the world's older population. This book, however, will focus exclusively on the issues associated with aging in America.

The challenges of population aging and the increasing length of life are tremendous. There are three major concerns: (1) Can society afford the growing numbers and proportions of older persons? (2) Will the prevalence of the aged lead to intergenerational conflicts? (3) Will stagnation of societal and economic progress result?

Daunting as population aging appears, one must not be swayed by gloom-and-doom prognosticators. In the United States, there are those who envision hoards of wealthy, robust, tax-evading retirees banding together with Medicare-dependent invalids to thwart economic growth and stymie the efforts of the next generation to realize the American dream. The new longevity may touch everything in society—family and community, productivity, public resource allocation, health and quality of life—and challenge us to develop new mind-sets, new institutions and social arrangements. But this should not be seen as an unwelcome development. In fact, the odds are in favor of the growth of a vital, active, experienced, engaged, and useful older population. Many will be healthy long past age seventy-five, and even among those who do not enjoy good health, the majority will still contribute to their families and society. More than 50 percent of persons over eighty-five living today, for example, are still independent.

This volume brings together some of the country's leading experts from the worlds of public policy, health care policy, economics, media, and advertising to consider the challenges and opportunities inherent in the growth of the number and proportion of older people relative to the population as a whole. Robert Myers, one of the pioneers of Social Security, debunks some of the myths surrounding the future of this program, pointing out that Social Security has been a flexible program since its inception and can continue to be so in the future. James Schulz of Brandeis University broadens the discussion and considers whether current economic and demographic trends foretell a future in which there will be intergenerational strife over limited resources and a shrinking economic pie. William Gale of the Brookings Institution analyzes whether baby boomers are saving enough for retirement, and Sara Rix of the AARP's Public Policy Institute examines retirement issues from another vantage point—current trends toward early retirement and the question of whether older workers' productivity can be preserved and enhanced to augment future labor force participation. Linda George of Duke University makes the important point that our understanding of financial status in later life remains incomplete without attention to subjective perceptions of financial well-being.

In the health care arena, Marilyn Moon of the Urban Institute analyzes Medicare's prospects for meeting the future health care needs of the older population. Robert Binstock of Case Western Reserve University takes on the issue of escalating health care costs and the extent to which medical services for the elderly contribute to these costs. Robyn Stone of the International Longevity Center-USA tackles the long-term care issues that are being faced today and that will become even more pressing in the future owing to the fast-growing population of people aged eighty-five and above. Charlotte Muller, also of the International Longevity Center-USA, considers the special health care and financial needs of older minorities and women. Women, who on average outlive men by seven years, are more prone to experiencing the medical and money-related problems often associated with very advanced age.

Lawrence K. Grossman, former president of PBS and NBC News, and John Zweig, chief executive officer of the WPP Group, write complementary chapters that consider how well the media and advertisers are responding to the demographic changes that are occurring now and will become even more dramatic in the future. The media and advertising industries are important opinion leaders in our country and therefore play a crucial role in shaping images of aging for the public. Both Grossman and Zweig note some positive trends in these areas and are optimistic about the future.

GERONTOLOGY, GERIATRICS, AND RESEARCH ON AGING

Our expanded life expectancy can be credited in no small part to the application of important scientific discoveries beginning in the latter part of the nineteenth century and continuing to the present. Early discoveries included the germ theory of disease, X rays, and inoculation against diphtheria. More recently, medical researchers have been discovering ways to retard age-related diseases and processes of aging. One example is the finding that exercise and weight training, supplemental calcium, and estrogen replacement for postmenopausal women can help prevent the loss of muscle mass (sarcopenia) and reduction of bone density that lead to mobility problems and osteoporotic fractures.

We can look forward to even more dramatic discoveries in the next century. For example, based on a theory first postulated by Barbara McClintock in the 1930s, scientists have proved that the end of a chromosome's telomere, which shortens after each cell division, is directly related to the longevity of a cell. It is not science fiction to imagine that in the twenty-first century such research will evolve into cures or treatments for age-related diseases, for instance, growing retinal cells to treat age-related macular degeneration, the number-one cause of blindness in older adults. Scientific research in the field of longevity, spurred by the promise of future breakthroughs, has helped to develop the related fields of gerontology and geriatrics.

Gerontology as a concept—indeed, the word itself—is a creation of the twentieth century. It was introduced in 1906 by Nobel Prize winner Elie Metchnikoff. Gerontology is defined as the study of aging from the biological, social, psychological, and economic perspectives, with other disciplines enlisted as needed. It did not become a substantial field of scientific investigation in the United States until the 1940s, and in the 1950s the first longitudinal U.S. studies of community-resident *healthy* older persons were begun at the National Institutes of Health (NIH) and at Duke University. These studies are significant because earlier investigations that concentrated on the aged were primarily observational, cross-sectional, and focused on chronic disease populations, especially in institutions. By overlooking the population of healthy aging persons, researchers unwittingly reinforced society's stereotype of all older persons as being frail, ill, and suffering from dementia.

The field of geriatrics is the application of medical knowledge to the diagnosis, care, treatment, and rehabilitation of older persons. The development of gerontology and geriatrics has helped to diminish stereotypes and create a better understanding of aging.

In an attempt to heighten public awareness of how commonplace are the negative attitudes toward older persons, the term "ageism" was coined in 1968. Ageism was defined as "a systematic stereotyping of and discrimination against people because they are old, just as racism and sexism accomplish this with skin color and gender. Old people are categorized as senile, rigid in thought and manner, old fashioned in morality and skills. Ageism allows the younger generation to see older people as different from themselves. Thus, they subtly cease to identify with their elders as human beings."[1]

A benchmark in the development of gerontology as a legitimate field of study was the establishment by Congress in 1974 of the National Institute on Aging (NIA). Since its inception, the NIA's mission has been to support high-quality gerontological research and to train highly sophisticated investigators.

However, notwithstanding the NIA and important contributions that have been made to the field of aging in the twentieth century, the future is not secure. The United States does not have enough people trained in geriatrics to meet current academic and practice needs. Although the overall patient population has become older, there is not yet even an officially recognized medical specialty for geriatrics. Among the 140 U.S. schools of allopathic and osteopathic medicine, only the Mount Sinai and the University of Arkansas Schools of Medicine have departments of geriatrics, which include a required rotation of medical students through their inpatient and outpatient clinical services, consultation services, and a teaching nursing home. The University of Oklahoma School of Medicine is in the process of creating a department of geriatrics. At last count, although forty-five medical schools have an elective in geriatrics, only 4 percent of their students register for the course. Twenty medical schools in the United States have significant geriatrics programs, some of which are strong in research, such as Harvard and the University of Michigan. In addition, the University of Southern California has a solid program in behavioral, social, and biological (particularly neurobiological) studies, but the program has virtually no relationship to the USC medical school.

In contrast, Great Britain has a department of geriatrics in every medical school, as do some Scandinavian medical schools. Japan too has been moving in this direction. Although this country needs an academic specialty of geriatrics, it does not need yet another potentially expensive practice specialty. Academic geriatrics would serve to integrate knowledge about aging and geriatric care into primary and specialty care medicine at the undergraduate, postgraduate, and continuing levels of medical education.

There are still more questions than answers. For example, what biological changes create a greater susceptibility to disease in people, and what causes failure to protect normal functions at the cellular and molecular level in the aged? How can the psychology of aging be advanced? Does personality change with aging? How do personality and ways of thinking, feeling, and behaving affect an individual's longevity? It seems clear that if the answers to these and other questions are to be found, we must strengthen our commitment to the advancement of longevity science in the twenty-first century.

PRODUCTIVE AGING

Every generation has produced its share of individuals who lived to great old age and continued to be productive virtually to the end of their lives. However, the experience of contemporary society is somewhat different, in part because of the invention of retirement. We are looking at the evolution of a new stage of life. No longer biologically fixed and immutable, old age has become a social and cultural construct that will undergo further transformation as the twenty-first century unfolds.

How should people conduct themselves in old age, having benefited from a long life? How should they fulfill commitments and obligations to other generations and to society at large? Should older people live in idleness? The new longevity calls for a reevaluation of social responsibilities and personal goals. It makes no sense to decry the aging population as a burden while ignoring its potential and restricting its productivity.[2] Today, people can look forward to twenty-five to thirty years of retirement. By the time baby boomers reach retirement age, economic circumstances will likely mandate that millions of them continue to work.

Older adults can make important contributions to society as paid or volunteer workers, and research shows that older workers in good health learn and perform effectively. Drawing upon their lifetime experiences, they could be placed at the disposal of the civil society, serving on juries or public school boards and otherwise directly assisting the community. "Retirees" already put in billions of dollars worth of community service. They mentor students and young workers, advise new businesses, visit homebound persons, and provide transportation and chore services for the disabled, among other activities.

Older persons are indispensable to contemporary society in their role as part-time and even full-time surrogate parents. One example of a community-based project that connects children and older adults is the Linkage House Intergenerational Program, located in the East Harlem section of New York. Linkage House is a partnership of four community organizations that collaborated to create a seventy-unit supportive living environment that links the generations through educational and recreational activities. Residents and other older persons serve as volunteer instructors and mentors for latchkey schoolchildren ages six to twelve.

Studies have shown a correlation between living a life of purpose and longevity. Eventually, retirement as we now know it may become an anachronism, as job sharing and part-time employment change the face of the workplace. Concepts of recreation are also undergoing revision, and scores of older adults are using leisure time to continue their education. Elderhostel in the United States and the "third age" universities in France are examples of education geared to mature students. Ecotourism, study tours, and language study have also become popular venues for continuing education. Information technology is particularly popular. Eighty-year-olds owning personal computers are now participating on the Internet. One can no longer think of education as being solely for children.

If the seventeenth century marked the discovery of childhood, according to historian Philippe Aries, then it is in the twenty-first century that the milestones of the life course and old age will be analyzed.[3] Our stereotypes of older persons no longer apply. The growing phenomenon of active, engaged, fruitfully occupied elders is less understood because it is so new and people have so little experience with it. It will have a profound effect on twenty-first century societies, though.

Old age is the five-star edition, the last version in the continuing invention of the self, marked by revisits to one's childhood and adjustments along the way. It can be the finest edition of all. To do the work of old age, aging persons must take responsibility for themselves, allowing themselves to be neither controlled nor cosseted by society.

Cicero said more than two thousand years ago: "For old age is honored only on condition that it defends itself, maintains its rights, is subservient to no one, and to the last breath rules over its own domain. For just as I approve of the young man in whom there is a touch of age, so I approve of the old man in whom there is some of the flavor of youth. He who strives thus to mingle youthfulness and age may grow old in the body, but old in spirit he will never be."

1

DISPELLING THE MYTHS ABOUT SOCIAL SECURITY

Robert J. Myers

C urrently, many prophets of gloom and doom are proclaiming that the Social Security program will cease operations within a few years. They argue that, over the long range, its costs will be "unbearable" and "crushing to the economy" and that it is just not sustainable. To all this, the following quotations from the New Testament's Book of Matthew are apropos: "Beware of false prophets, which come to you in sheep's clothing, but inwardly they are ravening wolves" and "Many false prophets shall rise and shall deceive many." This chapter shall demonstrate that such pessimistic prophecies abound and then point up their weaknesses. It will also try to separate fact from opinions.

Before discussing the many myths that are widely circulated nowadays, it is helpful to recount the fundamental purpose of the Social Security program (officially, the Old-Age, Survivors, and Disability Insurance program—or OASDI) and to appraise its financial status, both currently and over the long run. The actuarial cost data underlying the discussion are those from the 1996 OASDI trustees' annual report, which is the basis upon which much of the recent national debate and the report of the 1994–96 Advisory Council on Social Security (released in January 1997) have drawn. (The 1997–99 trustees' reports show about the same results as the 1996 one, although with a slightly more favorable outlook for preserving Social Security benefits.)

9

BASIC PURPOSE OF SOCIAL SECURITY

Over the years, the Social Security program has generally been considered an income maintenance program that provides an economic floor of protection for retirees or in the event of disability or death of the household's breadwinner. The program is intended to be almost completely financed by contributions (or taxes) from workers and employers and from a portion of the income taxes that are levied on Social Security benefits. It is not intended that the benefits of each worker be completely financed by that worker's own contributions and those on her or his behalf by the employer. Rather, it may properly be said that workers contribute toward their benefits but do not actuarially "purchase" them.

In any event, although the employer contributions represent part of employee remuneration, this does not mean that they are individually assignable as a property right to each employee. Rather, they can be viewed as being pooled for the general purposes of the program—that is, to deal with the burden of the benefits for high-cost groups, such as those near retirement age when the program began, low-earning workers, and those with dependents. This same practice is generally followed in benefit plans established by private employers. An outstanding example is the case in which an employer adopts a maternity benefits plan for the female workers instead of giving all workers a pay increase; the male workers cannot be said to have been inequitably treated even though they receive no benefits.

The Social Security program is *not* intended to be an investment program, under which all covered individuals get their money's worth in protection, no more and no less. To put it another way, each person does not get the same rate of return on contributions. In the same way, school taxes should not be looked at as an investment program (except, in the very broad sense, from the standpoint of the nation as a whole). The owner of a large mansion pays many times the school taxes that the owner of a modest dwelling (assuming the same family composition) does, yet receives only the same educational benefit. And the person who never has children does not get her or his money's worth at all. Nor can one equitably stop paying school taxes once all the household's children have become adults.

It is most important to note that those who retired during the early years of the program, and who received large "actuarial bargains" because of their relatively small total contributions, frequently had supported their aged parents, in whole or in part, in the era before Social Security benefits were available. Current workers, who pay relatively high Social Security contributions, rarely do this.

FINANCIAL STATUS OF THE
SOCIAL SECURITY SYSTEM

At the end of 1998, the assets of the Social Security program amounted to $762 billion. Virtually all of this was invested in federal government obligations that are counted as part of the national debt, and are redeemable at par on demand (plus accrued interest). The interest rate on these securities when they are issued, as set by law, is the average market interest rate on all federal bonds having a maturity date of at least four years from the end of the month prior to their issuance. The rate on such securities issued in 1998 varied from 4.875 percent in October to 6.000 percent in January, April, and May.

The intermediate-cost estimate in the 1999 trustees' annual report shows that trust fund balances will grow steadily over the next twenty-two years—by as much as $200 billion per year in 2008–2014—reaching a peak of $4.5 trillion in 2021 and 2022. Thereafter, if present law is not changed (though it is likely to be), the balances will decrease and become exhausted in 2034. Another way to look at the financial status of the trust funds is to consider the estimated actuarial imbalance over the next seventy-five years. According to the intermediate-cost estimate, this is 2.07 percent of payroll in the 1999 trustees' annual report, meaning that the employer and employee tax rates would each have to be immediately increased by about 1.04 percent in order for the program to be fully financed on its own.

It can hardly be said that an increase of such small magnitude would be "unbearable" for the public to preserve what is generally considered to be such a valuable program. The drawback is that extremely large fund balances would be built up in the next three or four decades and then drawn down thereafter. This would create almost insufferable problems during both periods. During the buildup period, the sizable excesses of income over payouts would be "scored" as income to the government for purposes of measuring the general budget deficit and would make the deficit appear much smaller than otherwise (or would show apparent surpluses). At the same time the national debt would tend to rise (because the investments of the trust funds are counted as part of it). Thus, the real budget deficit would be "masked," and less effort might be made to reduce it. On the other hand, during the later period of declining balances, the Treasury Department would have gigantic problems in selling the corresponding large amounts of government securities to the general public in order to redeem trust fund investments that were being liquidated.

The doomsayers often confuse the issue of whether workers get a good rate of return on their contributions by quoting the combined employer-employee tax rate without saying so, or similarly by using the high-cost estimate and/or including the Medicare hospital insurance tax rate without so indicating. It is debatable whether the employer payroll tax should be considered for measuring rate of return as being individually allocated to each employee. On the one hand, it may be argued that the employer levy results in lower wages than would otherwise be the case. On the other hand, it is quite common in private employer benefit plans for many employees not to get their money's worth in terms of benefit protection under the plan because the value of their protection is lower than the average employer contribution rate; this almost always is the case for some participants in defined benefit pension plans, in medical care plans, in maternity benefits plans, and under workers' compensation. Further, these critics ignore that the Social Security program is not "set in concrete" and that its benefit and financing provisions can be altered—as has happened many times in the past.

The financing problem of the Social Security program shown by the intermediate cost figures would not occur under the low-cost scenario, but would, of course, seem worse using the high-cost estimate. The assumptions used in the low-cost estimate are reasonable, although it is not too likely that the actual experience will conform to them all. The doomsayers, however, do not choose to recognize the possibility that there may actually be no long-range financing problem. Fiscal prudence dictates that remedial action be taken soon, although the changes legislated should be designed to be put in effect only many years hence when it is clear that there is a long-range problem—and, if there really turns out not to be, then action can be postponed or modified.

The outlook regarding one critical assumption is somewhat favorable—namely, the annual rate of increase of the consumer price index. In December 1996, an advisory commission chaired by Michael Boskin of Stanford University concluded that, for years, the annual rate of increase of the CPI had most probably been overstated by 1.1 percentage points. If such is the case, then, owing to this alone, the long-range deficit of the Social Security program under the intermediate-cost scenario would be reduced by two-thirds, and the point of exhaustion of trust fund balances would be deferred until the 2050s. Moreover, any program changes needed to close the gap would be relatively small.

However, the measurement of the CPI and its annual changes is not at all as precise a matter as, say, measuring the temperature at a specific place and time. The imprecision results from disagreement about how to take into account such elements as improvements in quality, substitution of one item in the market basket for another when their prices move at different rates (and consumers shift their purchases accordingly), and—with respect to Social Security benefit formulas in particular—the composition of the group to whom the cost-of-living adjustment (COLA) is applicable. As to the last of these, a "proper" market basket for beneficiaries aged eighty-five or over would be quite different from that for young survivor beneficiary families or for the working-age population overall.

It has been pointed out that each of the members of the Boskin Commission had previously taken the general position that the CPI overstated inflation significantly and that the commission did no new research on the subject. Other economists do not hold the commission's view and instead believe that only a small amount of upward bias in the CPI may be present—in the area of perhaps 0.25 percentage points per year. A few economists even believe that the CPI may understate inflation for the purpose of setting Social Security COLAs, especially considering the heterogeneous nature of the group that the Social Security beneficiaries constitute.

If COLAs are reduced as a result of the CPI being revised, as the Boskin Commission recommended (or if the 1.1 percent decrease in measured inflation is arbitrarily factored into the COLA the way some have proposed), but in reality the CPI is substantially accurate, the poverty rate for aged persons—especially the oldest ones—would be increased catastrophically from its present, low level.

Interestingly, some of the proponents of revising drastically the CPI also assert that the Social Security program is not financially viable over the long run. Here they are "walking on both sides of the street at the same time!" If their proposed change in the CPI were accepted, the problem of the long-term sustainability of the Social Security system would diminish almost to the point of extinction.

CURRENT-DAY MYTHS ABOUT SOCIAL SECURITY

Over the years, a number of myths have been voiced about the Social Security program. These are worth examining because they are used at times to denigrate the program, to greatly reduce confidence in its prospects for survival, and to press for its dilution (or even elimination) through so-called privatization.

1. "Everybody pays for his or her own benefits—and all get a great buy."
As mentioned, Social Security is not intended to function on a basis of individual equity by any means. At the start, the program was described as one under which individual accounts would be established to record each person's lifetime covered earnings, from which the amounts of the benefits would be determined. Although this was a completely accurate statement, it gave the false impression that the "account" was the accumulation of the person's contributions (and the employer's as well) and that this "purchased" the benefits. Also, it was well known that for those retiring in the early years of the program's operation, cumulative benefits over a few years would exceed the contributions made. This transitional situation favoring retirees in the early years of the program gave rise to the "great bargain" aspect of the myth, even though careful consideration would easily lead to the conclusion that, as time went by, the relationship between cumulative benefits and contributions would gradually and steadily become "worse." But because the program is not intended to work on an investment principle, this really is not relevant.

2. "Instituted to supplement private pension plans."
It is often said that the Social Security program was initiated to supplement private pension plans. This obviously is not so because in the early 1930s relatively few such plans existed. Instead, Social Security serves as a foundation on which private pension plans can be successfully built.

3. "Financed on a pay-as-you-go basis."
It is frequently asserted that, under the original 1935 Social Security Act, the program was intended to be funded on a pay-as-you-go basis. That this is not so can be seen from the fact that the original implementation strategy contemplated the buildup and maintenance of a relatively large fund balance, such that in 1980 interest earnings would finance about 40 percent of the annual benefit expenses. Thus, the funding basis was really "permanent partial funding," or limited self-support. The 1939 amendments to the Social Security Act moved in the direction of lower partial funding, but still did not make for a pay-as-you-go system. Strangely, some people have the notion that the original act was fully funded, just like any "proper" private pension plan, and that the 1939 amendments changed this to pay-as-you-go financing.

It is still widely asserted that, in the future, funding of the Social Security program will be on a pay-as-you-go basis. This is not the case. Actuarially speaking, the current funding basis can be described as "temporary partial-reserve funding." In 1983, amendments were enacted, featuring a level contribution (or tax) rate from 1990 onward—to finance fully the steadily increasing obligations over the seventy-five-year valuation period. The result according to the intermediate-cost estimate would be to build up a huge fund balance, peaking at about 5.4 times annual expenditures in 2015–18 (as against a ratio of 1.5 in 1997). Thereafter, the fund ratio was expected to decrease, to 0.5 in 2060 (that is, a balance equal to only a half-year's spending requirement). This funding basis resulted not by design but rather as a consequence of a virtually level contribution rate financing rising payouts over the years. Under true, responsible pay-as-you-go funding, the fund ratio should never exceed 1.0 at any time in the valuation period; likewise, it should never be less than 0.5.

Legislation affecting Social Security since 1983 has not changed this funding basis. However, the actuarial cost estimates were revised, utilizing more pessimistic assumptions generally. The projected buildup of a large fund balance was moderated, but not eliminated, as a result of the more pessimistic assumptions, and the decline of the fund balance was shown to start sooner and become exhausted earlier in the valuation period.

4.   "Certain to become bankrupt in the near future."

As discussed, the current intermediate cost estimate shows that the trust fund balances will peak in 2021–22 and become exhausted in 2034. Some note that payroll tax income will fall short of meeting the obligations in 2013 and in each subsequent year (but this is of no real significance because interest income also must be taken into account). These points are cited as evidence of certain near future bankruptcy. Ignored is the possibility brought out earlier that the low-cost estimate, which shows no long-term problems whatsoever, may end up being the most accurate.

5.   "Unbearable cost over the long run."

Some pessimists assert that the cost of the program will ultimately (in fifty or seventy-five years) be as much as 40 to 55 percent of payroll and thus obviously unbearable. Such calculations, including the employer portion of the payroll tax and the cost of the Medicare hospital insurance program (and, sometimes, the cost of the supplementary medical insurance program expressed as a percentage of taxable payroll, even though it is not financed in that way), are based on the high-cost estimate. On this basis, there naturally would be a huge, long-range actuarial imbalance. This would undoubtedly be rectified well in advance by changes in benefits and financing.

Along these lines, the critics say that very large budget deficits and increases in the national debt will result. They never note that historically the Social Security program, because of its self-supporting nature, has not contributed at all to general budget deficits (if anything, it has hidden them) or the swelling of the national debt. And, as long as this principle is maintained by appropriate reforms to the taxation and benefit structure, it never will have such an effect.

6. "The trust fund investments are worthless IOUs."

Cynics denigrate the government securities in the trust funds as being valueless because they are nonmarketable IOUs; moreover, the government "has already spent the money on all sorts of things." Not so. Just as with any bonds issued by a private company or any deposit in a savings bank, the money involved—although having been "spent" toward the purpose for which the bond was issued in the first place or in the form of bank lending—represents a valid, interest-bearing debt. The characteristic of the trust fund securities being redeemable at any time at par—to some extent similar to the popular Series E government bonds widely sold to the general public—is, at times, more advantageous than being marketable.

7. "The interest on the trust fund investments is not usable."

Critics frequently say that the interest earned on the trust fund securities is somehow unusable. They insist that, in the next decade or so, when the income from payroll taxes exceeds expenditures, the interest will not be used, for any valid purpose, but rather merely designated as more "worthless IOUs." Furthermore, after that time they argue that new taxes or borrowing will be needed to pay such interest. They forget, though, that if the trust funds had not had the money available to purchase these securities then the general public would have had to have done so (because Congress had authorized the expenditures for which such money was used, but did not specify the sources of financing) and the same interest payments would have had to be made in all years in either case.

Because the Treasury checks for the periodic interest payments to the trust funds are mingled with the payroll tax receipts submitted by employers, it is usually impossible to determine which of these two sources of income is used to meet annual expenses and which is left over to purchase government securities. One instance, however, is quite clear. Like any good money manager, the trust funds invest daily any excess of income over disbursements. Then, at the beginning of each month, when about $30 billion of cash is needed to pay benefits, current investments are redeemed (by precise, equitable rules). However, somewhat less than $30 billion of securities actually has to be redeemed because the accrued interest on the redemptions makes up the difference.

8.   *"Chile has the perfect social security program."*
Many critics of Social Security who would like to cut it back by partially privatizing the program (or even eliminate it by fully privatizing) contend that Chile has been a great success in its replacement of a floundering, traditional social insurance system by a privatized program in the early 1980s. Under the new system, all employees except the armed forces must contribute 10 percent of their wages (up to a rather high maximum) for retirement benefits and about 3.5 percent for disability and survivor benefits and for administrative expenses. There is no employer contribution. The employee selects a pension company (of which there are about fifteen approved ones), to which the contributions are transmitted. Self-employed persons can voluntarily participate, but only about 10 percent do so. It is true that the Chilean program has been reasonably successful, but it was not the only solution that could have been adopted, and it is by no means perfect.

Furthermore, conditions in Chile were quite different from those in other countries, so that what worked out well there would not necessarily do so elsewhere. For one thing, Chile had large budget surpluses that could be used to finance the transition costs (notably, credits to workers for prior service) and the generous minimum-benefit provisions (for which financing from general revenues may turn out to be a serious problem over the long run). Other countries frequently have budget deficits and so cannot readily follow this course of action. Chilean government bonds all are price indexed and in recent times bore double-digit coupon rates. So, it is not surprising that the pension companies, with about 40 percent of their assets so invested (and with private bonds and bank deposits necessarily having to be competitive with respect to investment returns), have shown very successful investment results.

Still, coverage compliance in Chile is poor (although greatly improved over the old system) because many people who legally should be contributing—estimated officially at about 30 percent—do not do so, and many low-paid workers contribute less than they should because they will receive the guaranteed minimum benefit in any event. And the administrative expenses of the retirement benefits portion of the system are relatively high—about 13 percent of contribution income, as compared with less than 1 percent for Social Security in the United States.

9.   *"Social Security is a Ponzi, chain-letter, or pyramid scheme."*
Some prophets of doom allege that the Social Security program is a big hoax or lie, because it is merely a Ponzi, chain-letter, or pyramid scheme, which of its very nature will inevitably collapse in the end. Under such kinds of plans, operations could continue over long periods *only* if there were a geometrically increasing number of contributors each year—an impossibility, of course. The Social Security program is quite different, however. All that it requires for long-range financial stability (in addition to a reasonable, steady level of benefit amounts) is that the ratio of contributors (active workers) to beneficiaries will ultimately stabilize at a reasonable level. That aim will almost certainly be achieved under normal demographic conditions. At worst, it can be accomplished through deferred, gradual increases in the "full benefits" retirement age (now 65 and scheduled to rise to 67 by 2027), so as to recognize increasing longevity over time. Under the intermediate-cost estimate in the 1999 trustees' annual report, the contributors-to-beneficiaries ratio is shown to decrease from 3.3 in 1996 to 2.0 in the period 2035 to 2055 and level off at 1.8 in 2075. Under the low-cost estimate, the ratio is 2.4 in 2025 and afterward, while under the high-cost estimate, it dips to 1.3 in 2075 and remains there.

10.   *"Social Security is a poor investment for many persons."*
Many individuals—particularly those who are younger and higher-paid—complain that Social Security is a poor investment: even if the program is viable over the long run, they do not get their money's worth in benefits from the payroll taxes paid by them and their employers. Although strictly speaking this is not a myth, it is a gross misunderstanding of the basic purpose of the program. It must be kept in mind at all times that Social Security is not intended to be an investment program based on the individual's contributions and those of his or her employer. Rather, it involves broad social pooling to provide a floor of benefit protection against the risks of old age and disability or death of the breadwinner. Thus, it should be considered an income maintenance program.

If people were allowed to opt out of Social Security and make their own investments to protect against these risks, it is true that many would be successful, but others would not. Following the actuarial law of adverse selection (namely, that when persons can use individual choice to take a certain action, they will tend to do so to their own advantage), the relative cost of the program for those remaining in it would rise, and there would be an increased public assistance burden to sustain those who opted out and failed to make good investments. Such costs would have to be met by society as a whole and would largely fall on those who believed that they had "successfully" opted out to their own financial advantage.

CHANGES PROPOSED BY THE ADVISORY COUNCIL ON SOCIAL SECURITY

The Social Security Act provided that, every four years, an Advisory Council be established to report on the status of the program, especially its financial condition (but recently, the law has been changed so that there will be no more such councils in the future). The 1994–96 council is divided into three groups with regard to the question of how to solve the system's long-range financing problem.

Consideration of the council's three general approaches is worthwhile and will be included in the next section. None of them are, on balance, desirable for various reasons. Even more important, the most extreme one is not enactable since this proposal would increase the national budget deficit, as it is computed under the unified budget concept, by at least $150 billion per year for the next decade or two—which is completely contrary to what both political parties are aiming to do. In some instances under all three approaches, the national debt would be increased greatly, and payroll and other taxes would have to be hiked steeply.

POSSIBLE CHANGES TO SOLVE SOCIAL SECURITY'S FINANCING PROBLEM

Among the many solutions, either partial or complete, proposed by Advisory Council members or others are the following:

1. *Increase the payroll tax rate immediately.* As indicated earlier, this would be undesirable because it would result in a huge fund buildup and a concomitant "masking" of the real budget deficit.

2. *Cover compulsorily all new state and local government employees.* This
    was proposed by all three Advisory Council groups and is a good idea,
    supporting the principle that universal coverage of workers is desir-
    able. At present, about 75 percent of all state and local government
    employees are covered under the Social Security program; those
    whose states or municipalities have their own retirement system are
    covered as a result of the state or local government having elected
    coverage, while all others are covered compulsorily.

3. *Subject all Social Security benefits to equitable income taxation.* This would
    be done in the same manner as other retirement pensions are taxed,
    rather than taxing the benefits of only high-income persons as is the
    current practice (but the majority of beneficiaries would still not
    wind up paying any income tax), with the proceeds reverting to the
    OASDI trust funds. This was proposed by all three council groups. It
    would be desirable because it is only logical that all retirement income
    should be taxed in the same, equitable way.

4. *Correct the technical flaws in the consumer price index, which overstate
    inflation.* This was proposed by all three groups. It is obviously always
    desirable to do things in as technically correct a fashion as possible
    (although not to make arbitrary changes in the CPI for other rea-
    sons). This is a complex matter, and there is no consensus on the rel-
    ative merits of various "fixes."

5. *Partially privatize the investments of the trust funds by investing a portion
    of them in common stocks on a nonselective, indexed basis.* This was pro-
    posed by one Advisory Council group. However, it is undesirable
    because of the general budget effect (showing larger budget deficits on
    the unified budget basis), the resulting need for more investment in
    government securities by private sector investors after trust fund
    moneys are shifted to Wall Street, and the strong possibility of a polit-
    ical weakening of the "automated, unbiased" investment procedure
    (investing only on an indexed basis), so that "socialism by the back-
    door method" would result as the government obtained control of a
    significant portion of private industry.

6. *Partially privatize the benefit structure by transferring a portion of employ-
    ee payroll taxes to individual investment accounts administered by private
    sector organizations such as mutual funds and by reducing Social Security*

benefits accordingly. Partial privatization through accounts was proposed, in differing degree, by two groups, with one even suggesting increasing payroll taxes and issuing more government bonds. This is most undesirable for many reasons: the deleterious effects on the general budget, taxes, and the national debt; the difficulty of equitably annuitizing the proceeds of the individual accounts (if this is indeed attempted), especially in regard to women, with their longer life expectancy; the great difficulty of fairly and rationally coordinating young survivor and disability benefits with total retirement benefits; and the higher administrative expenses (especially for the small accounts of low-earning or occasional workers).

7. *Decrease benefit amounts by lengthening the period over which the "average earnings" for retirement benefits are calculated from thirty-five to thirty-eight years.* This was recommended by all three council groups. It is undesirable because under today's labor market conditions it would particularly adversely affect women workers and all who have only sporadic work histories.

8. *Decrease benefit amounts gradually for high-earning workers by changes in the benefit formula.* This was recommended by one Advisory Council group. However, it seems undesirable to reduce further the component of fair treatment for all, which would cause high earners to complain even more about "not getting their money's worth" and to exert political pressure to opt out of the program.

9. *Increase the "full benefits" retirement age.* Beginning in 2003, retirement age is set to rise slowly under law until reaching sixty-seven for the year 2027 and after. Such change could be extended gradually, increasing steadily by two months a year from 2003 until normal retirement age reaches seventy in 2037. Alternatively, following the scheduled increase to age sixty-seven, there could be indexing thereafter based on life expectancy at retirement age. This change is desirable on the grounds that, as people live longer, they will most likely be in better health and able to work longer. It will be more understandable to the public than a mere reduction in the benefit level. The early retirement age should be increased in tandem from sixty-two. Increasing the full-benefit retirement age should be seen not as a "real" reduction in benefits, but rather as keeping up to date the total amount of lifetime benefits that will be receivable on average.

It is widely recognized that increasing the full-benefits retirement age may cause problems for persons who cannot afford to retire but cannot find a job either. This holds particularly true for those who, despite lower mortality rates and longer life expectancy, are not in good health and are thus unable to work longer. Employers will need to make serious efforts to deal with this situation as it evolves over time, and the government should encourage employers to do so. If not, then other steps concerning benefit and financing provisions will need to be taken. However, the increases in the retirement age should be legislated far in advance, so that people are well aware of them and they can readily be adjusted if circumstances require it.

A SOUNDER SOLUTION TO SOCIAL SECURITY'S FINANCING PROBLEM

The problem of financing Social Security essentially can be solved in the traditional, time-tested way of combining, more or less equally, benefit/cost reductions and tax revenue increases—all to be implemented in a deferred, gradual manner, although enacted into law in one shot.

Along with three relatively noncontroversial changes discussed previously (covering state and local government employees, equitable income taxation of all Social Security benefits, and adjusting the Consumer Price Index if need be) the full-benefit retirement age should be increased to seventy by 2037, and the employer and employee tax rates should both be raised by 0.3 percent in 2015 and then again in 2020, 2025, and 2030, making for a total increase of 1.2 percent on each side. Although in some quarters any proposal to increase taxes is virtually equivalent to blasphemy or to advocating economic collapse, such small, intermittent increases—even if the employer passes them on to workers in the form of lower wage increases—would not be harmful in the circumstances of slow but continuous growth in real wages that will almost certainly prevail over the long run in this country. This package of changes would definitely restore the long-range actuarial balance of the Social Security program according to the intermediate-cost estimate.

If the correction in the method of computing the CPI were as large as some experts recommend—resulting in annual increases about 1.1 percentage points lower—the changes advocated could be scaled back considerably, possibly necessitating only the raising of the full-benefit retirement age (and then not to as great an extent). It is not at all certain that the CPI should be "corrected" by such a large amount, however.

Finally, it would be a good idea to adopt a compulsory individual savings account plan to supplement a reformed and fiscally sound Social Security program. This would involve an additional employee contribution rate of, say, 2 percent of each paycheck. This money would be directed, at each individual's choice, to an appropriate, government-regulated private organization, such as a mutual fund, insurance company, or bank. The only exception would be that persons with low total earnings (perhaps less than $5,000 per quarter) would be exempted, by having their contributions refunded because the small amounts involved could not be handled at all in a cost-effective manner. Although the proposed compulsory savings plan would not help low earners, they are adequately provided for under the regular program (because of the heavily weighted benefit formula). Such a supplementary program would not only raise the retirement benefits protection significantly (to the extent that it did not merely substitute for voluntary private savings) but would also bolster our chronically low national savings.

2

MEDICARE, MEDICAID, AND THE HEALTH CARE SYSTEM

Marilyn Moon

T he future of the public health insurance programs that serve older
Americans has never been in greater doubt. It has become fashionable
to argue that public programs in general are not as efficient as those in the
private sector, and that we would be better off as individuals to rely upon
private initiatives and our own resources rather than to support public
institutions. This attitude affects Medicare and Medicaid, the two major
public programs that serve people over the age of sixty-five and younger
people with disabilities. High health care costs and disproportionate
increases (compared to the growth of the population as a whole) in the
number of persons eligible for these programs have made them the fastest-
growing components of the federal budget, lending credence to armchair
critics who take such growth rates as proof positive of their failure. Further,
with the aging of the population and the resulting higher costs projected
as necessary to sustain older Americans, these programs are likely to
become more expensive over time.

The key question to be answered is how to provide affordable health
insurance protection to older Americans in the face of high health care costs
and an aging population. Any true solution to this challenge cannot just
shift the problem elsewhere—that is, moving health care out of the public
sector but leaving major problems in its wake. It is important to recognize
that, if the consequences of ever-increasing expenditures on health care for

This chapter was originally released as a Century Foundation white paper in 1998.

seniors are ignored, other needs for this age group and for other vulnerable groups in the population may not be met. Serious efforts to slow health care spending need to be undertaken, and some positive steps in this direction occurred with passage of the Balanced Budget Act of 1997. Finally, changes in one public entitlement program like Medicare will interact in important ways with two others, Social Security and Medicaid. While reforms may be undertaken separately, it is essential to consider the other major programs for seniors at the same time and to recognize the potential impact of Medicare on the rest of the health care system as well.

Medicare, the health insurance program for the acute care needs of those aged sixty-five and older, is the primary focus of this paper. Medicare provides the basic insurance protection for older Americans, more than 97 percent of whom qualify for the program. Medicaid, which serves low-income Americans of all ages, is also important for the elderly, filling in crucial gaps in coverage. In other words, Medicare does not offer a fully comprehensive set of acute care benefits, so Medicaid supplements that coverage for about one in every seven low-income seniors. But, perhaps most important, the Medicaid program serves as the major source of public support for the long-term care needs of everyone, particularly those aged sixty-five and over.

Can these programs survive? And should Americans seek to preserve them essentially as they are today or to change them dramatically over time, perhaps ceding responsibility to the private sector? Is Medicare now a health care dinosaur that needs to be substantially revamped? The most honest answer to these questions is likely to be equivocal since it is extremely difficult to look into the future some thirty or forty years and have a sense of what our health care system will or should look like. There are likely to be substantial changes both in how care will be provided to individuals and how systems of payment and oversight will be organized in the next century. Nonetheless, a number of basic principles can be summoned for thinking about how to shape the future.

The underlying assumption of this chapter is that Medicare and Medicaid serve valuable roles in protecting elderly and disabled persons—population groups that the market has never been anxious to serve in toto. The federal government thus should continue to play an active role in meeting the health care needs of these two groups. Moreover, efforts that simply remove the burdens from the federal government are not "solutions" since the one in every eight Americans who depends upon Medicare will still need to get care somewhere. And, before moving to more substantial restructuring of the two main public health programs, it is important to be sure that the "reforms" indeed strengthen Medicare and Medicaid rather than undermine them. If Medicare is a target only because it is where the money is, then any reduction in spending is as good as any other. This is certainly not the case.

HOW SERIOUS ARE THE PROBLEMS FACING MEDICARE AND MEDICAID?

Although, as mentioned above, Medicare does not provide a fully comprehensive benefit package, most of the recent criticisms leveled at the program are associated with its rapidly rising costs and whether they can be successfully brought under better control—that is, slowed to a rate more in keeping with other public programs and the pace of general revenue growth. There is some urgency in dealing with the Medicare program today because of projections of financing shortfalls for the Part A (Hospital Insurance) trust fund. Although the recently passed Balanced Budget Act of 1997 extended the life of the trust fund by a number of years, the situation is unlikely to improve further on its own; by 2015 or just a bit later, the lack of resources in the Part A trust fund will create a major imperative to deal with the financing of the program.[1] This financing shortfall serves as a convenient rationale for criticizing the program.

Two impulses are driving up the costs of Medicare. First, for many years health care spending has been rising more rapidly than spending on other goods and services, and faster than wages and other sources of income. As a society, we have implicitly signaled how much we value health-related goods and services, consuming ever more each year. New technology, for example, tends to add new procedures, tests, and drugs to existing treatments, generally driving up their price. Thus, technology, much more than the aging of the population or the price of care, is responsible for increased health care costs over time.[2] This is not just a Medicare problem, nor is it just a problem associated with a government program. And although other countries spend less on health care than the United States, they too have been experiencing increasing rates of growth in this area.

The second reason for higher costs is the expansion in the number of beneficiaries covered by Medicare. Although much higher rates of growth will occur beyond 2010, the number of persons served has already grown at a faster rate than the general population since Medicare's inception in 1966.

This disproportionate growth among the elderly over the past thirty years in part reflects the increased life expectancy of the covered population—a sign of success, not failure. Both the current increase in the number of beneficiaries and the large rise expected in the future mean that America will have to face the expenses of an aging population either through a public program like Medicare or privately. The fact that about one in every four Americans will be either over the age of sixty-five or disabled in the year 2030 poses challenges throughout our economy and society.

Another reason for the present crisis facing Medicare's Part A trust fund rests with the revenue side of the program. The basic payroll tax rate for Part A has not risen since 1986. Between 1986 and 1997, spending per capita on Medicare Part A rose by 131 percent and the number of beneficiaries increased from 31 to 38 million.[3] It should come as no surprise then that Medicare now faces a financing shortfall.

Growth rates in the portion of the Medicaid program serving older persons have also been very high and affected by the same forces influencing Medicare. In addition, a large number of older persons continue to have resources that are limited and whose growth is generally outstripped by the costs of care. As a consequence, even if they are not initially entitled to support from the Medicaid program, which is limited to those with low incomes, older persons may become eligible after high health care costs cause them to "spend down" their assets. A major acute care episode or, more often, need for long-term supportive services can result in even middle-income seniors qualifying for help under the Medicaid program.

Despite these rising costs, there remain substantial unmet needs for the aged population and for younger groups in society as well. In seeking just to hold the line on Medicare and Medicaid spending for elderly persons, much less consider expanding it, concerns will inevitably be raised about competing demands on resources from advocates for other groups such as children. Some of these concerns may be well founded. For example, since Medicaid serves both young and old, and because many states— which share in the cost of Medicaid—would like to limit their expenditures on the program, more dollars for long-term care services may translate into fewer expansions of coverage for children. But this concept of a trade-off can be posed as a convenient excuse for making cuts rather than a commitment to a quid pro quo. For example, in the Balanced Budget Act passed in the summer of 1997, the $115 billion in cuts in the Medicare program did not lead to comparable increases in programs for children but rather to just $24 billion for a children's health care initiative.[4] The rest of those savings will be used for a wide array of other expenditure increases and tax cuts. Beware the admonition that more (or less) spending on one group automatically translates into less (or more) on another.

The bottom line is that we Americans are likely to spend more on health care in the future for the seniors in our population. That is not necessarily bad. Moreover, it is likely that much of this spending can and should remain in the public sector. Even granting this endorsement of Medicare, however, it must be acknowledged that a number of reforms are needed now. In addition, other, tougher changes will also need to be examined in the future. Any discussion of reform could be divided into short- and long-term issues, but a better alternative is to examine reform in terms of those approaches that affect per capita expenditures on health care for the elderly and those that deal with the increasing numbers of older Americans over time.

SLOWING THE GROWTH IN MEDICARE SPENDING

The goal of any policy to slow growth should be to do so in ways that do not adversely affect quality and access and that do not inordinately shift burdens to those who cannot readily absorb changes for the worse. Any analysis of proposals for change should heed these admonitions before making judgments about the proposals' desirability.

High rates of per capita spending growth have come about because Medicare has been subject to the same influences affecting health care spending for all Americans. In fact, between 1983 and 1993 Medicare's per capita growth was below that of private insurance.[5] Only between 1994 and 1997 has the private sector been able to point to lower growth rates, and since private insurance started from a substantially higher base in terms of payments to providers of services, it can find ways to cut spending more easily than the leaner Medicare program. The evidence is mixed concerning whether the two sectors have reached comparable levels of payouts, and whether it might be reasonable to expect equal rates of growth over time if both private and public agencies were effective in holding down costs. The most recent indicators of the costs of private insurance indicate that after the very low growth rates of 1994 through 1996, premiums and health care costs are again accelerating.[6]

THE DRIVERS OF HEALTH CARE COST GROWTH

Health care cost increases are a function of the price charged by providers for services, the basic efficiency of the delivery system, and the number of services delivered. It is in these three areas that potential savings can be sought that will help to slow growth.

Medicare has always been competitive in terms of holding down the price it is willing to pay for services, particularly in the key areas of hospital and physician payment. Studies have consistently indicated that Medicare pays hospitals below their costs on average,[7] and the fees that Medicare pays for physician services tend to be below even what insurers who demand discounts pay.[8] In fact, many private sector plans have adopted the reforms that Medicare pioneered for hospital and physician payment. In other areas, such as home health and skilled nursing facilities, Medicare needs to do better.

To assess how efficiently health care is delivered under Medicare involves examining various aspects of the program's performance. Medicare scores very well in terms of administrative expenses, averaging less than 3 percent of the cost of providing care.[9] Its costs are held down by law and largely kept separate from the trust funds that have been established to pay benefits. This track record is substantially better than that of the private sector, where group insurance administrative expenses run at about 8 percent of the cost of care and managed care plans often average 15 percent or more.[10] But it is possible to spend too little on oversight and management, resulting in other inefficiencies. This is particularly a danger with regard to fraud and abuse in the program. Until 1996, Medicare had few resources to devote to such activities. After remedial legislation, the program can now use trust fund dollars to finance investigations that promise to save the program money. Some highly publicized crackdowns in the area of home health care in 1997 stemmed in part from increased vigilance. However, many analysts are skeptical that such crackdowns alone will make major inroads in reducing the growth in health care spending. Often what gets reported as "fraud and abuse" is merely a result of the difficulty in knowing when care is appropriate and necessary, or the failure to file required paperwork certifying its necessity. For example, a recent hearing touting the problems in Medicare's home health benefit cited a number suggesting that more than 40 percent of the value of spending on such services represented fraud and abuse. A close reading of the documents, however, suggests that these were after-the-fact reviews that found missing signatures and poor documentation and judgment about when care was needed.[11] Nonetheless, data available for 1998 indicate some inroads from this initiative.

Costs imposed by insurers on the providers of care can also contribute to inefficiency, as can rules that lead to redundant activities or provision of services. Medicare has been criticized in these areas, both for overly rigid rules in certain cases and poor oversight leading to fraud and abuse in others. Moreover, boundaries between programs like Medicare and Medicaid encourage gaming, where one program seeks to shift the burden onto the other, leading to poor coordination and, likely, inappropriate care. Poor coordination of care may mean provision of too many services. Further, unnecessary reporting and other requirements can result in burdens on health care providers and patients. The development of managed care organizations ideally addresses some of these issues, although many loosely organized groups focus more on managing costs than on managing care. Poorly managed care can mean subpar service and undesirable rigidities in providing access to care.

The most important source of growth in health care costs, however, has arisen from the increased use of services, in terms of both the number of services used and especially the greater sophistication of new technology, often referred to as the "intensity" of service use. Truly reducing health care spending growth means tackling issues such as the diffusion of new technology.[12] But this will be a difficult assignment for Medicare and the rest of our health care system. There is little expert knowledge to help in sorting out appropriate and inappropriate care. Studies that have looked at the problems have concluded that there is a substantial amount of overuse of care.[13] But difficulty arises in pinpointing where it is occurring and how to control it. Even the development of general guidelines for treatment of certain conditions has proved to be controversial. Absent good efficacy and quality studies, many Americans (both providers and patients) view unlimited access to tests and procedures as a primary way to ensure quality. Particularly when services are noninvasive and hence not harmful, the path of least resistance is to do more tests and procedures rather than take a wait-and-see stance in the treatment of problems. Americans have a strong belief in and taste for high technology. And there is little reason to believe that technologies now under development will be substantially cost saving in nature.[14]

One of the critical issues here is who patients trust to help them make decisions on the use of services. In the "old days" of fee-for-service medicine and little oversight by insurance companies and other payers, the decision was largely left to physicians and patients. Their inclination, it is generally believed, was to use too many services. But, as yet, there is no agreement on how additional oversight or control for cost savings purposes should be established or on when or how it will be determined that "enough" care is being provided. Even traditional indemnity insurance, where patients simply submit bills for reimbursement, now often requires preadmission screening and other approvals before care will be covered. Medicare itself relies on a number of such pre- and postcare reviews to limit its liabilities. The development of managed care to coordinate and limit explicitly, where necessary, use of services has come under increasing fire as rules such as length of hospital stays and denial of referrals to specialists have become more commonplace. This is also an area where policing fraud and abuse may clash with what Americans desire to consume. Who should be in charge of determining what care is needed and when?

Another place where some have suggested savings may be possible is in malpractice reform to encourage physicians to refrain from practicing "defensive" medicine, in which tests are ordered to protect against possible lawsuits. The evidence on whether fear of malpractice suits leads to wasted resources is mixed; the real issue is whether Americans are ready to reduce their reliance on technology and abandon an attitude that more is always better. Until that changes, neither managed care, nor litigation reforms, nor practice guidelines, nor other policy changes will likely make many inroads into slowing the cost spiral.

One emerging field of research does suggest some relief from rising health care expenditures, however. In addition to improvements in mortality, the extent of illness and particularly disability among the elderly now also seems to be declining at each age level.[15] If this holds true over time, then the task of slowing the rate of growth of spending may be eased, specifically with regard to costs of Medicaid long-term care. It is too early to assume, however, that this alone can solve the problems facing Medicare and Medicaid.

THE LIKELY IMPACT OF THE BALANCED BUDGET ACT ON SLOWING MEDICARE'S GROWTH

A number of changes just enacted in the Medicare program could substantially slow growth in per capita spending. Limits on payments to hospitals and physicians and more careful management of home health care, outpatient hospital services, and other Medicare-covered services will take us part of the way toward a long-term solution. Many of the provisions of the Balanced Budget Act should help, but it will take some time to determine the extent of their effectiveness since they will be phased in over the next five years. Cost cutting in the private sector opened up some opportunities for additional Medicare savings since, in most parts of the country, Medicare is no longer viewed as an inadequate payer as compared to private insurers or managed care organizations. Consequently, the budget act's language on health care will reduce payments to many providers of Medicare services, including hospitals and doctors. Preliminary estimates indicate that this may slice by nearly half the long-run financial imbalance in the Part A trust fund.

In addition to price cutting for inpatient hospital services and physician payments, the Balanced Budget Act established a more ambitious set of reforms in a number of other areas where the traditional Medicare program has long paid on the basis of what providers report it costs to offer the care (leaving providers with little or no motivation to become more efficient in delivering care). A number of Medicare's fee-for-service benefits will be transformed into prospective payment systems, setting a fixed price for services: home health services, skilled nursing facility care, outpatient hospital services, rehabilitation hospital services, and eventually some others as well. These are areas that have been growing very rapidly in recent years, in part because our changing health care system is encouraging care to be delivered in less intensive settings, thereby reducing reliance on inpatient hospital care. To some considerable degree, the growth in these less intensive settings is certainly desirable. Nonetheless, the rapid expansion of these services has outpaced Medicare's ability to oversee such care. Reforms that promise to improve incentives to offer care more economically as well as revamp the payment mechanism were a welcome part of the new legislation. But these are more goals than reality at this point, and already many providers are complaining about these new controls and payment levels.

The example of home health services is perhaps most telling. Traditionally, home health agencies billed for their costs (subject to an upper bound), and there has been almost no oversight on length of visits or number of services provided. Before the Balanced Budget Act, beneficiaries did not even get an explanation-of-benefits notice that could serve as a check on whether care was delivered to them. The data that are available suggest that less-skilled health aide services provided by for-profit agencies are where much of the explosive growth is occurring in home health, prompting many analysts to suggest payments are too high and oversight too lax. Establishing improved payment mechanisms and starting movement away from a per visit basis, as called for in the budgetary legislation, should help. Medicare will also be required to develop new normative standards to provide guidance about the necessity of services, and beneficiaries will receive notice about services billed on their behalf. But after a *decline* in home health spending in 1998, many agencies are clamoring for relief from those changes

Reforms in home health care and elsewhere do not have to be made via a fixed payment (capitated) approach or through reliance on private plans in order to be effective. In fact, one problem with capitation approaches is that, since so little is known about what care is necessary and appropriate, the incentives to underserve will likely be strong. Many of the innovations in the private sector do not rely upon fixed budgets or capitation in any event. Rather, they apply strict (and sometimes arbitrary) principles for coverage of services and use sophisticated computer programs for profiling use of services.[16] Innovations from the private sector such as selective contracting—placing limits on which providers of services can participate or precluding providers who abuse the system—could be applied in areas where Medicare is criticized for paying for unnecessary services and at prices above what many other payers have negotiated. Many of these techniques can be readily adopted with some investment in the necessary tools and training.

But, as a public program, Medicare faces more obligations and demands for accountability, which makes it difficult to adopt all the tools available in the private sector. For example, when managers of private plans decide they do not like the way that a physician or other provider is delivering care, they can simply choose not to contract with that provider any longer. They can, in other words, be arbitrary in their responses and move quickly to confront problems they see. Medicare is always likely to be much more bound to due process rules and other constraints. This means that the program will miss some opportunities to save from halting inappropriate use of services, but it also means that it will sometimes do better by its clients in giving providers the benefit of the doubt. There are both advantages and disadvantages in the flexibility that the private sector can offer.

What about moving more quickly to encourage beneficiaries to participate in Medicare's private plan options, particularly those that rely upon managed care? In theory, this could allow even more rapid savings from some of the recent innovations in the private sector. But, at present, Medicare does not take advantage of such enrollments because of its inability to set appropriate ground rules for payments to private plans. Thus, a number of structural reforms in how Medicare pays plans, how it adjusts for different types of beneficiaries and different locations, and what controls it places on plans need to be undertaken. The Balanced Budget Act contained changes in this area, but the overall effect is to grant more opportunities to expand private plan options prematurely, before some of the tougher issues on payment and oversight of such plans are resolved. Further, a number of these new options will go well beyond managed care and allow plans with a less proven track record to try to demonstrate improvements in the way that care can be delivered. Thus, Medicare will save less as a result of the expanded role for the private sector than it might have with a more careful strategy.

At present, private plans are, on average, paid too generously by Medicare. As a result, the program is said to lose money on each new enrollee. While there is some dispute over this claim, according to most of the relevant evidence such overpayments are indeed a serious issue.[17] Simple arithmetic indicates that losses on each enrollee cannot be made up by having ever larger numbers of beneficiaries participate. Moreover, it is unfair to beneficiaries at large to sustain a higher payment for those in private plans; doing so simply allows these plans to offer generous additional benefits that may attract more enrollees. If the plan payments are later reduced, the disruption to beneficiaries who have changed physicians and learned a new system will be considerable. It is much better to have beneficiaries face a level playing field now rather than later; thus, the sooner that private plan payments can be adjusted the better. The Balanced Budget Act is reducing payments on a gradual basis. The danger is that this is allowing plans and beneficiaries—who gain from the higher payments—to marshal opposition over time, as evidenced by calls in 1999 for a rollback in these payment changes.

As a further difficulty, reducing premium payments may slow enrollment growth if plans scale back on extra benefits that now serve as an enticement. If private plans are to serve as the future of Medicare and offer savings to the program, Medicare must save money on each enrollee *and* there must be high rates of participation in the program. This is a dilemma without an obvious solution.

The Balanced Budget Act will also have a major impact by broadening the types of plans that can compete for Medicare beneficiaries. Private, fee-for-service plans will be permitted. In addition, new arrangements such as provider-sponsored organizations—groups of hospitals and doctors that form their own plans—will also be allowed to set up shop. These new plans, which attract healthier beneficiaries, would add to Medicare's costs rather than help generate savings. Medicare's monthly payments to such private plans for healthy beneficiaries are too high; consequently, each new enrollee in a private plan will actually cost Medicare more than if that person had remained in the traditional program. Although these new plans could have started in January 1999, there have been few companies seeking to offer such plans thus far.

Nonetheless, the legislation may have moved prematurely to expand private plan options. Piecemeal reforms have been adopted without thinking through their implications. With no good vision of what the future can and should look like, the policy changes made in 1997 may yet create problems that will be difficult to undo later.

The organization of plans into arrangements such as the Federal Employees Health Benefits Program (FEHBP) is sometimes proposed as a further step toward encouraging more competition among plans. FEHBP allows federal employees to choose among a broad range of alternative insurance plans. But it is not this structure that ensures savings; competition among private plans does not magically lead to lower costs. Rather, to offer lower premiums or more benefits (and assuming that skimming off the good risks is precluded) plans would have to become very efficient and make tough choices regarding provision of care. Further restructuring of Medicare in the direction of relying on competing private plans should be postponed until savings or other advantages from the private plans now operating under Medicare become apparent. As yet the evidence does not support the unbridled enthusiasm of some for restructuring Medicare into an FEHBP-type system.

Issues facing Medicaid are somewhat different. As a joint federal/state program, there is a great deal of variation in the quality and availability of benefits to eligible populations. And while some savings can certainly be sought from this program, they are unlikely to be anywhere near in magnitude to what is being considered for Medicare. Improved coordination of acute and long-term care benefits between the two programs is certainly needed and could probably result in some savings, but savings would better be directed at unmet needs. Changes in the Medicaid program were a much smaller part of the Balanced Budget Act, and it is not clear what the legislation's impact will be on that program.

ASKING BENEFICIARIES TO PAY MORE OF THE COSTS OF THEIR CARE

Another way to slow the growth in per capita spending by the federal government is to ask beneficiaries to pay more of the costs of their care, and this was also a feature of the Balanced Budget Act. Most observers of Medicare believe that more changes will be considered in this area over time. But it is important to recognize at the outset that if costs are merely shifted from one part of the economy to another, this does not reduce health care spending; rather, it merely changes how the burden is distributed. This may be appropriate, but it is an approach quite different from finding savings from increased efficiencies or better targeting of care.[18]

Beneficiaries are now liable for about 20 percent of the current costs of Medicare (not counting contributions in payroll taxes that fund Part A). The Part B premium, which is set at 25 percent of the costs of the physician and other ambulatory services covered by this part of the program, constitutes about 9.5 percent of the expenditures on all Medicare services. And cost sharing accounts for about another 10 percent of the bill for Medicare-covered services. The Part A deductible and coinsurance levels for hospital care ($768 and $192 respectively in 1999) are quite high as compared to private insurance. And since Medicare beneficiaries are much more likely to be hospitalized than others, these burdens are particularly large. On the Part B side, the deductible is relatively low at $100, but the 20 percent coinsurance with no upper limits (that is, "stop loss") also makes Medicare cost sharing more onerous than for most private, employer-provided insurance plans.[19]

Any new requirements on beneficiaries to help pay the costs of Medicare should recognize the already high burdens borne by the elderly and disabled. In 1996, out-of-pocket costs and premiums averaged $2,605 for all persons over sixty-five residing in the community, and the 10 percent of beneficiaries with the highest out-of-pocket costs averaged about $8,802 per capita in 1996.[20]

Consequently, the average, noninstitutionalized elderly beneficiary in fee-for-service Medicare spends about 21 percent of income on health care. And with income below 125 percent of the poverty line, he or she will spend more than 30 percent on health care. These amounts have grown over time as the costs of health care have outstripped growth in the well-being of the aged. Most older Americans continue to live on very modest incomes. Although poverty rates have come down substantially over the years for the elderly, about 40 percent of seniors living outside of institutions still have incomes below twice the poverty level.[21]

The most common proposal to require beneficiaries to pay more has been to raise the Part B premium—the strategy used by the Balanced Budget Act. Its chief advantage is that this is a straightforward option that raises substantial revenue and does not unduly affect those in poor health. The basic problem with a premium increase, however, is that it generates a disproportionate burden on those with low and moderate incomes. For example, a single woman with an income of $10,000 now devotes 5.1 percent of her income to the Part B premium. The increase in the premium passed with the budget act would keep the requirement that the premium cover 25 percent of Part B costs, while shifting some home health services that are now included in Part A to Part B, thus raising the level of the premium. By 2007, if this woman's income rises at about the same rate as expected Social Security benefit increases, the premium will consume 9.4 percent of her income.[22] This is because health spending is still expected to grow faster than the incomes of seniors and because a greater share of all Medicare expenditures will be used in calculating the premium.

This problem limits the range and magnitude of all options that ask beneficiaries to pay more. One solution is to combine such changes with enhanced protections for low-income beneficiaries to shield them from higher costs. For example, the existing Qualified Medicare Beneficiary (QMB) and Specified Low-Income Medicare Beneficiary (SLMB) programs run through Medicaid could be expanded to make people further up the income scale eligible. This was initially set as a condition of the budget agreement announced in May 1997, but the final law does not go nearly far enough to shield those with low incomes. The new low-income protections will last only for five years and are subject to an annual cap that is high enough to cover only about one-third of all those who would otherwise be eligible. Thus, although participation in the QMB and SLMB programs is currently low, limiting their success, they are still more generous than the new extension of protections in the Balanced Budget Act.[23]

Another option likely to be raised in the future is moving to an income-related premium for Part B, with higher-income persons paying a greater share of Part B costs. Tying premiums to income makes good sense on grounds of equity but may be difficult to achieve in practice. Administrative costs would likely have to rise substantially in order to establish such a system (or it could be run through the IRS, an option that is likely to be politically unpalatable).

But, most important, such approaches do not generate much in the way of new revenue. Consider, for example, the distribution of income for the elderly. Only 1.1 percent of aged singles have incomes above $75,000—an initial threshold commonly suggested for an income-related premium. Dropping that threshold to $50,000 brings the share up to only 3 percent. Such proposals usually have higher thresholds for couples, whose incomes are higher on average. But again, the cutoffs would usually include only a small number of such persons. Consequently, even large increases in the Part B premium for high-income seniors would raise only modest amounts of new revenue. There simply are not enough high-income elderly persons to enable this option to "solve" the problem, unless the threshold is moved down to a relatively low level—where it is no longer a "high-income" premium. Nonetheless, this option is likely to be part of a long-term strategy for reforming Medicare.

An alternative to raising premiums would be to treat Medicare benefits—all or in part—as income and subject to the federal personal income tax. If, for example, half of the average insurance value of benefits were added to the incomes of the elderly and disabled, these benefits would be subject to tax rates that would vary according to other income received. This would naturally result in a progressive tax on Medicare benefits, and since it would use an average insurance value, taxes would not be higher on those with health problems. This is analogous to taxing Social Security, although more complicated because these benefits are received in kind and are not traditionally viewed as income. Taxation of benefits would not only raise revenue to help fund the current program (or expansions) but also make beneficiaries more acutely aware of the "value" of Medicare benefits over time. Finally, to protect those with low incomes, taxation could be restricted to those whose incomes are above some threshold (as is now the case with Social Security).[24]

Cost-sharing changes are also sometimes advocated as a means for increasing what beneficiaries are required to pay. But such cost sharing is already very high, and this might further disadvantage those who stay in the traditional Medicare program. Further, as more and more people sign up for private plans, the effectiveness of cost sharing as an incentive to use fewer services would be blunted. A higher Part B deductible and an added home health copayment are the most likely options if cost-sharing increases were to be considered.

Some piece of a long-term solution probably will (and should) include further increases in contributions from beneficiaries beyond what was included in the Balanced Budget Act. The question is how to implement this fairly, and at what point in the process changes should be made.

VOUCHERS AND PRIVATIZATION

The most dramatic way to reduce per capita costs of health care would be to limit directly what the federal government would pay, shifting the risks of higher costs over time onto beneficiaries. Advocates of a private approach to financing health care for Medicare enrollees argue for a system of vouchers in which eligible persons would be allowed to choose their own health care plan from among an array of private options, allowing for various combinations of benefits, which could be supplemented by other resources to make up a comprehensive package. (Indeed, the conferees' report on the Balanced Budget Act makes the claim that a first step has already been taken in this direction.)[25]

While competition among plans to attract enrollees might help to lower prices, the only certain way for Medicare to reduce costs under a voucher scheme would be to fix the payment level (presumably with appropriate adjustments for beneficiaries' health status) and set its rate of growth over time at a level low enough to ensure savings to the federal government. Vouchers are not necessary in order to offer choice to beneficiaries, but they are a means of achieving predictable savings. By placing a cap on the rate of growth of the benefit, vouchers effectively shift the risk to the private insurer or to the enrollee, or both. If a plan is not successful in holding down costs and Medicare's contribution is fixed, the most likely response is to raise the premium contribution required of enrollees. Essentially this would serve as a premium increase on beneficiaries.

One serious problem with vouchers is that the market would begin to divide beneficiaries in ways that put the most vulnerable ones—those in worse health and with modest incomes—in jeopardy. If vouchers result in high-cost, "Cadillac" plans, or if other types of specialized plans like medical savings accounts skim off the healthier, wealthier beneficiaries, many Medicare enrollees who now have reasonable coverage for acute care but who are the less desirable risks would face much higher costs owing to market segmentation. A two-tier system of care could result, in which modest-income families are forced to choose plans that offer fewer benefits or substantially more restrictions.

The problem of market segmentation is likely to get worse, not better, over time without very strict oversight. Improvements in tests and screening may make it easier to know earlier and with more detail what problems people will develop as they age. A private market left on its own would almost surely discriminate against those whose tests show they have certain genetic markers or otherwise are at high risk for illnesses that are expensive to treat. Even with controls, clever marketing strategies may be employed to achieve the same result. Furthermore, individual self-interest would cause the healthier among us to look for less costly insurance. Thus, it is not just discrimination by insurance companies but also the natural inclinations of consumers that lead markets of this type to fail to serve everyone. Any move to rely on the private market carries pitfalls. And voucher plans, whose intent is often to lessen government intervention, are likely to foster such game playing.

On balance, vouchers offer less in the way of guarantees for continued protection under Medicare. The problems of making tough choices and the financial risks would be borne by beneficiaries. The federal government's role in influencing the course of our health care system would be substantially diminished. For some, this represents a major advantage of such reforms. But the history of Medicare demonstrates that the public sector has often played a positive role, first insuring those who could not find insurance coverage in the private sector and then leading the way in many cost containment efforts. But the most troubling potential for voucher schemes is that the principle of offering a standard benefit would be seriously undermined, dividing up the market into ever smaller risk pools. If privatization is carried to its ultimate extreme, Medicare could cease to be social insurance and instead become simply a publicly mandated private insurance plan. Such a strategy would not only privatize, but also "individualize" the program, reflecting an "every person for himself or herself" approach. While this is one possible vision for Medicare's future, it is certainly not a preferable one.

DEALING WITH AN AGING POPULATION

Enacting reforms to help Medicare slow its rate of growth in per capita costs is a manageable—although politically challenging—task. But after 2010, the financing challenges will loom even larger when, in addition to health care cost issues, the first of the baby-boom generation become eligible for Medicare. By 2030, under current law, Medicare will be the primary insurer for one in every four Americans. To deal with a society in which a substantially larger share of the population is older means that a broader set of policy options needs to be on the table for discussion, including an evaluation of revenue sources and changes in program eligibility. It will not be possible with the current financing structure for the program to serve all who are potentially eligible to participate. Even a slower rate of growth in spending cannot fully resolve the demographic issues. To deal with the specific implications of population increases, the policy options are essentially whether to find ways to limit the number of persons eligible or to increase the contributions that taxpayers must make. Both of these are issues of who will pay.

PUTTING BENEFICIARY GROWTH IN CONTEXT

One should not treat these demographic trends as creating insurmountable challenges. A statistic often used to discuss the magnitude of the problems facing Medicare is the ratio of workers to retirees—that is, the number of people contributing to the system compared to the number receiving benefits. In 1995, there were about 3.9 workers for every beneficiary. That number will fall steadily as the baby boomers begin to retire, to 2.2 workers per beneficiary in 2030.[26] Appropriately, many analysts point out that this substantial decline will place higher burdens on workers over time.

But there are also other, less dramatic ways to view these numbers. In 1995, 37 million people received Medicare, as compared to about 144 million workers paying into the system. This means that, on average, each 100 workers had to support the health needs of 126 workers and Medicare beneficiaries. By 2030, each 100 workers will need to support 146 workers and beneficiaries. That constitutes about a 16 percent rise, a substantial increase in the burden on workers, but one that is certainly within our abilities to absorb as a society—and one that is well below projected increases in per capita incomes over the same period.

OPTIONS FOR REDUCING THE NUMBER OF ELIGIBLES

The two major options usually suggested for reducing the numbers of persons eligible for Medicare are raising the age of eligibility or moving to a means-tested program in which eligibility is limited to those with resources below a certain level. Both have advantages and disadvantages.

One of the justifications for raising the eligibility age—aside from the primary one of saving the system money—is that the average age of retirement should increase to take into account the enhanced life expectancy of the population. Since Medicare was introduced in 1966, life expectancy for sixty-five-year-olds has grown by a little less than three years.[27] As people live longer, they receive Medicare benefits for a greater portion of their lifetimes. Increasing the age of eligibility could go partway toward restoring the worker/beneficiary ratio that obtained in 1966. In fact, such an approach has already been adopted under the Social Security amendments of 1983, which established a schedule whereby the age of eligibility for full Social Security cash benefits would increase from age sixty-five to age sixty-seven by the year 2022.

Medicare is different from Social Security, however, in that, even with Social Security's changes, early retirement will still be possible at age sixty-two. For Medicare, eligibility is all or nothing. Looking at the needs of special groups, though, suggests that savings from raising the eligibility age would be less than many people expect—probably less than 5 percent of total spending could be saved by raising the eligibility age by two years.[28] A number of those in the sixty-five to sixty-seven age group would likely remain eligible or would require special treatment in some other way. Those who were previously eligible because of disability would be unlikely to be dropped from the rolls. The costs of the dually eligible who also receive Medicaid would be fully shifted to that program, with important consequences for federal spending. In this case, spending burdens would simply be moved to a different program.

Raising the age of eligibility for Medicare would create problems. Not all Americans are equally healthy at age sixty-five. While some remain in the labor force or have generous retiree benefits at that age, others struggle to make it to the time when they can qualify for Medicare. As yet, increasing life expectancy has not in practice been translated into later retirement by workers. To make the policy option of postponing eligibility less burdensome on individuals who would be out of the labor force before becoming eligible for Medicare, reform to ensure access to the purchase of affordable private insurance would be critical—reform that has proved difficult to implement for the under sixty-five population. Without such reform, those with health problems might find it difficult to obtain insurance at any price. This is currently a problem for many persons in their early sixties.

Alternatively, Medicare could allow individuals between ages sixty or sixty-two and age sixty-eight to buy into Medicare. This would be analogous to the early retirement option under Social Security available at age sixty-two. Medicare would be available for those who must retire early. If this were combined with some low-income protections and phased in slowly, the objections of critics could be effectively answered. But such a feature would be expensive and would further reduce savings to the program.

Another possible (and dramatic) change would be to means-test Medicare fully, that is, make it available only to persons whose resources are below some prescribed limit. Higher-income elderly and disabled persons could be offered the option of buying into the system at a nonsubsidized rate or could be precluded from participating altogether.

While financing for Medicare technically is based on a flat payroll tax and hence is criticized as being too high on modest-income workers, figuring in the distribution of benefits measured against contributions makes the program appear more equitable. For example, contributions from a salaried individual making $100,000 per year total $2,900, as compared to the $580 put in for a worker earning $20,000 per year—both for the same benefit package. It is not hard to conclude that eliminating high-income earners from eligibility could undermine some of the strong political support that Medicare has traditionally enjoyed. It would eliminate the image of Medicare as a program where everyone pays but everyone also benefits. It would constitute a major shift in the philosophy of Medicare from a universal to a "welfare"-based program.

A major, practical concern with this proposal is where the cutoff for eliminating the federal subsidy should be set. At what income is an elderly person capable of footing the bill for the full costs of Medicare? The Medicare premium for both Parts A and B totaled $5,754 in 1997. Other out-of-pocket spending and premiums for private insurance to cover gaps would average in excess of $1,500. Together the bill for more than $7,200 would consume a substantial share of the income of most enrollees. Per capita income for the average elderly person stands at about $12,000.[29] Certainly, at least half of the elderly, and likely many more, would thus not be good candidates for paying for all of their own care.

If policy were set so that the average expenditures on health care should not total more than 15 percent of an individual's income, the cutoff for eligibility for Medicare would be set at more than $48,000. This would mean that very few elderly persons would be excluded from the program. In 1995, only 3.4 percent of Medicare beneficiaries had per capita incomes exceeding $50,000.[30] To get a higher share of the population excluded from the program via means testing (and hence generate more savings), the cutoff would need to begin at much lower incomes, where such restrictions would generate substantial hardships.

Finally, if more people must rely on the private sector for insurance, the same types of problems will arise as were considered in the discussion of vouchers. This is not a minor issue. A substantial percentage of persons aged sixty-five and sixty-six currently would be unable to buy insurance in the private market. Health care problems often render people "uninsurable" in the eyes of a market seeking to maximize profits. The easiest way for insurers to keep costs low is to provide insurance only to those who are least likely to need health care. Substantial consumer protections to ensure that insurance is available, or that those who lose eligibility for Medicare retain the ability to buy into the program, are essential. Rather than splitting up the risk pool that now successfully serves nearly all persons over sixty-five, it may be desirable to address demographic concerns in other ways, most likely through a combination of higher contributions by beneficiaries and new revenues designated to support the program.

ASKING TAXPAYERS TO INCREASE SUPPORT FOR MEDICARE

In addition to asking beneficiaries to bear more of the costs of their care, new revenues affecting all taxpayers will be needed to finance the Medicare program over time. It is not reasonable to require a program that gradually doubles the share of the population it serves to do so with the same tax base as before. In fact, efforts to hold the line on Medicare spending ought to be considered very successful if real per capita spending can be stabilized through a combination of reforms in the efficiency of service delivery and higher beneficiary contributions. That would still leave the need to expand the tax base that supports the program as the baby-boom generation begins to retire.

Legitimately, many policymakers have raised concerns about the level of the payroll tax. But Medicare could be supported with other revenues or a small payroll tax increase plus other revenues. The right mix depends upon how, as a society, we decide to share these burdens. Moreover, the proper balance of beneficiary and taxpayer obligations needs to be weighed in the context of combined Social Security and Medicare reform. If changes in Social Security can be done within the existing tax framework, that leaves more room for modest increases in revenues to support Medicare. If Social Security benefits are substantially reduced, though, beneficiaries will be less able to afford premium or other increases in their Medicare contributions. And if payroll taxes are raised for Social Security, it will be difficult to do so to help support Medicare as well.

OTHER ISSUES FOR HEALTH POLICY
AND THE ELDERLY

Thus far, this discussion has focused on ways to limit spending on and increase revenues for Medicare in order to keep the program viable and yet make it more affordable in the context of the demands of an aging society. Will there be room for other spending on behalf of the elderly and other groups? How will changes in Medicare and Medicaid affect the rest of society? At this point, these issues are barely on the radar screen of public discourse, but they should be given thorough consideration as well.

LONG-TERM CARE AND OTHER UNMET NEEDS

One of the most important—and most disliked—public programs aiding older Americans is Medicaid's long-term care benefit. To obtain coverage, a person must have already faced financial disaster, depleting most assets and income. Only then will Medicaid help. Because the program is structured around certifiable desperation, many Americans seek ways around the rules, adding to dissatisfaction with the program because of a perceived lack of fairness in its application. Many states have opted to have their medical programs provide inadequate care for those who remain at home. For these and other reasons, improvements in long-term care protection have long been at the top of the wish list of many elderly advocacy groups. But expanding benefits further to those over age sixty-five in the face of other demands is a tough sell and likely to become even harder as the numbers of the very old increase.

Can long-term care insurance be expected to fill in the gaps? The problem for the private sector is to guess at what costs and needs will be in twenty years. Insurance companies face the dilemma of either pricing conservatively and thus discouraging sales, or canceling policies later if costs rise faster than anticipated. If policies do not sufficiently keep up with the costs of long-term care, they may not protect even those who do buy insurance. Already anecdotal evidence is beginning to show that people who have insurance cannot afford the cost sharing and extra costs beyond what the insurance is offering. For these and other reasons, many Americans have hesitated to buy policies. Consequently, it seems unlikely that long-term care insurance will expand sufficiently to satisfy the unmet need, even with recent changes in tax policy intended to stimulate sales.[31]

Improved public programs to deal with long-term care will be feasible only if the current costs of Medicare and its projected expenditures can be brought under better control. Only then will politicians be willing to consider substantive upgrades. In the meantime, it may be possible to achieve modest improvements within the context of Medicaid, particularly if less expensive forms of long-term care and better coordination of acute and long-term care services can be accomplished. If Medicaid is successful in this, limited expansions in coverage might be viewed as permissible without breaking the bank.

IMPACTS ON THE REST OF HEALTH CARE

Another major issue is the size of the Medicare and Medicaid programs relative to the rest of the health care system in the United States. Health care costs for elders are, and likely will continue to be, substantially higher than those faced by younger persons. Right now the parts of Medicare and Medicaid that go for health care for the elderly total about 21 percent of health care spending. If out-of-pocket and private supplemental insurance expenses are added, the share for looking after the elderly rises to more than one-third of all health care spending. Imagine what is in store once all members of the baby boom pass the age of sixty-five: at that stage, persons over the traditional retirement age will represent one in every five Americans. Spending on the elderly in these two programs could very well top half of all health care outlays. This means that the government potentially has enormous leverage and could influence the whole health care delivery system even beyond what has already occurred. The private sector, which is now seeking to preclude any cross-subsidization of the major government programs even while seeking deep discounts from hospitals, doctors, and other health care providers, may feel threatened. This could create unhealthy competition to shift costs between the public and private sectors rather than cooperation to find viable solutions to the problem of rising health costs.

On the other hand, if reforms of Medicare and Medicaid were done well, they could serve as a model for the rest of the health care system. But this will occur only if policymakers use opportunities to strengthen the public programs rather than just cut them. Two areas that need to be managed well if these programs are to serve their intended populations effectively are: 1) finding the right balance between preserving program integrity and offering a reasonable choice of plans and adequate protection for beneficiaries, and 2) finding better ways to protect and reassure consumers regarding the quality of care they receive. If Medicare offers a full choice of plans to beneficiaries, it could set an example as an individually based system of managed competition; if not done well, it could result in fragmentation of the risk pool and a failure to provide for the most vulnerable. The evidence on how well Medicare can do in managing private plans is not very encouraging at the moment, but no one involved in the program can roll back the clock and ignore the developments that have changed the way health care is delivered. For the elderly and disabled, Medicaid reforms will need to occur only after Medicare's changes are adopted if the two programs are to work well together. In the meantime, improvements in the efficiency and coordination of long-term care services should be a high priority for Medicaid. The future will depend upon how judiciously Americans move to reform and revise Medicare and Medicaid.

3

LONG-TERM CARE: COMING OF AGE IN THE TWENTY-FIRST CENTURY

Robyn Stone

INTRODUCTION

Long-term care is a policy issue that emerged as a major public concern over the past three decades and that promises to be a significant challenge for the United States and the world in the next century. In 1995, approximately 13 million Americans of all ages were reported to require some level of long-term care, but this figure belies the much larger number of relatives, friends, and others who were faced with similar care decisions. It is known, for example, that 95 percent of disabled elderly living in the community receive unpaid assistance from family members and other "informal caregivers"; almost two-thirds rely exclusively on unpaid help, primarily wives and daughters.[1] Many more relatives provide indirect help, including arranging for long-distance care and even providing unpaid assistance to disabled elders living in nursing homes.

These estimates, however, pale in comparison to the demand for long-term care expected with the aging of the baby boomers. Between now and the year 2040 the elderly population in the United States will more than double; for the first time in history, one out of five Americans—77 million people—

49

will be sixty-five years or older. What is even more dramatic is the tripling of the eighty-five and over population, with an estimated 14 million "oldest old" living in the United States in 2040.[2] Even if recent projections of declines in disability rates among the elderly are borne out over time,[3] the sheer volume of very elderly individuals, who are the most likely to be chronically disabled, will undoubtedly increase the demand for long-term care.

At the same time, there is likely to be a smaller pool of family care-givers—adult daughters in particular—available to provide the bulk of the informal long-term care. As more women enter and remain in the labor force, have children later in life, and find their adult children in their twenties and thirties returning to the nest, competing demands on their attention are like-ly to put a substantial strain on the mainstay of the long-term care system.

Given this demographic imperative, the major issues to be addressed are how to design and implement a system of long-term care that best meets the needs of the elderly and their families and how to pay for such a system. The questions are not new; in fact, they have been on the policy agenda for the past thirty years without successful resolution. The aging of the baby boomers, however, will raise the stakes of the debate and place a premium on solutions that society has heretofore been able to push off to the next generation.

This chapter will present a brief history, evaluating the current status of long-term care in the United States and highlighting the implications of selected demographic and policy trends for the financing and delivery of long-term care in the future. It then examines the diverse characteristics of the long-term care population. This is followed by a discussion of the state of domestic long-term care financing and delivery and a summary of the emerging policy alternatives. The chapter concludes with some reflections on possible directions for long-term care policy and practice and a set of prescriptions for the design of an "ideal" system.

WHAT IS LONG-TERM CARE?

Long-term care encompasses a broad range of services needed by individuals with a chronic illness or other disabling condition over a prolonged period of time. Long-term care needs are highly correlated to, but not synonymous with, medical conditions such as arthritis, paraplegia, diabetes, dementia, traumatic brain injury, or chronic mental illness. These services focus pri-marily on supportive functions that provide assistance with daily activities in order to rehabilitate, or to minimize or compensate for loss of independent functioning (physical and/or mental) owing to an underlying condition or disability. The repertoire of services includes assistance with basic activities of daily living (ADLs) such as bathing, dressing, eating, or other types of personal care and instrumental activities of daily living (IADLs) further categorized as (a) household chores, such as meal preparation and cleaning; (b) life management, such as shopping, money management, and medication management; and (c) transportation.

While primarily low-tech, long-term care can also respond to the need for high-tech medical interventions such as intravenous drug therapy, ventilator assistance, and wound care. Long-term care can be provided by unpaid family members or friends (informal caregivers) or by specially trained and licensed professionals and paraprofessionals (formal caregivers).[4] Services can involve hands-on and standby or supervisory human assistance as well as the use of assistive devices and technology.

Long-term care is provided in a range of settings, depending on the needs of the individual, the availability of informal support, and the source of reimbursement. At the most restrictive end of the continuum is the nursing facility or nursing home, where both skilled and unskilled custodial care are provided as well as room and board. Home and community-based care is a catchall phrase that refers to a wide variety of noninstitutional long-term care options. Residential care (for example, board-and-care homes, assisted living facilities, adult foster homes) falls within this category, although the boundaries between institutional and noninstitutional settings are far from clear-cut. In the ideal, residential care, which combines room and board with some level of protective oversight and care, is viewed as an option for individuals who may not require nursing home-level assistance but who are no longer able to remain in their own homes. Other home and community-based care settings include adult day care and one's own home. Within the home setting, care is further differentiated between *home health care*, which includes some level of skilled nursing and supervised custodial care, and *home care*, which typically includes personal care services (bathing, dressing, toileting) and homemaker chore services such as meal preparation and laundry.

A Brief History of Long-term Care Policy

Before the advent of Medicare and Medicaid, public long-term care was, for the most part, available to charity cases living in almshouses, on poor farms, or in homes for the aged, and to some lucky few living in the community who received care from visiting nurses. The 1960s ushered in a new era of long-term care. Medicare provided limited, postacute skilled nursing in nursing homes and short-term home health benefits for qualified elderly and disabled beneficiaries. In contrast, Medicaid, the federal/state program of health care for the poor, provided coverage for more long-term, custodial care to financially eligible elderly and disabled nursing home residents.

During the 1970s, the old adage "services follow the dollars" became a reality with the development of a very sophisticated and powerful nursing home industry. The 1980s and early 1990s witnessed tremendous growth in home care, catalyzed by a loosening of the Medicare regulations and definitions of coverage. In 1995, approximately $106.5 billion was spent on long-term care, with 57.4 percent financed publicly through Medicaid, Medicare, and other state and local funds.[5] Despite the growth of the formal sector, however, informal caregivers have remained the dominant providers of long-term care, with 90 percent of America's long-term care beneficiaries receiving some form of support from, and two-thirds depending exclusively on, family and friends for their long-term care services.[6]

As long-term care became more formally recognized, many consumer advocates, particularly those focused on the personal care, custodial, and supportive functions of these services, expressed increasing concern about the overmedicalization of long-term care. In the 1970s and early 1980s there was a strong movement toward a social model of care, emphasizing the need to ensure that long-term care services not be controlled by hospitals, physicians, and other health professionals. It was argued that long-term care consisted primarily of services outside the traditional health care system and that providing such care within the medical framework would be inappropriate, costly, and perhaps iatrogenic. Furthermore, the medical model failed to recognize the central role of the family and the importance of attending to the needs of the informal caregivers as well as the care recipient. The bifurcation of acute and long-term care into medical and social paradigms was reinforced by a system of governmental and nonprofit agencies that developed at the state and local levels to meet the nonmedical, human services needs of the elderly. As part of this development of state units on aging, area agencies on aging, senior citizen centers, and other organizations, a new industry of managers, primarily social workers and socially oriented nurses, emerged to coordinate home and community-based services.

By the late 1990s, some began to question whether the pendulum had swung too far in the direction of the social model of long-term care.

Most people with long-term care needs have chronic conditions that require a range of medical and social interventions. The dichotomy between the health care and long-term care systems, further exacerbated by fragmentation of the sources of funding, is now seen as an impediment to quality management of care. The boundaries between acute, subacute, postacute, and long-term care have become very fuzzy, as changing financial incentives and the continual metamorphoses of delivery systems (for example, managed care, provider service organizations) have shifted people who need considerable attention to presumably less costly settings, typically from hospitals to nursing homes or home care.

As the twenty-first century approaches, we have come full circle in terms of recognizing that acute and long-term care needs are inextricably tied. Policymakers and practitioners are experimenting with integrated approaches to providing care to people with chronic illness and disability. In order to achieve such integration, some have argued that the dollars must follow the person rather than being tied to one setting or service approach. While intuitively appealing, achieving such a goal, as will be discussed later in this chapter, depends on the streamlining of funding sources as well as major restructuring of care delivery and radically different training of the workforce.

WHO NEEDS AND USES LONG-TERM CARE?

The long-term care population is diverse in terms of age and the scope and degree of disabling condition. Of the estimated 12.8 million Americans reporting long-term care needs in 1995, 57 percent were over the age of sixty-five. Another two out of five were working-age adults, and 3 percent were children.[7] The prevalence of functional limitations increases substantially with age. Among the 229 million Americans under the age of sixty-five, only 0.1 percent were institutional residents, and 2 percent were living in the community with limitations in terms of either ADLs or IADLs. [8] In contrast, among the 34 million elderly in 1995, 5 percent—1.7 million people age sixty-five or over—were nursing home residents and 12 percent—4 million people—were living in the community with defined limitations. The prevalence rate is significantly higher for the oldest old. Among those age eighty-five and over, for example, 21 percent were in nursing homes in 1995, and another 49 percent were community residents with long-term care needs.[9]

Preliminary analyses comparing samples of elderly nursing home residents from the 1987 National Medical Expenditures Survey and the 1996 Medical Expenditure Panel Study[10] suggest some important changes in the characteristics of this population over the ten-year period. The population in 1996 is significantly older, with the proportion of those eighty-five and older increasing from 43.5 percent in 1987 to 49.3 percent. Nursing home residents are also more likely to be married, with that proportion increasing from 13.3 percent in 1987 to 16.7 percent in 1996. The institutionalized elderly in 1996 tend to be more severely disabled than those in the 1987 sample: the proportion with five ADL limitations was up from one in three to more than one in two. In addition, the nursing home population appears to be more cognitively impaired, with a much lower proportion of those surveyed in 1996 recognizing staff and a much higher proportion having difficulty making decisions.

Approximately 81 percent of the elderly with specific impairments live in the community, and these tend to be much less disabled than those in nursing homes.[11] Three out of five are disabled only in IADLs and approximately 17 percent are considered severely disabled with limitations in three or more ADLs. According to recent, unpublished data from the 1994 National Long-Term Care Survey (NLTCS),[12] more than one in three (37 percent) of functionally impaired elderly living in the community report some level of unmet need (needing but not receiving help) or undermet need (need more help than currently receiving). The vast majority of this group are people with unmet needs in the areas of meal preparation, outdoor mobility, and money management. Only 1.4 percent report unmet needs and another 13.1 percent report undermet needs in the ADL category. Comparative analyses of previous waves of the NLTCS indicate a decline in the proportion of disabled elderly reporting unmet ADL needs from 5.2 percent in 1984 to 2.6 percent in 1989 to 1.4 percent in 1994.

While preliminary, these findings are intriguing because they suggest that most elderly with long-term care needs believe those needs are being sufficiently addressed. It is important to remember, however, that most of the care is being provided "free" by family and friends, and that future declines in the availability of caregivers may contribute to an increase in perceived unmet need. This research also raises some interesting possibilities for channeling resources more effectively and efficiently to the community-dwelling, disabled elderly population with unmet or undermet needs. For example, would it be possible for publicly funded home and community-based care programs to build unmet and undermet need into their eligibility criteria? If assessment tools could be developed, it would help state and local governments to channel resources first to those with the most need.

WHO PAYS THE LONG-TERM BILL?

As noted, the vast majority of long-term care is provided "for free" by unpaid, informal caregivers, primarily family and friends. In fact, 5.4 percent of disabled elderly living in the community receive only formal, paid care.[13] The importance of having an informal support system is underscored by the fact that 50 percent of the elderly with long-term care needs and no family network are in nursing homes compared to only 7 percent of those who have access to family caregivers.[14]

While a cross-sectional view of the elderly indicates that a minority are in need of long-term care services at any one point in time, the risk of having to resort to such services after age sixty-five is substantially higher. The proportion of elderly likely to use nursing homes ranges from 39 percent to 49 percent depending on the database; estimates of those living at least two years in a nursing home after age sixty-five range from 16 percent to one in four.[15] One recent simulation model[16] found that elderly persons are more likely to use home care than nursing home care over their remaining lifetimes (72 percent versus 49 percent). The average nursing home use over a lifetime is one year, and the average home care use is a little more than two hundred visits. It is important to note that many users receive care for only short periods of time, while a small proportion requires substantial amounts of long-term care services.

Long-term care costs make up a relatively small but growing proportion of personal health care expenditures, increasing from less than 4 percent in 1960 to more than 11 percent in 1993.[17] The financing of long-term care services is a patchwork of public (federal, state, and local) funds and private dollars, primarily out-of-pocket spending. It should be cautioned that the estimated $106 billion reported as spent on long-term care in the United States in 1995 does not include monetization of the vast amount of informal care provided, including the opportunity costs of forgone wages.[18] Public resources accounted for 57.4 percent of reported long-term care expenditures, with Medicaid being the largest payer (21.1 percent federal and 16.7 percent state dollars) followed by Medicare (17.8 percent) and other federal and state funds (for example, from the

Department of Veterans Affairs, the Older Americans Act, the federal social services block grant, state general assistance). Private insurance accounted for only 5.5 percent of the expenditures, while one out of three dollars was attributable to out-of-pocket expenses.

MEDICAID

Medicaid, the federal/state health insurance program for the poor, is the major public program covering long-term care for the elderly and nonelderly disabled. Despite the public's tremendous interest in and demand for home care, Medicaid continues to exhibit a strong institutional bias; of the almost $50 billion Medicaid spent on long-term care services in 1995, $40 billion supported nursing homes and institutions for the mentally retarded, with the remaining $9.9 billion paying for home and community-based care. There has, however, been tremendous growth in the home and community-based care sector; while total Medicaid long-term care spending increased by 8.6 percent between 1993 and 1994, non-institutional spending grew by 26 percent.

It is important to recognize that while concerns have been raised about devolution of authority for acute health care from the federal government to the states, this is not as much of a concern with respect to long-term care. States have always been the major public vehicle for long-term care policy, and there is tremendous inter- as well as intrastate variation in policies and programs. Montana had the highest Medicaid nursing home expenditures per capita in 1994, while Arizona ranked lowest. Arizona also had the lowest per capita expenditures for home and community-based care, while New York's spending ranked highest.[19] In fact, 35 percent of all Medicaid spending on home care in the United States in 1995 occurred in New York.[20]

While the institutional bias prevails in most states, there has been significant movement to level the playing field between nursing home placement and home and community-based care options. In 1994, forty-five states regulated the growth of new nursing home beds with certificate-of-need requirements and other mechanisms.[21] Several states, most notably Oregon and Washington, have explicitly recognized nursing homes as the setting of last resort and have intentionally reduced the number of nursing home beds. In Oregon, for example, the ratio declined from forty-seven per thousand elderly in 1982 to thirty-five per thousand in 1995. With an aggressive home and community-based care policy since the early 1980s, the state has successfully placed many seriously disabled elders and younger disabled as well in alternative assisted-living facilities and adult foster homes. Oregon also has a strong case management program, which allows many disabled beneficiaries to remain in their own homes.

In addition to the federal Medicaid dollars that states match and the relatively modest sums available for personal care services through the Older Americans Act and the social services block grant, many states augment the spending from Washington or create their own separate programs with state funds. Pennsylvania and New Jersey, for example, have relatively large state home and community-based care programs that are supported in large part with lottery revenues. A number of local communities also have been successful in raising funds for long-term care services. Hamilton County, Ohio (the Cincinnati area), supports its disabled elderly through a county levy that the local area agency on aging was successful in getting legislated several years ago.[22] In 1997, the agency's Elderly Services Program was spending $17 million for homemaker services, personal care, home-delivered meals, case management, adult day care, and transportation for its frail elderly living in eighty-eight neighborhoods throughout Hamilton County. The agency in this locale was successful in convincing citizens—elderly and nonelderly—that a levy for long-term care services was necessary, given continuing cutbacks in federal funds, and that the dollars would benefit the entire community.

MEDICARE

Medicare has generally not been a major payer in coverage of long-term care. Many have argued that one of the reasons the elderly have not prepared themselves for long-term care expenses is that they believe Medicare will cover those costs. Medicare covers primarily acute care costs, with skilled nursing facility and home health care benefits intended as short-term coverage to meet the post-acute care needs of beneficiaries following a hospital episode. However, the popular notion that Medicare covers long-term care has more validity now than in the past. Through a series of regulatory and administrative changes since 1989, Medicare has come to support more long-term, nonskilled personal care.[23]

Medicare spending for home health services increased nearly tenfold between 1987 and 1995.[24] A combination of a lawsuit and administrative changes in 1989 led to a slackening of denial rates and looser interpretations of both definitions (like "homebound") and benefits (for example, management and evaluation) by fiscal intermediaries. Most of the growth came in the form of an increase in the number of visits, particularly home health aide visits—the low-tech, personal care type of services usually regarded as long-term care. It is estimated that visits per person served represented 49 percent of the growth in Medicare's home health spending between 1990 and 1996.[25] Furthermore, the 10 percent of the Medicare home health users with more than two hundred visits in 1994 were responsible for 43 percent of the program's spending on home health care in that year. The length of the typical home health care episode has increased substantially, with a small but growing proportion of users receiving continuous care for two years or more. Recent research has found that these beneficiaries tend to be more disabled than those with shorter, postacute episodes and to be receiving more unskilled home health aide visits.[26] These findings support the concern expressed by some policymakers that a small but relatively expensive subpopulation of Medicare home health users are inappropriately receiving traditional long-term care through the program.

There is also some evidence to suggest that states are substituting Medicare for Medicaid in order to reduce state costs for long-term care.[27] In Mississippi and Tennessee, total Medicare spending on home health care in 1995 was, respectively, thirty-one times and thirty-six times higher than Medicaid spending on home and community-based care. In contrast, in New York, the most generous state for Medicaid personal care in the country, Medicare spending on home care was only a quarter of similar Medicaid spending. This state "Medicare maximization" behavior was substantiated through a series of case studies in which the state officials interviewed acknowledged that there was budgetary pressure to help elderly Medicaid clients become eligible for Medicare home health benefits.[28]

Congress and the Clinton administration have responded to the tremendous growth in the Medicare home health benefit by enacting provisions in the Balanced Budget Act of 1997 that significantly reduce payments to home health agencies, implement a new prospective payment system of reimbursement as of 1999, and crack down on fraud and abuse. Given these changes, it remains to be seen how much state substitution of Medicare for Medicaid will occur in the future.

The other Medicare growth area where the lines between acute and long-term care have become fuzzy is subacute care. There is no consensus about the definition of subacute care, although it is described by proponents as a set of intensive and coordinated treatments and services provided to postacute care patients for the purpose of minimizing or even bypassing expensive hospital stays. Whether subacute care is an innovative service delivery mechanism or a marketing strategy by sophisticated providers to repackage long-standing postacute care services (for example, a skilled nursing facility, rehabilitation facility, or home health service) is a subject of much discussion.[29] Subacute care may refer to certain types of services (rehabilitation),[30] patients (for example, those who no longer require acute services),[31] or levels of care (classified as between acute hospital care and skilled nursing care).[32]

The use of Medicare nursing facilities increased substantially between 1990 and 1993, up from twenty-two per thousand beneficiaries to thirty-one per thousand beneficiaries.[33] Gage and colleagues found that increases in Medicare expenditures for these services were attributable in part to administrative and legislative changes and in part to the provision of subacute care services for more medically complex cases in nonacute care settings.[34] The question remains whether subacute care is, as Manard and others concluded after a series of case studies, "old wine in new bottles."[35]

PRIVATE, LONG-TERM CARE INSURANCE

Private, long-term care insurance finances only a small proportion of the long-term care bill; in 1995, private insurance covered less than 6 percent of nursing home and home care costs.[36] The market has grown over the past decade, with the number of policies sold increasing from 800,000 in 1987 to 4.3 million in 1995. A 1995 Health Insurance Association of America survey indicated that the number of companies has fluctuated somewhat over the years, with 121 insurers selling long-term care insurance in 1994.[37] The vast majority of these products are individual policies; approximately 12 percent of the policies sold in 1994 were employer-sponsored and another 8 percent included long-term care as part of a life insurance policy.[38] The small group market is primarily employee-paid, voluntary coverage with level premiums and no employer contributions.

Controversy surrounding private long-term care insurance has raged over the past decade, with the corporate sector arguing that public programs will never be able to meet the demand and consumers and regulators expressing concern about affordability and fraudulent marketing practices. It is somewhat of an academic debate to argue over what proportion of income or assets people will or should be willing to spend for long-term care insurance.[39] One estimate suggests that a single person should have at least $40,000 in liquid assets to consider purchasing insurance.[40] A recent *Consumer Reports* article on long-term care[41] suggests that only about 10 to 20 percent of the elderly can afford insurance and notes that premiums for two "adequate" policies bought at age sixty-five total $3,500 per year or 13 percent of the median annual income for elderly married couples. Given the uncertainties about the risks of needing long-term care and the generally lengthy period between purchase and claim, questions about the optimal age of purchaser, scope and nature of coverage, and inclusion of inflation and nonforfeiture protections will continue to remain the subject of intense discussion and disagreement among insurers, regulators, and consumer advocates.

One interesting experiment in combining public and private policies is the Partnership for Long-term Care, a demonstration program sponsored by the Robert Wood Johnson Foundation to promote the development of private funding sources for long-term care.[42] The Partnership, implemented in four states—California, Connecticut, Indiana, and New York—uses private insurance to cover the initial costs of long-term care, with Medicaid paying for services after the private insurance coverage is exhausted.[43] Two models have been developed: a Dollar-for-Dollar Disregard model in California, Connecticut, and Indiana, and a Total Asset Disregard model in New York. In the first model, consumers purchase an amount of private insurance coverage equal to the amount of assets they wish to protect. When the private benefits are exhausted, the amount of private insurance that was paid out for qualified services is disregarded in determining eligibility for Medicaid. The New York model requires that consumers purchase three years of private nursing home or six years of home care coverage, and all of the insured's assets are protected once the private benefits have been exhausted.

One of the major limitations in evaluating private, long-term care insurance (as holds true for the development of the market itself) is the frequently significant lag time between the purchase of a policy and a claim. Consequently, the Partnership demonstration has yet to supply empirical evidence as to the successes or failures of the project. Recent research, however, provides interesting information on the purchasers of these products.[44] Partnership purchasers were older, had smaller families, and were much more highly educated than the comparison sample of individuals age fifty-five to seventy-five who were not covered by Medicaid. They were more likely to be female, white, in reportedly good or excellent health, and in a relatively high-income bracket. The Partnership sample was also more inclined than the comparison group to disagree with the statement

"Medicare currently provides sufficient coverage for long-term care" and much less prepared to believe that government will pay for long-term care if needed in the future. This study identified the Partnership purchasers as a self-reliant group, in which decisions to purchase were based on maintaining independence and preserving income and choice rather than the desire to leave an inheritance.

EMERGING TRENDS IN LONG-TERM CARE

At the outset of the twenty-first century, policymakers, practitioners, and consumers recognize the dual—and sometimes conflicting—needs to rein in long-term care costs while maintaining and even improving quality of care. These two objectives have led to the emergence of several trends in the financing and delivery of long-term care that have important implications for the new millennium, when the aging of the baby boomers will probably increase the demand for a broad array of long-term care services.

MANAGED CARE

Managed care has become one of the buzzwords of the 1990s, characterized as either the panacea for this country's exploding health care costs or the nemesis of quality care for the chronically disabled.[45] While definitions vary, the major dimensions of managed care generally include (1) some form of capitation payment to plans or systems of providers; (2) the assumption of full or partial risk by the plans or providers; and (3) a gatekeeping mechanism to assure the delivery of the most efficient and appropriate type and level of care. Managed care has been sold as a way to save money for plans, consumers, and payers, but the exponential growth of proprietary health plans with profits and shareholder obligations as the bottom line has raised serious concerns about the extent to which quality of care has been traded off in the name of cost savings.

While off to a somewhat slow start, Medicare managed care now covers approximately 14 percent of the beneficiaries.[46] There is evidence, however, that plans have been "cherry-picking" healthy elderly, with one study reporting that this kind of selection resulted in the Health Care Financing Administration (HCFA) paying almost 6 percent more for Medicare HMO enrollees than if they had remained in fee-for-service plans.[47] Given that they favor a healthier than average population, it is not surprising that most managed care plans have not covered long-term care. In addition to their belief that the capitation payments are not sufficient to cover the costs of long-term care, most plans and provider networks do not have the trained workforce to offer long-term care.

There are, however, a number of initiatives at the federal, state, and provider levels in various stages of development to manage long-term care and integrate acute and long-term care services. While most are in their embryonic stages, they do promise help in addressing the financing and delivery concerns of an aging population.

INTEGRATION OF ACUTE AND LONG-TERM CARE SERVICES

While there is no general agreement on how integration of acute care and long-term care should proceed, retention of the following elements is critical:

◆   broad and flexible benefits for all types of care;

◆   far-reaching delivery systems that have the capacity and experience to go beyond traditional HMOs to community-based long-term care, case management, and specialty providers;

◆   mechanisms for actually integrating care (such as care planning protocols that would assist physicians and other providers in tailoring a set of services to each individual across a range of settings from the hospital to one's own home; interdisciplinary care teams including physicians, nurses, therapists, and social workers; centralized patient records);

◆   overarching quality systems with a single point of accountability; and

◆   integrated financing with flexible funding and the incentives to align payers and eliminate cost shifting.[48]

Despite the rhetoric of integration, the dearth of experimentation in this area is not surprising. One of the primary barriers to integration of acute and long-term care is the fragmentation of funding sources, particularly Medicare and Medicaid. Since most acute care is covered by Medicare and most long-term care is covered by Medicaid, it is difficult to coordinate services because the programs have different coverage rules and opportunities for flexibility. Furthermore, since the federal government is responsible for Medicare and the states are responsible for Medicaid long-term care, this impedes the ability of state programming to develop integrated programs for their long-term care populations.

A second is concern about financial risk and fear on the part of plans and providers about the special challenges of trying to integrate acute and long-term care for high-risk, high-cost people. There is no valid and reliable risk adjustment methodology or other technique to ensure that payments are adequate to cover the costs of providing care to people with chronic illness and disability.

Perhaps the most overlooked barrier is the lack of knowledge, information, and training needed by health and long-term care providers to offer, coordinate, and manage this array of services. There is no recognized authority in our current health care system for managing care across time, place, and profession, and little acknowledgment that individuals with chronic disabilities move back and forth between physicians, hospitals, nursing homes, and their own homes.

Most of the research on integration of acute and long-term care has been conducted through several federal demonstration projects. The Social HMO (SHMO), ongoing since 1985, adds community care services and short-term nursing home care to a Medicare-HMO acute care plan. The program focuses on providing a broad cross section of the Medicare-eligible population with acute care and *limited*, community-based long-term care coverage. The Program of All Inclusive Care for the Elderly (PACE) represents a public approach to providing long-term care to frail elders who are Medicaid eligible and nursing home certifiable. The distinguishing features of PACE are pooled Medicare and Medicaid funding and providers who assume full financial risk by accepting one lump-sum payment for each participant; integrated delivery of acute and long-term care services with adult day care as the focal point; case management through interdisciplinary care teams (from the physician to the van driver); and an aggressive attempt to keep individuals out of nursing homes using community-based care alternatives.[49]

To date, findings from the demonstrations have been equivocal at best,[50] and not very enlightening despite the long history of these projects. Researchers have, for example, pointed to the failure of the SHMOs to actually integrate care among acute and long-term care providers. Gruenberg and colleagues found that in comparing PACE enrollee costs with those of a national sample of fee-for-service Medicare beneficiaries, the PACE program provides Medicare with a 9 to 34 percent saving depending on the analytical assumptions and sites selected.[51] Shen has shown that inpatient hospital utilization rates for frail, elderly PACE enrollees are much lower than those for a comparably frail population outside the program.[52] Others, however, have referred to PACE as a "boutique" model that has tended to serve an average of just two hundred clients per site and that may have engaged in client "skimming."[53]

At the same time, these models are intuitively appealing and have helped shed light on better ways to coordinate care across a broad range of services and systems. The Balanced Budget Act of 1997 makes PACE a permanent Medicare provider, and many state officials, often without much empirical evidence in hand, have expressed the desire to create PACE-like systems in their communities. HCFA is currently supporting a second generation of SHMOs designed to improve on the first-generation models.[54] Rather than minimizing the possibility of getting a "sicker than average" enrollee population by establishing enrollment categories by disability level from least to most severe, the new models will establish reimbursement rates based on an individual's impairment and illness profile at the time of enrollment and annually thereafter. In addition, the new generation will establish state-of-the-art geriatric health programs that apply to all enrollees, not just those with long-term care needs. This demonstration will focus on coordinating acute care with a set of flexible, user-friendly, efficient long-term care services.

The EverCare model of managed care for nursing home residents, originally operated as a subsidiary of the United Health Care Corporation, also shows promise for an integrated approach to serving the most disabled and expensive long-term care population. Through Medicare and Medicaid waivers, HCFA is currently testing this model in nine sites. Teams of geriatricians and nurse practitioners provide more intensive primary care services to nursing home residents than is the norm and also serve as liaisons with long-term care providers in the institutional setting.

Motivated by escalating Medicaid budgets and growing numbers of aged, blind, and disabled enrollees, many states have expressed interest in the integration of acute and long-term care. They are particularly concerned about their "dual-eligible" population—those eligible for Medicare and Medicaid who account for about 17 percent of the state Medicaid enrollees and 30 to 35 percent of program expenditures.[55] While nineteen states had some type of integration initiative as of 1995, several are experimenting with some innovative financing and delivery strategies for meeting the acute and long-term care needs of their Medicaid elderly and younger disabled. Arizona's Long-Term Care System is a mandatory Medicaid managed care program targeted to people whose needs qualify them for long-term care services. Medicaid acute, long-term care, and behavioral health services are integrated, but Medicare funding is not explicitly incorporated in the program. However, it implicitly achieves a degree of integration at the contractor level because Medicare services are usually delivered through that contractor and reimbursed on a fee-for-service basis.

Minnesota was the first state to receive Medicare and Medicaid waivers explicitly to integrate acute and long-term care for the dual-eligible elderly in seven counties in the Minneapolis-St. Paul area. The Minnesota Senior Health Options (MSHO) program offers an integrated package of acute and long-term care services through a choice of three managed care plans with voluntary enrollment. Plans are at risk for the first 180 days of nursing home costs and then are reimbursed on a fee-for-service basis, with the plan continuing to provide all services. MSHO offers financial incentives for plans to use home and community-based care services in lieu of institutional services.

Colorado received Medicaid and Medicare waivers in July 1997 to enroll all Medicaid beneficiaries, including the dual eligibles, in an integrated managed care plan in Mesa County. The state will contract with Rocky Mountain HMO to provide all primary and acute care services. Long-term care services will be managed through a subcontract with the Mesa County Department of Social Services, a single-entry point agency that currently manages the Medicaid community-based waiver and state-funded, long-term care services.

MaineNet is being developed in three rural counties, areas with very low managed care penetration. Given the lack of HMOs in northern Maine, the state will require elderly and younger physically disabled Medicaid enrollees to join an integrated service network (a version of a provider service organization) for all Medicaid-funded acute and long-term care services. The state has proposed in its waiver application to HCFA that Medicare services be delivered through a primary care case management component. The same primary care physician would order both Medicare and Medicaid services, thus helping to coordinate care. As an incentive, beneficiaries who agree to use this arrangement would receive monthly points, redeemable for supplemental benefits such as eyeglasses.

Texas Star+Plus is a proposed pilot project (the waiver application has been submitted to HCFA as of this writing) in the Houston area that will enroll 60,000 aged, blind, and disabled beneficiaries, including 31,000 dual eligibles, into one of three managed care plans. (Two have or will have established Medicare risk mechanisms.) Medicaid enrollment is mandatory; beneficiaries may also choose to receive their Medicare coverage through one of the two Medicare risk plans participating in this pilot project. They will receive an unlimited prescription drug benefit as an incentive to enroll in the full acute/long-term care package.

It should be noted that, with the exception of Arizona and Minnesota, all of these programs are in the planning or early implementation phase. In addition, all but Arizona limit their initiatives to selected local areas within the state. Furthermore, none of the states have fully integrated the financing and delivery of services. Both the Robert Wood Johnson Foundation and HCFA are sponsoring evaluations of these programs and demonstrations in other states, but the results of these studies will not be available for some time. In the meantime, the rhetoric of integration will continue, as policymakers, providers, and researchers struggle with honing the details.

ASSISTED LIVING

Another trend that is receiving increased attention from policymakers as well as private developers and consumers is assisted living. One of the major problems in this regard, however, is the lack of a consistent definition among providers, regulators, and policymakers. Some would argue that assisted living is just a 1990s term for a long-term care setting that has been around for centuries, another example of "old wine in new bottles." Homes for the aged, frequently associated with nonprofit fraternal and religious organizations, proliferated in the nineteenth and early twentieth centuries to respond to the room and board needs of poor and/or indigent, infirm elderly. Over the past three decades periodic attention has been focused on scandals surrounding the treatment of residents in board-and-care homes, a version of homes for the aged that also became a refuge for the chronically mentally ill in response to the deinstitutionalization frenzy of the 1960s.

In the 1980s the term "residential care facility" became fashionable as a catchall for places providing room, board, and some level of protective oversight. Hawes and fellow scholars have estimated that about a half-million people live in residential care facilities or board-and-care homes in the United States.[56] Perhaps twice that number are living in unlicensed facilities.[57]

It is somewhat ironic that homes for the aged, board-and-care homes, and other types of residential care were replaced by the more modern, hospital-like "medically oriented" nursing home, only now to be seen again as more desirable alternatives because of their ostensibly less institutional character and an emphasis on a social rather than a medical model. A number of states (such as Oregon, Washington, Florida, Colorado) have been aggressive in attempting to use residential care as a less costly substitute for institutions. One recent study estimates that between 15 and 70 percent of the nursing home population could live in residential care.[58] Kane has questioned the judgment of hospital discharge planners who refer disabled elders to nursing homes rather than alternative arrangements because of the twenty-four-hour care available.[59] She notes that, in reality, remarkably little nursing care is provided in nursing homes. For example, a survey of nursing home residents in six states found that 39 percent of the nursing home residents received no RN care over twenty-four hours, with the RN time per resident averaging 7.9 minutes and the nursing assistant time averaging 76.9 minutes daily.[60] Despite these arguments, it is important to note that the empirical research has been equivocal on the issue of the "substitutability" and cost savings of residential care relative to nursing home placement.[61]

What appears to differentiate assisted living from the general concept of residential care and the somewhat pejorative label "board and care" is a matter of philosophy and emphasis on care as well as housing.[62] Some have suggested that assisted living is the rich person's residential care while board and care is for poor people who rely on federal Supplemental Security Income (SSI) and state supplements (SSP) to cover the costs. A recent survey of assisted living regulations in the fifty states indicates that four states (Alabama, Rhode Island, South Dakota, and Wyoming) use the terms interchangeably.[63] For the other states, the three characteristics differentiating assisted living from other residential care models are:

- an explicit focus on privacy (for example, the ability to lock doors; having a separate bath), choice, and independence;

- an emphasis on apartment settings shared by residents who choose to live together; and

- the direct provision or arrangement of personal care and some nursing services and a focus on various levels of disability and need.

While assisted living is emerging as a phenomenon that warrants serious consideration by policymakers, providers, and consumers, there are a number of impediments to its development that need attention. Currently, the market for assisted living is primarily the well-off elderly, with little available to moderate- or low-income consumers. This gap is due, in part, to the inadequacy and limited sources of public financing (primarily SSI and SSP) that could otherwise help to subsidize the room, board, and care costs for financially strapped individuals and their families.

Other impediments include concerns expressed by state policymakers and potential private providers about balancing consumer choice and privacy with health and safety and their fears concerning liability. One of the major issues reflecting this concern is the degree to which states are willing to moderate their nursing practice acts to allow delegation of certain tasks such as medication administration, wound care, and changing catheters.[64] A number of states (Oregon, Kansas, Texas, Minnesota, New York) have introduced delegation provisions, but the latitude and interpretations vary tremendously. Not surprisingly, these initiatives have met with serious resistance by many of the nurses' organizations, with the professional turf considerations as significant as the care issues.

In addition to these barriers, there is also some question as to the extent of care that is actually being provided in assisted living facilities. As providers look for new markets and reimbursement strategies, there has been concern that many skilled nursing facilities will simply lay down carpet, install some doors with locks, and hang out the assisted living shingle. Anecdotal information also suggests that while many assisted living facilities market themselves as care providers to the cognitively impaired as well as those who have no cognitive deficits, they strongly "encourage" discharge of such residents at the first sign of dementia.

It is difficult to predict the future for this segment of the long-term care continuum. As states move toward developing regulations for assisted living, it is important to recognize the negative as well as the positive implications for consumer choice, health, and safety. One key question that remains to be addressed is the extent to which it is desirable to emulate nursing home regulation, given the condition of the industry that was created in large part by that regulation.

CONSUMER DIRECTION

The 1990s may someday be referred to as the "coming of age" of the health and long-term care consumer. While the focus on consumer choice is a relatively recent phenomenon on the acute care side, it has a longer history in long-term care primarily thanks to the disability and independent living movements of the 1960s and 1970s. Catalyzed by younger physically disabled persons strongly opposed to institutionalization and desiring a range of home and community-based options with the client in control, a trend toward more consumer involvement and direction among the elderly has begun to take shape.

The fundamental underpinnings of consumer direction involved the ability of people with long-term care needs to assume a proactive role in choosing service modalities as well as in care delivery. Important characteristics include privacy, autonomy, and the right to "manage one's own risk." Consumer direction in long-term care is seen as a way of leveling the playing field between institutional and home and community-based care. It is also viewed by a growing number of policymakers as a potential mechanism for cost savings through efficiencies in both the allocation of resources and in care delivery.

Policy options span the continuum from consumer involvement in care planning and decisionmaking to the ultimate in consumer direction—providing cash benefits to beneficiaries and allowing them to purchase their own services. Much of the consumer-directed activity at the state level has taken place through Medicaid home and community-based waiver (where states are allowed to waive certain federal Medicaid requirements to enable them to offer home care in lieu of nursing home care) and state-funded personal assistance services programs. California, for example, has a large independent provider program for elderly and younger disabled home care clients. Rather than receiving case-managed services through an agency, participants have the option of hiring and firing their own workers. As employers, they have the ability to direct their own care and to be more personally responsible for the quality of the care provided. The state supports a registry of home care workers but also allows clients to hire their own family caregivers. The U.S. Department of Health and Human Services has funded a three-year evaluation of this program to examine the impact of the independent provider model versus an agency model on costs and quality for care recipients and workers.

At least thirty-five states have programs that provide some form of financial payment to relatives and other informal caregivers of persons with disabilities of all ages for homemaker, chore, and personal services.[65] Programs may compensate for work done or only for the out-of-pocket expenses incurred by caregivers.[66] Wage programs provide compensation directly to the caregiver, although most programs provide neither full-time employment nor fringe benefits to persons caring for one or two recipients. Allowance programs provide a flat grant geared to the family or caregiver's need and in relation to the care recipient's condition. Caregivers may be eligible for aid because of their categorical eligibility for income assistance, their shared household status with the recipient, or their simply being related to the disabled persons.

The concept of direct cash payments for long-term care services, including payments to caregivers, has been much more controversial in the United States than in other countries. Germany's 1994 Dependency Insurance Act, for example, provides universal coverage of long-term care for disabled people of all ages with the options of cash, vendor payments or a combination of in-kind and cash benefits.[67] Statistics for the first year of program operation indicate that 80 percent of care recipients with the lowest level of impairment and nearly two-thirds of the severely disabled opted for cash benefits. Since the value of the program's cash payments is considerably lower than the monetary-value of vendor payments, the overwhelming use of the cash option helped Germany's care funds to keep their budgets within the prescribed limits.

The Medicaid program precludes direct cash payments to care recipients. However, through a joint demonstration and evaluation grant from the Department of Health and Human Services and the Robert Wood Johnson Foundation, four states (New York, New Jersey, Arkansas, and Florida) are applying for a Medicaid waiver to experiment with "cashing out" the home and community-based care benefit. The states are currently in the process of designing their respective programs, establishing the cash payment rates, developing the marketing strategy for enrolling a treatment and control group (those receiving case-managed agency services) of Medicaid eligibles, developing a counseling program to help cash recipients make choices about use of their dollars, and creating a quality monitoring system that balances consumer autonomy with safety and potential fraud and abuse concerns.

As the notion of an informed consumer becomes the centerpiece of new managed care initiatives based on the concept of choice, it will be interesting to see how rhetoric is translated into reality in the long-term care arena. Historically, U.S. policymakers have been comfortable with a cash benefit model for certain subpopulations (the working disabled, veterans). They have been less sanguine about direct payments to "undeserving" individuals such as Supplemental Security Income beneficiaries, as is reflected in recent congressional actions to cut back on such benefits for certain groups of disabled children. Concerns about misuse of dollars as well as potential liability in the face of unforeseen mishaps have impeded the growth of the movement toward placing control in the hands of care recipients in the United States. On the other hand, younger people with disabilities have begun to join forces with advocates for the aging to fight for more choice and autonomy in the areas of personal care and assisted living.

Consumer direction is not an option for all people with long-term care needs, but it may prove to be an effective and efficient way to allocate precious resources to an important subset of this population. Depending on the perspective from which they are observed, consumer-directed programs can be seen as either a relatively safe and inexpensive way to satisfy consumer needs and allow payment of relatives and friends for important services or a vehicle for depressing health professionals' wages, exploiting workers, and jeopardizing the health and well being of vulnerable consumers who may not be able to supervise their own care adequately.[68] Although little empirical research has tested the validity of either viewpoint, several important studies in this area may shed some new light on the potential and pitfalls of this emerging practice.

SINKING OR SWIMMING INTO THE FUTURE

Taking into account the rapidly changing health and long-term care environments, it is very difficult to predict what kind of financing and delivery system or set of systems will prevail in the future. There are, however, several givens as the twenty-first century approaches. The first is the major demographic shift that is about to overtake this country and the world. As noted in the introduction, the number and proportion of elderly citizens— particularly the very old—will increase dramatically, and with it the demand for long-term care.

Another constant is the pivotal role of family and friends in providing long-term care assistance to disabled elders. Policy discussions about the future of financing and delivery of care in the United States continue to focus on how to support informal caregiving, with the implicit or explicit objective of avoiding any substitution of formal, paid care for family care. What may change is the nature and character of the informal networks available to provide those services. In the short term, there will be more adult children than are available to help the current cohort of elderly because of the very low fertility rates of the "Depression Mothers." As the year 2025 gets closer, however, the potential pool of caregivers will begin to decrease. Coupled with more women remaining in the workforce and the trend toward delayed childbearing, a "sandwich generation" will increasingly have to juggle the multiple demands of work, child care, and elder care.

It is also clear that the pendulum is swinging in the direction of a more holistic approach to service delivery for the long-term care population that recognizes the acute, chronic, and nonmedical needs of the disabled elderly and their families. This approach recognizes that long-term care is more than services; where people live and how their environment can be accommodated are also important. The residential aspect of long-term care has always been explicit in nursing home policy (that is, paying for room a nd board as well as services), but housing (including the cost of room and board and environmental adaptations) must also become integral to the financing and delivery of home and community-based care options.

Despite thirty years of discussion, experimentation, and innovation, the same questions remain pertinent to the long-term care arena—What system is best for the United States? How much will it cost? Who will pay? There have been continuous debates about the advantages and disadvantages of a social insurance model that would provide universal coverage for some or all of the long-term care population.[69] The thwarted Clinton health care reform effort in 1994 included a home and community-based care program for people of all ages; the benefits would have been capped and administered through block grants to the states. This somewhat limited program, without a nursing home benefit, would have cost the taxpayers $58 billion over a five-year period.

The extent to which private, long-term care insurance will resolve at least part of the financing dilemma remains to be seen. As noted previously, the limitations of the individual market and the failure of a group market to form do not bode well for private sector ventures. On the other hand, future cohorts of elderly, particularly the "young old," will be more highly educated and wealthier than the current generation and may be more likely to purchase such insurance. Younger people as well may see private insurance as a wise investment if the premiums are low enough. One long-term care insurance product—the disability model—needs to be given serious consideration. Currently offered by a few insurers (for example, UNUM, Aetna), this option provides the claimant with a set dollar amount tied to level of disability rather than access to a set of discrete services. Given the rapidly changing nature of delivery systems and the increasing focus on consumer choice, such an approach might appeal to individuals who want to know what their premiums are buying thirty years hence and want the maximum flexibility that a cash alternative would provide.

While there is no clear recipe for balancing public and private financing options, several elements are essential to the design and implementation of a long-term care system for the future. First, the system should address the long-term care needs of people of all ages, recognizing that services and other accommodations must be tailored to people with varying degrees of physical and mental impairment. Second, the long-term care system must be sensitive to the needs of the family as well as the person needing care. Although formal care should not, and probably will never, replace the efforts of family and friends, the repertoire of services should build their contributions into the process and ensure that family and friends are supported.

The long-term care system should recognize the wide array of options available to meet the residential and care needs of the individual. Further, it should take into account that these needs do not necessarily increase in a linear fashion. The system must be flexible enough to contend with the acute, chronic, and nonmedical needs (such as housekeeping and transportation) of the long-term care client that may fluctuate over time. Those who prefer more self-direction should have that option, although it is important that they recognize the trade-offs involved in managing their own risk, including the possibility that their health and safety could be jeopardized.

In the ideal world, the dollars, whether public or private, would follow the person rather than the provider. Individuals and their families would have the ability to make choices that include their preferences and values, within the financial constraints set by public programs and their own private resources. Such a vision, of course, would require major restructuring of our current public health system so that funding streams (Medicare, Medicaid, state funds) become truly seamless. While not essential, it would also be beneficial for individuals, their families, and other surrogate decisionmakers to have access to care managers or intermediaries who could assist the long-term care client in navigating the system and making the best choices.

Like it or not, long-term care is coming of age and will be one of the major challenges of the twenty-first century. Our society can wait for the crisis to hit, or we can be proactive in developing a financing and delivery strategy that learns from the successes and failures in this country and other nations, that strikes the right balance between public and private resources, and that recognizes that the long-term care client and family must be in the driver's seat.

4

OLDER PERSONS AND HEALTH CARE COSTS

Robert H. Binstock

Health care costs for older people are an ongoing public policy concern in the United States. The size of both aggregate present costs and projected future costs fuels this concern. Persons aged sixty-five and older account for roughly one-third of annual U.S. personal health care expenditures.[1] In 1997 this amounted to about $323 billion out of $969 billion overall.[2]

Public expenditures on the health care of older people have been escalating rapidly in recent years, through Medicare—the national health insurance program for people aged sixty-five and older (as well as for persons who receive federal disability payments and those who have end-stage renal disease)—and Medicaid, the federal/state grant-in-aid program that finances much of the long-term care of older persons. Medicare outlays are projected to continue to swell from $211 billion in fiscal year 1998 to $444 billion in 2009.[3] From 1989 to 1996 combined Medicaid and Medicare outlays for the long-term care of older people increased by 112 percent for nursing homes and 452 percent for home care.[4] For the period 2000–2010, expenditures from the two programs are projected to go up by 40 percent for nursing homes and 60 percent for home care.[5]

Reining in Medicare and Medicaid expenditures on older people became a major item on the national policy agenda starting in the mid-1990s, as Republicans and Democrats alike began acting on the principle

---

This chapter was originally released as a Century Foundation white paper in 1998.

that the annual budget of the federal government should be brought into balance. This concern for balancing the budget has weighed heavily in proposals to make structural changes and large reductions in Medicare and Medicaid spending. The Balanced Budget Act of 1997, for example, included a $115 billion cut in projected Medicare spending from 1998 through 2002 as well as a number of changes designed to set a fixed annual budget for reimbursement for the care of many individuals who participate in the program.[6]

Growing attention to the aging of the baby boom generation, a cohort of 75 million persons born between 1946 and 1964, has also focused a great deal of public attention on the health care costs of older people. When baby boomers reach the ranks of "the elderly" we will have become what many have termed an "aging society." By the year 2030, the number of persons aged 65 and older will have more than doubled, from 31 million in 1990 to about 70 million, and the elderly will comprise 20 percent of the population.[7]

Analysts are projecting enormous costs for health care when the baby boom reaches old age. One study estimates, for example, that by 2040 the national cost of nursing homes will increase nearly threefold in constant, inflation-adjusted dollars.[8] A major factor in calculating such estimates is the projected demand for long-term care in the years ahead. The Congressional Budget Office,[9] using 2000 as a baseline year, has estimated that total national costs of long-term care will almost double by 2020 and nearly triple by 2030.

Such projections, of course, are based on assumptions that the financing and organizational features of health care for the elderly in the third and fourth decades of the twenty-first century will be the same as they are today. But extrapolation from existing arrangements is a poor mode of prediction. Especially in the health care arena, both public policy and market forces are already bringing about rapid change.

Nonetheless, health care costs of the elderly in the twenty-first century have been depicted by a national commission as an unsustainable economic burden for our nation.[10] Biomedical ethicist Daniel Callahan has promulgated an apocalyptic view of the health care costs of older people. He has depicted the elderly population as "a new social threat" and a "demographic, economic, and medical avalanche . . . one that could ultimately (and perhaps already) do [sic] great harm."[11]

This chapter attempts to sort out some of the myths and realities of health care costs and aging. It begins with a discussion of the health care needs of the elderly in the future. Then it explores two common myths. One is that population aging in itself has a major impact on national health care costs. The other is that old-age-based health care rationing would save significant amounts of expenditures on health care. Next, the chapter examines contemporary structural changes in the financing and organization of health care for older people that are designed to control spending, and the risks that these changes pose to the health care of older persons. Finally, it considers whether future adaptations in the financing of care will be politically feasible given that older people are reputed to be a powerful and self-interested force in American politics.

HEALTH CARE NEEDS OF THE ELDERLY POPULATION IN THE FUTURE

Undergirding concerns about health care expenditures on the elderly in the future are expectations that the absolute number of older persons needing health care will increase markedly. In addition to the sheer size of the baby boom, such estimates are based on the fact that the older population will be older on average than it is today and on the comparatively high rates of disease and disability experienced by the very old.

The older population is, in itself, aging. Persons of advanced old age will more than double when the baby boom becomes elderly. The population aged seventy-five and older will have grown from 13 million in 1990 to 32 million by 2030, and those aged eighty-five and older will have tripled from 3 million to 9 million.[12]

Prevalence rates of morbidity and disability increase markedly in advanced old age. For example, while 22.6 percent of the population aged sixty-five to seventy-four experiences difficulties with activities of daily living, the rate is 44.5 percent among those aged eighty-five and older. Similarly, the rate of Alzheimer's disease rises sharply in the older age ranges. According to recent estimates, 6 percent of people between the ages of sixty-five and seventy-four have Alzheimer's; among those age eighty-five and over, as many as 50 percent show signs of it.[13]

A reflection of such prevalence rates in advanced old age can be found in the present rates of nursing home use among different old-age categories. About 1 percent of Americans aged sixty-five to seventy-four years are in nursing homes; this compares with 6.1 percent of persons seventy-five to eighty-four and 24 percent of those aged eighty-five and older. Similarly, disability rates increase in the advanced old-age categories among persons who are not in nursing homes, from nearly 23 percent of

those aged sixty-five to seventy-four who experience difficulties with activities of daily living to 45 percent of those aged eighty-five and older.

When members of the baby boom are in their late sixties and early
seventies, they may have better health, on average, than that experienced
by preceding cohorts when they were at the same ages. This general expectation is based on numerous causes that have been unique to the baby
boomer's life course experiences, including: (1) generally better prenatal
care, optimum preventive practices in childhood such as immunization
for common serious illnesses, better nutrition, and lower accident rates; (2)
more healthful work environments with lower work-related injury rates,
reduced exposure to known carcinogens, and the spread of employer-related wellness and stress reduction programs; and (3) better health practices
throughout adult life, such as lower rates of smoking, more participation in
exercise programs, and greater attention to preventive measures relevant
to many chronic diseases.

Nonetheless, the mere increase in the number of persons of advanced
old age suggests a substantial expansion of the aggregate health care needs
of older people. For instance, the number of diagnosed incidents of cancer is projected to increase markedly in the next several decades.[14] The
growth in long-term care needs will be tremendous. Whether rates of
disability in old age will increase or decline in the future is a matter on
which experts disagree. Assuming no changes in the age-specific risks of
disability, Cassel, Rudberg, and Olshansky[15] calculate a 31 percent
increase between 1990 and 2010 in the number of persons aged sixty-
five and older experiencing difficulties with activities of living. Using
the same assumption, the Congressional Budget Office[16] projects that
the elderly disabled population will increase 40 percent between 2000
and 2030. Even those researchers who report a decline in the prevalence
of disability at older ages in recent years emphasize that there will be
large absolute increases in the number of older Americans needing long-
term care in the decades ahead.[17]

DOES POPULATION AGING INCREASE HEALTH CARE EXPENDITURES?

With the substantial increases in health care demand for older people
that will occur when the baby boom reaches old age, predictions that population aging will engender an enormous economic burden for the nation

appear to be intuitively sound. Yet, empirical evidence indicates that this will not necessarily be the case.

PRESENT IMPACT OF POPULATION AGING IN THE UNITED STATES

Although population aging is frequently cited as a major contributor to the growth of health care spending both in the United States and abroad,[18] empirical studies attempting to identify such a relationship have been relatively sparse. The few analyses that have focused on aging as a factor in U.S. health care cost increases have found that the impact of aging and other demographic changes on expenditures in recent decades has been dwarfed by the combined effects of such phenomena as increases in the intensity and utilization rates of health services, health-sector-specific price inflation, and general inflation.

A study by Daniel Mendelson and William Schwartz,[19] for instance, indicated that while population aging in the United States accounted for about one-fifth of the annualized rise in real expenditures for long-term care from 1987 through 1990 it was a relatively negligible factor in the rise of spending on hospitals, physicians, and other forms of health care. Moreover, this analysis found a steady reduction in the contribution of aging to health care costs between 1975 and 1990 and projected little impact of aging on costs through 2005.

Other analyses[20] have yielded similar findings regarding the minimal impact of aging and other demographic changes on growth in health care expenditures through the end of this century despite the fact that U.S. health care spending increased from less than 6 percent of the gross domestic product (GDP) in 1965 (when Medicare and Medicaid were established) to more than 14 percent of GDP in 1993.[21] Yet the authors of most of these studies boldly state that they expect population aging to be a major impetus pushing up U.S. health care costs in the early decades of the twenty-first century.

CROSS-NATIONAL OVERVIEW OF AGING AND EXPENDITURES

These empirical studies, however, have been retrospective or contemporary in focus. What will happen when the large baby-boom cohort reaches old age? Will demography be destiny with respect to health care expenditures?

One way to address this issue is to make a cross-national comparison. Analyzing data compiled by George Schieber, Jean-Pierre Poullier, and Leslie Greenwald,[22] one can see if there appears to be any relationship between population aging and the amount of national wealth spent on health care. The advantage of this approach is that it enables us to look at nations that already have proportions of older people in the general population that resemble what the situation in the United States will be like in the decades ahead.

Simple cross-national comparisons of expenditures and selected aspects of population aging suggest that little if any direct relationship exists between them. A comparison of aging and health care spending in 1990 is displayed in Figure 4.1, where twelve advanced industrial nations are ranked by their percentages of population aged sixty-five and older. Their respective proportions of gross domestic product (GDP) spent on

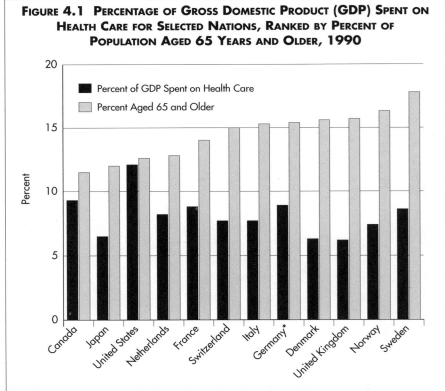

FIGURE 4.1 PERCENTAGE OF GROSS DOMESTIC PRODUCT (GDP) SPENT ON HEALTH CARE FOR SELECTED NATIONS, RANKED BY PERCENT OF POPULATION AGED 65 YEARS AND OLDER, 1990

* Both percentages are for the Federal Republic of Germany, 1988.

Source: Assembled by the author from data in George J. Schieber, Jean-Pierre Poullier, and Leslie Greenwald, "U.S. Health Expenditure Performance: An International Comparison and Update," *Health Care Financing Review* 13, no. 4 (1992).

health care in that year indicate no discernible pattern in comparative ranking or in relation to their proportions of elderly people. It is worth noting that the United States, the highest-spending country at 12.1 percent of GDP, is one of the lowest ranking of the dozen countries in the percentage of population aged sixty-five and older (at 12.6 percent). In contrast, Sweden, which ranks highest in the proportion of population aged sixty-five and older (at 17.8 percent), spent just a bit more than two-thirds as much of its GDP on health care as the United States.

Changes in expenditures and the demographics of aging over time are shown in Figure 4.2, which ranks the twelve nations in accordance with their rates of change from 1980 to 1990 in the proportion of population aged sixty-five and older. Again, the rates of change in national health expenditures for that period of time show no pattern of relations to change rates in the percentage of older persons. Perhaps the most striking illustra-

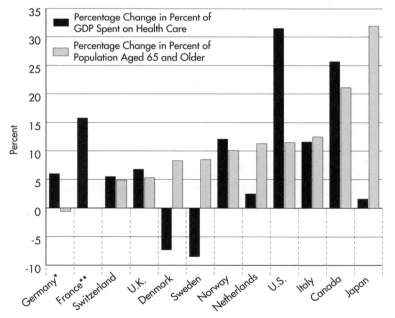

FIGURE 4.2 CHANGE IN PERCENTAGE OF GROSS DOMESTIC PRODUCT (GDP) SPENT ON HEALTH CARE FOR SELECTED NATIONS, RANKED BY PERCENTAGE CHANGE IN PROPORTION OF POPULATION AGED 65 AND OLDER, 1980–1990

* Both percentages are for the Federal Republic of Germany, 1980–1988.
** No change, 1980–1990, in % 65+.

Source: Author's calculations from data in George J. Schieber, Jean-Pierre Poullier, and Leslie Greenwald, "U.S. Health Expenditure Performance: An International Comparison and Update," *Health Care Financing Review* 13, no. 4 (1992).

tion of the absence of relationships between the two variables is provided by the cases of Japan and the United States. Japan is notable among the industrial nations of the world for its extremely rapid contemporary rate of population aging, with its proportion aged sixty-five and older increasing by 31.9 percent from 1980 to 1990. Yet it experienced only a 1.6 percent increase in the proportion of GDP spent on health care during the decade. In contrast, the United States is notable for its high rate of increase in health care costs, which was 31.5 percent during the ten-year period, or about twenty times the increase in Japan. But its population aged sixty-five and older increased at a rate of about one-third that of Japan's.

One might argue that an older age group—say, age eighty and beyond—should be used for such cross-national comparisons. After all, as discussed before, it is well established that this and other age groupings within the elderly population have higher rates of morbidity and health care utilization than persons aged sixty-five to seventy-nine. Hence, the proportion of persons aged eighty and older, and the rate of increase in their share of a nation's population, might be more appropriate dimensions for examining relationships between aging and national health expenditures than comparisons based on age 65 and older.

But Figures 4.3 and 4.4 (see pages 83 and 84), depicting cross-national comparisons based on cohorts aged eighty and older, show no more salient a relationship with expenditures on health care than is evident for the comparisons based on age 65 and older. Once again, specific cases underscore the absence of relations between population aging and health care spending. In Figure 4.3, for example, Sweden's proportion of population aged eighty and older is 55 percent greater than that of the United States. Yet Sweden's proportion of GDP spent on health care is but three-quarters of the U.S. proportion. Similarly, in Figure 4.4, note that the United States shows the highest rate of spending growth and the lowest rate of increase in the proportion of the population aged eighty and older. In contrast, Japan has the highest rate of increase in the share of its population represented by those aged eighty or over but a low rate of expenditure increase (only 12 percent as rapid as that of the United States).

HEALTH CARE SYSTEM CHARACTERISTICS

Before abandoning the notion that there is a definite correspondence between population aging and pressures on national health care spending, it is worth considering whether specific features of various health care systems

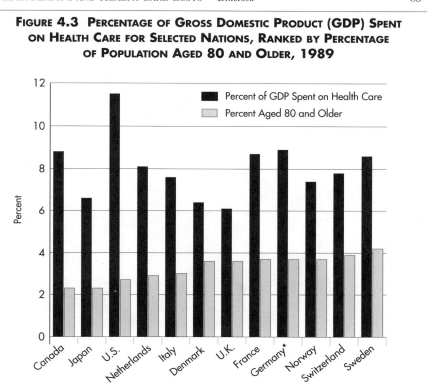

FIGURE 4.3 PERCENTAGE OF GROSS DOMESTIC PRODUCT (GDP) SPENT
ON HEALTH CARE FOR SELECTED NATIONS, RANKED BY PERCENTAGE
OF POPULATION AGED 80 AND OLDER, 1989

* Both percentages are for the Federal Republic of Germany, 1988.

Source: Assembled by the author from data in George J. Schieber, Jean-Pierre Poullier, and
Leslie Greenwald, "U.S. Health Expenditure Performance: An International Comparison and
Update," *Health Care Financing Review* 13, no. 4 (1992).

may account for some of the counter-intuitive results that appear in the
cross-national data, masking the impact of aging in itself. Consider, for
instance, certain contrasting characteristics of the health care systems of
Great Britain and the United States.

In Great Britain people of all ages are publicly insured through the
National Health Service. But, as chronicled by Henry Aaron and William
Schwartz[23] and others, customary practices within the National Health Service
lead to the rationing of care for older persons. In the United States, by virtue
of the Medicare program, people aged sixty-five and older are the *only* age
group that has universal public insurance for—and thereby, universal access
to—health care. These characteristics of the two systems could at least partially
account for the contrast between the two nations in their average spending on

**FIGURE 4.4   CHANGE IN PERCENTAGE OF GROSS DOMESTIC PRODUCT (GDP)
SPENT ON HEALTH CARE FOR SELECTED NATIONS, RANKED BY PERCENTAGE
CHANGE IN PROPORTION OF POPULATION AGED 80 AND OLDER, 1980–1989**

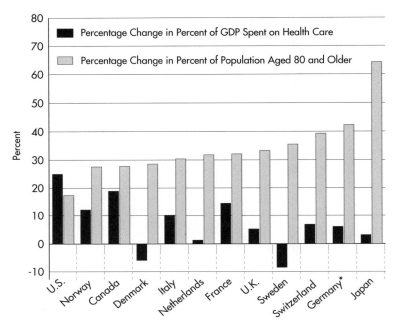

* Both percentages are for the Federal Republic of Germany, 1980–1988.

Source: Assembled by the author from data in George J. Schieber, Jean-Pierre Poullier, and
Leslie Greenwald, "U.S. Health Expenditure Performance: An International Comparison and
Update," *Health Care Financing Review* 13, no. 4 (1992).

health care for elderly versus nonelderly citizens. In Britain the elderly/
nonelderly per capita spending ratio is 2.8; the U.S. ratio is 4.1, or 46 percent higher.[24]

The practice of rationing care for the aged may also partially explain
(refer to Figure 4.1) the seeming anomaly that Great Britain has a relatively high proportion of older people but the lowest overall health care
bill among the advanced industrial states. (Probably stronger explanations are that the National Health Service operates within a strict budgetary allocation and makes comparatively limited use of high-technology
interventions.) Similarly, the Medicare program may contribute to the
United States' being the highest spender for health care overall, in spite of

having relatively few elderly. Heavy U.S. reliance on the marketplace and high-technology treatment, however, are likely much more important.

An effort to move beyond such speculation toward more comprehensive and systematic interpretations regarding the effects of specific health system features was undertaken by Deborah Chollet[25] in an analysis of the relative impact of aging on per capita health care spending in six nations (Canada, France, Germany, Netherlands, Great Britain, and the United States). She undertook this difficult challenge by constructing an econometric model that used a variety of independent variables for each nation—measures of administrative centralization in the health system, system capacity, system use, per capita gross domestic product, and proportion of the population aged sixty-five and older. Although a detailed account of this analysis is beyond the scope of this discussion, her findings are of interest.

In the context of her particular model Chollet provided evidence that population aging in selected countries may have an impact on levels of national health care spending, but the workings of such a relationship are unclear. She found the responsiveness of spending to population aging (expressed as the "age elasticity" of national spending) to be high in Great Britain and still higher in the United States, even though they have markedly different levels of spending and systems of health care. The other four countries showed only slight expenditure sensitivity to population aging, substantially lower than for Great Britain and the United States. Her general explanation for differences in aggregate national spending lay in varying health care capacities, as measured by the nations' respective numbers of hospital beds and physicians per capita.

Chollet remained cautious, however, about attempting to explain the comparatively high but different levels of age elasticity found in Great Britain and the United States. She interpreted Britain's low aggregate national expenditures as associated strongly with its limited system capacity and then conjectured that its high age elasticity may result from the possibility that population aging generates successful "public pressure" for increased services from that restricted system. She concluded by simply observing that the dynamics of susceptibility to population aging in Great Britain and the United States may "differ greatly."

DEMOGRAPHY IS NOT DESTINY

Several observations seem warranted from the evidence presented in this multicountry exploration. First, simple cross-national comparisons—inevitably involving health care systems with markedly different features—

do not provide convincing evidence that substantial or rapid population aging cause high levels of health care spending. Second, health care costs are far from "high" or "out of control" in many nations that have comparatively large proportions of older persons or that have experienced rapid population aging. Third, the structural features of health care systems—and behavioral responses to them by citizens and health care providers—are probably far more important determinants of a nation's health care expenditures than population aging and other demographic trends. The amount of expenses that are "caused" by population aging can be controlled by policy changes, and such changes need not be ones that deny or limit care for older persons. As Reiner Leidel concluded in a prospective study of population aging and national health care expenditures in Germany, "neither the growing number of elderly nor their share in health care and its expenditures gives any reasons to provoke discussions on discriminatory measures such as rationing by age."[26]

Political leaders and policy analysts in the United States and throughout the world might do well to give less attention than they have to foreboding scenarios generated through simple demographic projections—that is, to cease engaging in what has been variously termed "voodoo demographics"[27] and "apocalyptic demography."[28] Rather, they might focus greater attention on social values regarding how various groups within their nations—the young and the old, the rich and the poor, the spectrum of ethnic groupings—are provided or denied appropriate health care now and in the future, and the implications of such differential treatment for health and the quality of life in their societies.

THE SPECTER OF OLD-AGE-BASED RATIONING

Both the public and private sectors of the U.S. health care system are already undergoing rapid structural changes, and they will undoubtedly continue to do so in the early decades of the twenty-first century as the baby-boom cohort grows older. One type of change that has been advocated and discussed prominently for some years is rationing health care on the basis of old age.

Public suggestions that limitations should be placed on the health care of older people began to emerge in the early 1980s. In a 1983 speech to the Health Insurance Association of America, economist Alan Greenspan, now chairman of the Federal Reserve Board, pointedly wondered "whether it is worth it" to spend close to one-third of Medicare funds annually on just 5 to 6 percent of Medicare insurees who die within the year.[29] In 1984 Richard Lamm, then governor of Colorado, was widely quoted as stating that older persons "have a duty to die and get out of the way."[30] Although Lamm subsequently said that he had been misquoted on that occasion, he continues to propound his view in a somewhat more delicate fashion.[31]

Throughout the past ten years, discussion of this issue has spread to a number of forums. Ethicists and philosophers have been generating principles of equity to undergird "justice between age groups" rather than, for instance, justice between rich and poor, or justice among ethnic and racial groups,[32] in the provision of health care. Conferences and books have explicitly addressed the subject with titles such as *Should Medical Care Be Rationed by Age?*[33]

The most prominent exponent of old-age-based rationing has been biomedical ethicist Daniel Callahan, whose 1987 book entitled *Setting Limits: Medical Goals in an Aging Society* received substantial popular as well as academic attention. He proposed the official use of "age as a specific criterion for the allocation and limitation of health care" by denying life-extending health care—as a matter of public policy—to persons who are aged in their "late 70s or early 80s" or have "lived out a natural life span."[34] Although Callahan described "the natural life span" as a matter defined by each person's biography rather than biology, he used chronological age as an arbitrary marker to designate when, from a biographical standpoint, the individual should have reached the end of a natural life.

Setting Limits provoked widespread and continuing discussion in the media and public forums throughout the country, and it directly inspired a number of books[35] and scores of journal articles dealing with the topic of old age and rationing health care. Today the notion of limiting the health care of older people in one way or another is surfacing with increasing frequency in national magazines and newspapers, while Callahan continues to promote his old-age-based rationing agenda.[36]

THE ECONOMICS OF OLD-AGE-BASED RATIONING

Proponents of old-age-based rationing have attempted to justify their proposals on economic (and, in some cases, ethical and moral) grounds. Yet, curiously, the various proposals for rationing have not attempted to identify the magnitude of savings to be achieved. Would such savings be of economic significance in the overall context of health care costs? For illustrative purposes, one can construct an example.

For a number of years about 28 percent of annual Medicare expenditures have been on those program insurees who die within a year.[37] On the surface, this sounds extraordinarily wasteful. But relatively few of the 4,500 cases of Americans aged sixty-five and older who die each day[38] involve high costs. The vast majority of these deaths among older people are relatively low cost; they do not occur as the final episode in a heroic, spare-no-expense effort to save lives. Proponents of old-age-based rationing have neglected the numerous low-profile cases in order to focus their attention on high-cost, high-tech, life-saving interventions that turn out to be futile.

How much money would be saved if society were to deny care to prospective *high-cost* Medicare decedents (although, clinically, it is rarely possible to make highly reliable prospective distinctions between high-cost survivors and decedents)? Even if it were ethically and morally palatable to implement a policy that denied treatment to such high-cost patients and thereby eliminate "wasteful" health care, the dollars saved would be insignificant in the larger context of national health care costs.

High-cost Medicare decedents, as reasonably defined, annually account for 3.5 percent of Medicare expenditures.[39] In 1996, when Medicare expenditures were $198 billion,[40] a policy that denied these cases treatment would have saved $7 billion. Viewed in isolation, this is a substantial amount of money. But saving such an amount would have a negligible effect on the overall budgetary situation, reducing national health care spending in that year from $907 billion[41] to about $900 billion, or by 0.8 percent.

In another approach, Ezekiel Emanuel and Linda Emanuel[42] have estimated the savings that could be achieved if living wills, durable powers of attorney, hospice care, and the elimination of aggressive care could be effectively implemented for all persons aged sixty-five and older who will die within the year. They calculate that such methods to reduce the use of aggressive, life-sustaining treatment would save, hypothetically, 6.1 percent of annual Medicare expenditures. In 1997 this would have yielded $12.9 billion, or 1.3 percent of total national health care expenditures.

In short, the impact on national health care costs would likely be negligible if the United States were to try to save money by limiting aggressive, high-cost care for older patients who are going to die within a year. Even if one considers these amounts significant for any given year, such savings will not restrain the rate of growth in health care spending over time. Increases in service intensity, utilization rates, and health-sector-specific price inflation are vastly more significant contributors to annual health care cost increases.

These facts about the economic insignificance of "futile care" are not widely known and appreciated.[43] Yet, even if they come to be understood, it seems very likely that issues of high-cost, acute care for those older persons who *survive*, as well as those who die, will continue to be debated in the years immediately ahead. A substantial agenda of research needs to be implemented to inform such debates about specific types of aggressive care for patients of advanced old age. At the moment, the conventional wisdom is that extraordinary amounts of money are expended on aggressive care for persons aged eighty and older. Yet, for example, coronary artery bypass graft surgery on persons in that age range accounts for only 0.6 percent of Medicare Part A reimbursements, and hip replacements for this age group make up just 0.3 percent.[44]

THE RISKS OF STRUCTURAL CHANGES TO CONTAIN COSTS

A number of structural changes in Medicare and Medicaid are under way to contain public expenditures on these programs. Although these cost-containment measures and other contemplated reforms in Medicare do not involve old-age-based rationing of the kind proposed by Callahan and others, they do pose distinct risks for older persons in terms of access to and quality of health care. The dangers of such risks need to be carefully and forcefully monitored.

The general approach with respect to Medicare is making a transition from the program's traditional, open-ended, fee-for-service approach to paying for health care to a situation in which much of Medicare operates with fixed budgets that cap program costs. The primary strategy now in place for carrying out this approach is to encourage both the proliferation of and enrollment in Medicare managed care plans that receive a flat, per capita fee for providing health care for each beneficiary enrolled in the plan. About 13 percent of program enrollees are already in Medicare HMOs, and the number is expected to grow in the years immediately ahead as the federal government promotes the growth of Medicare managed care contractors.[45] The financial incentives offered to managed care organizations, however, lead to the undertreatment of patients.[46]

Studies have already indicated that outcomes for older people who are poor and have chronic diseases and disabilities are worse in HMOs than when care is provided through fee-for-service payments.[47] Even relatively healthy older persons in HMOs seem to have been underserved in certain respects.[48]

Another strategy, currently in a demonstration phase, is to establish individual, tax-exempt Medical Savings Accounts (MSAs) that include high-deductible (as high as $6,000) health insurance policies. Each MSA plan participant receives an annual sum from Medicare and can use it to purchase health care. Unused balances in such accounts can be retained, spent, or invested by the Medicare participants, and can even be passed on through inheritance.

Most policy analysts expect that relatively healthy and wealthy older people will opt for MSAs. But there is a distinct possibility that poorer, older people will select the MSA option, too.

The sum to be paid into MSAs by Medicare (as much as $5,000 in some urban areas) might be perceived as a substantial cash windfall by older people who are either below the poverty line, which is $9,220 for an elderly couple,[49] or perhaps only a few thousand dollars above it. Those poorer old people who elect the MSA may well forgo needed medical care in order to preserve the windfall, even though as a group they tend to be relatively unhealthy.[50]

The growth of Medicare managed care also has important implications for long-term care. In the same manner as the implementation of Medicare's prospective payment system in the mid-1980s led hospitals to discharge patients as quickly as possible, the incentive systems of Medicare HMOs lead them to transfer patients from acute care to subacute care in nursing homes and at home expeditiously, at the lowest possible cost. And within subacute care (in nursing homes and at home) settings the incentive is to transfer patients to still lower levels of care, where the cost of providing treatment is substantially lower, as quickly as possible.

As they compete for Medicare enrollees, those managed care organizations that do not own the appropriate long-term care services for which Medicare's capitation payment makes them responsible make contractual arrangements—especially with large for-profit nursing home chains—to providers of such care, which shifts financial risk to the latter. Reportedly, substitution of subacute care for hospital days by managed care organizations enables them to reduce their costs by 50 percent or more.[51] Hence, the incentives for providers of long-term care shift from the traditional reimbursement-driven basis, which encourages more provision of services, to a cost-control basis emphasizing less.[52] The quality of care under such arrangements will be a major issue to study in the years immediately ahead.[53]

In addition, from the mid-1980s to the present there has been a series of experimental and demonstration programs that attempt to minimize expenditures and improve quality of care simultaneously by integrating acute care and long-term care, and Medicare and Medicaid financing. These programs include social/health maintenance programs (SHMOs), the On Lok program in San Francisco and its replication through Programs of All-Inclusive Care for the Elderly (PACE), the Minnesota Long-Term Care Options Project (LTCOP), the Arizona Long-Term Care System (ALTCS), and EverCare.[54] Research on these programs has provided valuable preliminary evidence on issues of quality of care and cost saving under such arrangements.[55] Indeed, the Balanced Budget Act of 1997 terminated the demonstration phase of the PACE program and transformed it to full status as a Medicare option. Integrative programs of this sort are likely to proliferate and expand substantially, and additional research on the quality of care they offer should be an ongoing, top priority.

These contemporary changes in health care policies affecting older persons are relatively modest with respect to cost containment and revisions in organization and financing. As the baby boom edges even closer to old age, the structural changes undertaken to contain health care costs for treating the elderly are likely to be far more radical. If so, the danger mounts that older people will have less access to appropriate health care and experience poorer quality of care.

A FINAL NOTE: STRUCTURAL CHANGE AND THE POLITICS OF AGING

Most journalists, and many scholars who are experts in subjects other than politics, fear that older people will constitute a sufficiently powerful political force in an aging society to ensure, *selfishly*, that their needs will be met through the auspices of government, at the expense of other societal needs. Consequently, in the view of these commentators, it is impossible to refashion health policies on aging (as well as Social Security) substantially because of the political power of older people. Economist Lester Thurow, addressing the economic implications of an aging baby boom, has expressed what is perhaps the strongest statement of this view to date:

No one knows how the growth of entitlements for the elderly can be held in check in democratic societies. . . . Will democratic governments be able to cut benefits when the elderly are approaching a voting majority? Universal suffrage . . . is going to meet the ultimate test in the elderly. If democratic governments cannot cut benefits that go to a majority of their voters, then they have no long-term future. . . . In the years ahead, class warfare is apt to be redefined as the young against the old, rather than the poor against the rich.[56]

Central to this viewpoint is a so-called senior power model of politics that assumes the political behavior of older people is dominated by self-interests and, furthermore, they all perceive their interests to be identical. Applying this model, one expects older people to be homogeneous in political attitudes and voting behavior and, through sheer numbers, to be a powerful, perhaps dominating force.

The senior power model, however, is neither empirically valid nor conceptually sound. Consider Sweden, for example, which currently has the highest proportion of people aged sixty-five and older, about 18 percent. During the past two decades there have been substantial cutbacks in Sweden's benefits to the aging as part of a general retrenchment of that nation's welfare state.[57]

Studies involving many different birth cohorts in the United States have established that the attribute of old age has little impact on political attitudes.[58] Attitudinal differences between age groups are far less impressive than those *within* age groups. Numerous polls have shown that older people are nearly indistinguishable from younger adults (both the middle-aged and younger categories) on most issues—including aging policy toward the elderly. In fact, socioeconomic characteristics and partisan attachments are the best predictors of political attitudes among adults of all ages.

When it comes to the voting behavior of older people, the same holds true. There are no opportunities, of course, for people to vote on specific national policy propositions such as those affecting Social Security and Medicare. Analyses of voting returns in presidential and congressional elections, though, show no indication that the aged are a single-issue—or several-issue—constituency.[59]

Although older persons vote at much higher rates than other age groups, they do not vote as a monolithic bloc any more than middle-aged or younger persons do. In fact, the elderly distribute their votes among candidates in about the same proportions as do younger citizens,[60] even when issues involving Social Security and Medicare are prominent in election campaigns.

Consider, for instance, the 1984 campaign, when Ronald Reagan was running for reelection to the presidency. In his first term he had led a

Republican-dominated Congress to delay for a year the annual cost-of-living adjustment in Social Security benefits, and he had proposed substantial further reductions in benefits. Throughout the election campaign, Democrats portrayed Reagan as an archenemy of Social Security. Yet the percentage of older people voting for Reagan increased from 54 percent in 1980 to 60 percent in 1984; the level of support that Reagan received from older voters in 1984 was actually one percentage point higher than the 59 percent he received from the electorate as a whole.[61]

Similarly, consider the 1996 presidential election campaign, in which discussions of Medicare were more prominent in speeches and political ads than they had been in a long time. On the one hand presidential and many congressional candidates labored hard to convey the impression that they had been trying to "save" Medicare and would continue to do so in the future. On the other hand they tried to label their opponents as potential destroyers of Medicare, or as indifferent to the fate of the program and those it serves.[62] Yet, once again, older persons distributed their votes among the candidates in roughly the same proportion as did younger ones. President Clinton received 48 percent of older persons' votes; the overall percentage for Clinton was 49 percent.[63]

That the attitudes and votes of older persons distribute in the same fashion as those of the rest of society should not be surprising. There is no sound theoretical reason to expect that a birth cohort—composed of all religions, ethnic groups, economic and social statuses, political attitudes and affiliations, and every other characteristic in society—would suddenly become homogenized in its political behavior when it reaches the "old age" category. Moreover, as Nobel laureate Herbert Simon has pointed out, the very assumption that mass groupings of citizens, such as elderly people, vote primarily on the basis of self-interested responses to a single issue or cluster of issues is, in itself, problematic.[64] To the extent that policy issues might have an impact within *heterogeneous* groups such as older persons, self-interested responses to any single issue are likely to vary substantially. A proposed reduction in Social Security benefits, for example, may be of grave concern to a poor older person but not to a wealthy one.

The senior power model also assumes that old-age-based political organizations and interest groups that purport to represent all older people are powerful in affecting old-age policy and will become more so in the future. Here again the evidence suggests otherwise.

Social Security, Medicare, and other major old-age programs in the United States have been enacted and amended over the years through the initiatives of political elites, not interest groups.[65] And important retrenchments and reforms in policies toward the elderly have been accomplished despite the opposition of old-age groups. To be sure, policymakers prefer to have the assent of these organizations when changes are under way. But the old-age interests have not proved to be a formidable obstacle when they oppose such reforms.

In the United States, for example, we have experienced more than a decade of policy reforms in old-age programs, which the old-age interest groups have viewed with disfavor.[66] Among these reforms, the major ones took money out of the pockets of older Americans. For instance, the Social Security Reform Act of 1983 made 50 percent of Social Security benefits subject to taxation for individuals with incomes exceeding $25,000, and for married couples, in excess of $32,000. The Tax Reform Act of 1986 eliminated the extra personal deduction that had been available to all persons sixty-five years old and over when filing their federal income tax returns. The Omnibus Budget Reconciliation Act of 1993 made 85 percent of Social Security benefits subject to taxation for individuals with incomes surpassing $34,000 and for married couples, more than $44,000. There have been other instances in the 1980s and 1990s as well in which the opposition of old-age interest groups has not prevented policy reforms in elder benefit programs.

Most notable of the "senior lobby" interest groups is the American Association of Retired Persons (AARP). It has 33 million members, an annual budget approaching $500 million, 1,700 employees, 4,000 local chapters, and extensive contacts with the White House and Congress.[67] The press describes AARP as the nine-hundred-pound gorilla of American politics that can get anything it wants.

Yet AARP has rarely tried to cohere the votes of its members, and has failed when it has attempted to do so. It has experienced strong protests and even resignations from within its heterogeneous membership whenever it has taken a reasonably specific position on policy issues, and it is very moderate in its political tactics. No massive rallies or protests. No significant mass media campaigns. In fact, AARP maintains its 33 million membership and large revenues through the material and associational incentives that it provides to its members, rather than through political incentives. The political activities of AARP are essentially marketing strategies and do not include controversial or militant tactics that threaten to jeopardize the stability of the organization's membership base and financial resources.

In summary, there is no evidence to date that senior power will, as Thurow and others suggest, imperil the future of democracy. Yet things could change. Some social scientists[68] have argued for several decades that by the twenty-first century an age-group consciousness would develop among older people, to the extent that they could behave in a cohesive political fashion to dominate the political systems and establish a "gerontocracy." Perhaps this could happen. Perhaps the class warfare between young and old that Thurow envisions could emerge.

Suppose, for example, that proposals for official old-age-based health care rationing become more prominent and reach the policy agenda as the baby boom approaches old age. If so, age-group consciousness might very well develop among older people, and they might act in a cohesive political fashion in attempts to counter such proposals. Similar radical proposals undermining policies that nurture the well-being of older people through income maintenance programs and various services could have the same kind of effect.

If the economy of the aging society is not productive, old-age-based health care rationing could very well be proposed by political leaders. Americans may find themselves contemplating the destruction of the fragile moral and ethical principles regarding the sanctity and dignity of human life, which most human cultures have developed laboriously over many centuries. This country could experience the ascendance of a *new* morality, in which older people are set aside categorically as unworthy of the humanistic protection and support that the United States has tried to make available to all of its citizens. In turn, this could lead down the clichéd "slippery slope" whereby various other categories of citizens— grouped perhaps by race, ethnicity, religion, or disabling conditions and diseases—are also deemed unworthy of lifesaving care.

The preeminent challenge for our nation regarding health policies toward older people in the twenty-first century will be to maintain, actively, a range of moral perspectives with which to frame our public policy issues and discussions. This would not mean being overly preoccupied by issues framed in terms of intergenerational equity—conflict between cohorts of the young and old. It *would* mean preserving notions of equity— in terms of rich versus poor, or the conditions of some racial and ethnic groups in comparison with others—among people of all ages.

5

THE DISTINCTIVE NEEDS OF WOMEN AND MINORITIES

Charlotte Muller

INTRODUCTION

W omen and ethnic minorities comprise the most vulnerable segments of the older population in this country. In addition to sharing a plethora of problems associated with growing old in our society, many suffer the disabling consequences of discrimination specific to their sex and ethnicity. This contributes to a poorer quality of life and lower standard of living for older women and minority individuals compared to the aging population as a whole. The imbalances between their needs and the resources allocated to them by society perpetuate a situation in which women and minorities are disproportionately represented among those who live at or near the poverty level as they age.

Minorities and women are affected by "cross-cutting issues," that is, clusters of variables that undermine the quality of their lives. These include employment and earning records that negatively affect a person's ability to receive an adequate pension and Social Security benefits, compromised health status and inadequate health coverage, lack of family support systems, and divorce or the death of a spouse. Issues such as these are frequently exacerbated by social taboos and fears that prevent older minorities and women from utilizing available assistance. In combination, these problems frequently have the effect of overwhelming the individual who must deal with them all at once.

One must ask: What in their communal life experience makes ethnic minorities and women so vulnerable in their later years? What are the special needs they have in common, and in what significant ways do these two groups differ from each other? How can our society today meet the challenges they present? Finally, how can society be structured so that later generations will not have to encounter the same barriers to better quality of life in old age?

WOMEN

WHO THEY ARE

Women constitute 55 percent of those aged sixty-five to sixty-nine, and their proportion rises to 72 percent for those aged eighty-five and over.[1] Since the start of the twentieth century, life expectancy at birth has risen dramatically for both men and women. It increased from forty-six years for men and forty-nine years for women in 1900 to seventy-two and seventy-nine years in 1991, indicating a widening gap in favor of women (see Table 5.1). Between 1950 and 1991 women consistently had a longer life expectancy at age sixty-five than men, and again the gap actually widened—with life expectancy at that age for men and women, respectively, averaging 11.5 and 12.2 years in 1900 and 15.3 and 19.1 years in 1991. While acknowledging the human progress that the numbers represent, people must be cognizant of the downside of living these extra years: the chronic problems of loneliness and income inadequacy that have often accompanied survival as widows.

Older women tend to be poorer than their male counterparts and are less likely to have accrued adequate benefits for retirement. If advanced age is a risk factor for poverty, it has a greater impact on women. The percentage of elderly persons who are below the poverty line increases after age seventy-five—going from 8 to 10 percent for men but jumping from 13 to 20 percent for women.[2] Furthermore, this statistic does not take into account the plight of the near-poor, that is, those with incomes between 100 and 125 percent of the poverty line. Although not statistically poor, many of them are unable to meet all their economic needs, especially if they have special medical, nutritional, or other requirements. Women on the cusp of the poverty line have few or no reserves for emergencies.

TABLE 5.1 LIFE EXPECTANCY AT BIRTH AND AT AGE 65, BY RACE AND SEX, 1900 AND 1991				
	REMAINING LIFE EXPECTANCY IN YEARS			
SPECIFIED AGE AND YEAR	WHITE		BLACK	
	MALE	FEMALE	MALE	FEMALE
At birth				
1900[1,2]	46.6	48.7	32.5	33.5
1991	72.9	79.6	64.6	73.8
At sixty-five years				
1900–1902[1,2]	11.5	12.2	10.4	11.4
1991	15.4	19.2	13.4	17.2

[1] Death registration area only: in 1900, this comprised ten states and the District of Columbia
[2] Includes deaths of nonresidents of the United States

Source: Robin A. Cohen and Joan F. Van Nostrand, "Trends in the Health of Older Americans: United States, 1994," National Center for Health Statistics, *Vital and Health Statistics* 3, no. 30 (April 1995), Chapter 3, Table 1, drawing from vital statistics data.

MARITAL STATUS

Marital status is an important determinant of financial security in old age for both sexes since it affects the sources of income to which individuals are entitled. Being without a spouse is predictive of a higher risk of poverty among the elderly. Since nearly three-quarters of nonmarried people over the age of seventy-five are female, gender in itself becomes a risk factor late in life. Nonmarried women are generally in the most precarious economic position. Sixty-one percent of these women receive less than $12,000 a year, whereas only 44 percent of nonmarried men and 10 percent of married couples have income that low. With very few exceptions, this single benefit is a Social Security check. Only 30 percent of nonmarried women have two or more benefits; in most cases, these are Social Security plus a private pension (see Table 5.2, page 100); moreover, nonmarried women are less likely than other groups to have earnings to supplement their public or private pension income (see Table 5.3, page 103).

TABLE 5.2
RECEIPT OF RETIREMENT BENEFITS, EARNINGS, AND INCOME FROM ASSETS BY MARITAL STATUS, AND SEX OF NONMARRIED PERSONS: PERCENTAGE DISTRIBUTION OF HOUSEHOLDS CONSISTING OF THOSE AGED 65 OR OLDER, 1994

RETIREMENT BENEFITS	TOTAL	EARNINGS		INCOME FROM ASSETS	
		YES	NO	YES	NO
ALL					
Number (in thousands)	23,887	5,049	18,838	16,010	7,877
Total percent	100	100	100	100	100
No benefit	6	11	5	4	12
One benefit	53	50	54	46	67
Social Security only[1]	51	47	52	44	66
Private pension annuity only	1	2	0	1	1
Government employee pension only[2]	1	1	1	1	1
Railroad retirement only	0	0	0	0	0
More than one benefit[3]	40	39	41	50	21
Social Security and federal pension only	3	3	3	4	2
Social Security and railroad retirement, state/local, or military pension only	7	7	7	9	4
Social Security and private pension only	27	26	27	33	15
Three or more benefit types	3	3	3	3	1
MARRIED COUPLES					
Number (in thousands)	9,734	3,361	6,372	7,655	2,080
Total percent	100	100	100	100	100
No benefit	5	9	3	3	11
One benefit	43	47	41	39	61
Social Security only[1]	41	43	39	36	59
Private pension or annuity only	1	2	1	1	1
Government employee pension only[2]	1	2	1	1	1
Railroad retirement only	0	0	0	0	0
More than one benefit[3]	52	44	56	58	29
Social Security and federal pension only	4	3	4	4	3
Social Security and railroad retirement, state/local or military pension only	8	8	8	9	3
Social Security and private pension only	35	28	38	38	20
Three or more benefit types	5	3	5	5	2

TABLE 5.2 (Continued)

RETIREMENT BENEFITS	TOTAL	EARNINGS		INCOME FROM ASSETS	
		YES	NO	YES	NO
NONMARRIED PERSONS					
Number (in thousands)	14,153	1,687	12,465	8,355	5,797
Total percent	100	100	100	100	100
No benefit	8	14	7	4	12
One benefit	60	57	61	54	70
Social Security only[1]	58	55	59	51	68
Private pension or annuity only	0	1	0	1	0
Government employee pension only[2]	1	0	1	1	1
Railroad retirement only	1	0	1	1	0
More than one benefit[3]	32	29	33	42	18
Social Security and federal pension only	2	2	2	3	1
Social Security and railroad retirement, state/local, or military pension only	7	5	7	8	4
Social Security and private pension only	22	20	22	28	13
Three or more benefit types	1	1	1	2	0
NONMARRIED MEN					
Number (in thousands)	3,310	536	2,774	1,959	1,351
Total percent	100	100	100	100	100
No benefit	8	10	6	6	11
One benefit	52	12	52	43	66
Social Security only[1]	50	19	50	40	65
Private pension or annuity only	1	3	1	1	1
Government employee pension only[2]	1	0	1	1	1
Railroad retirement only	0	0	1	1	0
More than one benefit[3]	39	28	41	51	23
Social Security and federal pension only	3	2	3	3	1
Social Security and railroad retirement, state/local, or military pension only	6	4	6	7	4
Social Security and private pension only	30	20	32	38	17
Three or more benefit types	1	0	1	1	0

continued on next page

TABLE 5.2 (Continued)

RETIREMENT BENEFITS	TOTAL	EARNINGS		INCOME FROM ASSETS	
		YES	NO	YES	NO
NONMARRIED WOMEN					
Number (in thousands)	10,843	1,151	9,692	6,397	4,446
Total percent	100	100	100	100	100
No benefit	7	12	7	3	13
One benefit	63	59	63	57	71
Social Security only[1]	61	57	61	55	69
Private pension or annuity only	0	1	0	0	0
Government employee pension only[2]	1	1	1	1	1
Railroad retirement only	1	1	1	1	0
More than one benefit[3]	30	29	30	40	17
Social Security and federal pension only	2	2	2	3	1
Social Security and railroad retirement, state/local, or military pension only	0	5	7	9	3
Social Security and private pension only	19	20	19	25	11
Three or more benefit types	1	2	1	2	0

[1] Social Security beneficiaries may be receiving retired-worker benefits, dependents' or survivors' benefits, disability benefits, transitional insurance, or special age-72 benefits
[2] Includes federal, state, local, and military pensions
[3] Includes a small number with combinations of pensions not listed

Source: Susan Grad, "Income of the Population 55 or Older" publication no. 13-11871, Social Security Administration, January 1996, Table 1.6.

A comparison of the categories of nonmarried older people (widow, widower, never-married or divorced men and women) reveals that older women bear the economic consequences of their marital status to a greater degree than men.[3] Widows are more likely to receive Social Security benefits than never-married or divorced women. In contrast, divorced women are the most likely to be either wage earners or self-employed. The never-married most often receive government pensions, primarily from schoolteaching.

TABLE 5.3
TOTAL MONEY INCOME BY MARITAL STATUS, SEX OF NONMARRIED PERSONS, AND SOCIAL SECURITY BENEFICIARY STATUS: PERCENTAGE DISTRIBUTIONS OF HOUSEHOLDS CONSISTING OF THOSE AGED 65 OR OLDER, 1994

| | Beneficiary units[1] | | | | | Nonbeneficiary units | | | | | |
| | ALL | MARRIED COUPLES | NONMARRIED PERSONS | | | ALL | MARRIED COUPLES | NONMARRIED PERSONS | | |
			TOTAL	MEN	WOMEN			TOTAL	MEN	WOMEN
Number (in thousands)	21,789	9,004	12,785	2,948	9,837	2,098	730	1,367	362	1,006
Total percentage	100.0	100.0	100.0	100.0	100.0	100.0	100.0	100.0	100.0	100.0
Income										
Up to $6,000	8.3	1.0	13.5	10.2	14.5	42.5	20.5	54.1	41.8	58.5
$6,000-$11,999	29.0	8.5	43.5	34.1	46.3	13.8	10.1	15.8	15.2	16.2
$12,000-$29,999	41.6	51.8	34.4	42.4	31.9	20.4	23.1	18.9	24.1	17.1
$30,000-$59,999	15.4	27.6	6.9	9.8	5.9	13.6	24.6	7.6	10.8	6.6
$60,000-$74,999	2.1	4.1	0.6	1.5	0.4	2.7	4.9	1.6	3.7	0.9
$75,000-$99,999	1.8	3.7	0.4	1.1	0.3	2.2	5.3	0.6	0.8	0.5
$100,000 or more	1.8	3.4	0.7	1.2	0.4	4.8	11.4	1.3	3.9	0.4
Median income	15,443	25,020	10,730	13,180	10,084	7,932	25,521	5,463	9,325	5,185

[1] Social Security beneficiaries may be receiving retired-worker benefits, dependents' or survivors' benefits, transitional insurance, or special age-72 benefits.

Source: Susan Grad, "Income of the Population 55 or Older" publication no. 13-11871, Social Security Administration, January 1996, Table 3.2.

The never-married are less likely to have asset income than widowed or divorced women. They are also less likely to be homeowners. Although most elderly people possess their own homes, the ownership rate varies by marital status and ethnicity. At all ages above sixty, it is more common for married couples to own their home than for a female living alone. For those between the ages of sixty-five and sixty-nine, 67 percent of women living alone are owners, compared to 91 percent of couples. As is the case with minority homeowners, the market value of the homes of elderly women living by themselves frequently diminishes because, among other reasons, there is not enough money for upkeep. The only types of income for which nonmarried women are on a par with nonmarried men are those derived from assets, but both groups are less likely than married couples to have such resources.

Security of retirement income is likely to be endangered by suggested approaches that would radically change Social Security financing and would oblige those who have little background to prepare themselves to make major investment decisions and to select a suitable saving rate (even if they have the income to do so). Forty percent of women in a recent survey are not saving for retirement, and among women who are, only 39 percent are confident that they are investing their money wisely. Few of the women surveyed are fully confident that they will be able to afford retirement, and African-American and Asian-American women are less confident than their male counterparts.[4]

Work

Women's special vulnerability as they age is associated with culturally prescribed roles and responsibilities that long discouraged paid employment during their child-rearing years. In addition, women who did participate in the paid economy were clustered in different occupations and industries from men, in what were generally considered "leftover" jobs that paid significantly lower wages. This phenomenon has been associated with discrimination against women in education and hiring, a lack of adaptation of industrial equipment to women, and a mind-set that differentiated "women's work" from higher-paying male occupations. Finally, the financial gains from higher education have been lower for women than for men, even after account is taken of the higher labor force participation rates of men.

Participation in the workforce before and after the normal age of retirement is of course beneficial to the income of elderly women. But this is not always possible. One of the determinants of whether or not older married women continue working is health—their own health and that of their spouse. Research by Marjorie Honig indicates that married women's health in preretirement years (fifty-one to sixty-one) affected the probability of continuing full-time work after age sixty-two. In addition, a Hispanic wife is more likely to plan to continue working if her husband's health deteriorates, but the opposite has been found to be true for a non-Hispanic, African-American wife, perhaps because fewer Hispanics expect Social Security benefits compared to African Americans.[5]

In recent years women have improved their financial status by entering better-paid occupations and compiling more continuous work histories, thus adding to their credits for retirement as well as offering more experience to employers.[6] Like the African-American and Hispanic communities, women have benefited from civil rights legislation and affirmative action programs and are becoming more widely accepted on an equal footing in the culture of the workplace.

The gender wage differential has been narrowing. This will be beneficial to women as they age, since it will enable them to accumulate more resources for retirement. However, the potential for voluntary savings may be undercut by the child care costs faced by single working mothers, who number 2.2 million, and by many married working mothers.[7] In addition, it must be noted that the shrinking of the gender wage differential is owed partly to the weakening of union protection for male workers in the lower range of the skills spectrum, with the effect of lowering their wages.

Overall, women cannot feel secure that their position in the workforce will steadily improve. The increase in the percentage of women with substantial work experience will eventually slow down. An adverse economy can reverse the progress of job opportunities and limit the potential for those with poor access to education. Almost 4.5 million women work in health care occupations.[8] As health management continues to stress cost control, constraints on rewards to health professionals may erode the financial security enjoyed by women working in this sector. Finally, legislation restricting public financing of family planning limits career options for poor women.

HEALTH CARE

Gender-specific health problems of older women are not necessarily worse than those of older men; however, age bias in considering treatment for women's health conditions can deprive older women of necessary services. One example is the age cap that was used in recommendations for the Pap smear test for early detection of cervical cancer. (That restriction has been lifted, and Medicare now covers the test.) Another is the discrimination women have experienced both before and after surgery for breast cancer. The Health Care Financing Administration recently acted to prevent HMOs and fee-for-service providers from limiting mastectomy for breast cancer to outpatient locations and from restricting hospital days after breast cancer surgery.[9] Postsurgery, it has been reported that older women are less likely than younger women with breast cancer to receive adjunctive chemotherapy and radiation treatment.[10] In response to these issues, the American Medical Association now recognizes that a female presence in the ranks of practitioners offers a safeguard against gender bias.[11]

When health problems common to both sexes are examined, it becomes apparent that women aged seventy and over suffer more than men from chronic conditions that limit their activity. Significantly, women and minorities also are more likely than white men to use outpatient clinics, which are generally considered inferior in quality to other health care institutions.

ETHNIC MINORITIES

WHO THEY ARE

Each minority community has unique cultural characteristics and they all live "as minority members in a majority culture."[12] Today, nine-tenths of the elderly are white, but the poverty rates for African Americans and Hispanics far exceed their representation in the population at large.[13]

The minority population is mostly African American (29.9 million) and Hispanic (21.9 million, who can be of any race but mostly consider themselves white). The Asian and Pacific Islander population numbers 7.2 million and the Native American population, 2.1 million.[14]

Increasingly, such figures are approximate because of substantial intermarriage and differences in self-reporting. Within these broad groups, certain subgroups are the most numerous. Mexican Americans (13.4 million) are about three-fifths of all Hispanics (61.2 percent), Puerto Ricans (2.7 million) are 12.7 percent, and Cuban Americans (1.1 million) make up 4.8 percent. Of the Asian/Pacific Islander population, those of Chinese,

Filipino, and Japanese origin together make up more than half (54.4 percent), with Chinese alone (1.6 million) amounting to 22.8 percent.[15]

African Americans, the largest ethnic minority in the society as a whole, predictably are also the largest ethnic minority among older citizens, constituting 8.1 percent of the U.S. elderly. By comparison, Asian and Pacific Islanders are 1.9 percent and Native Americans only 0.3 percent of the general population of older folk. Hispanics make up 4.6 percent of the U.S. elderly.[16]

Minorities have a younger age profile than the American population as a whole, of whom 12.8 percent were sixty-five and over in 1995. The highest percentage of elderly is found among blacks (8.2 percent), with Asian/Pacific Islanders, Native Americans, and Hispanics all having elderly populations constituting less than 7 percent of their communities.[17]

The generally younger age profile is the result of several influences, among them the fact that immigration is concentrated in younger groups, the short length of residence in the United States of many immigrant cohorts, and relatively high fertility—but it is also the result of the adverse influences of poverty, obstacles to timely medical care, and discrimination. The Native Americans, who include Eskimos and Aleuts, are among the poorest people in the United States. A substantial minority live on reservations or in Alaskan native villages. While life expectancy increased from fifty-one years in 1941 to more than seventy-one in 1987–89, few Native Americans are sixty-five plus; the older ones have an unemployment rate twice as high as whites and have high rates of work disability and malnutrition. Within the four minority groups, however, there is considerable variation in the percentage who are elderly. Cubans, with 15.8 percent aged sixty-five or over, have much higher rates than other large Hispanic groups. Japanese, who were less restricted by law in bringing families with them than other Asians, have higher percentages of elderly than Chinese and Filipinos.[18]

ECONOMICS

As with older women, the financial problems of minority elderly result in large part from their experiences in the working world, with low-paying employment restricting their ability to acquire pension rights, Social Security, or other income sources. Limited access to education, job training, and equal opportunities in the job market handicaps both minorities and women and creates difficulties as they reach retirement. Whereas women's child-rearing and family responsibilities present an additional barrier to maintaining a regular employment history, minorities frequently face language and cultural barriers. Minority women, of course, have the daunting task of overcoming the obstacles placed before both groups.

In 1994, median income was higher for white elderly than for blacks and Hispanics: for Social Security beneficiaries, $16,214 versus $9,030 and $9,788, respectively; for nonbeneficiaries, $9,998 versus $5,600 and $5,197 (see Table 5.4). Among beneficiaries, blacks had the lowest median income, and among nonbeneficiaries, Hispanics had the lowest. But the differences between the minorities paled in comparison with the separation between both and the white medians.

Assets. Demographic groups with low incomes on average are not likely to have substantial financial assets. A recent report from the Rand Corporation cited a statistic that for every dollar in wealth held by a household maintained by a white person aged fifty-one to sixty-one, an African-American household in the same age cohort had twenty-seven cents and a Hispanic household thirty cents.[19] Minority households generally command little in the way of surplus income that can be accumulated as assets in preparation for retirement. In addition, immigrants may be constrained from saving for their own retirements because they are committed to supporting their elders who lack entitlements.

A majority of whites, African Americans, and Hispanics own their own homes. However, depressed market values caused by changes in taxes and public services, shifts in neighborhood demographics, and the difficulties older owners experience in finding the money to maintain their homes adequately can significantly decrease their home equity. Home ownership is the only major financial asset of 67 percent of African Americans, compared to 42 percent of whites and 58 percent of Hispanics.[20] These assets can and should be preserved and enhanced by public investment in neighborhoods and urban services.

Social Security. Older Americans who are African-American or Hispanic are less likely to receive Social Security than whites (see Table 5.5, page 111). There are many reasons why some members of minority groups fall through this minimal financial safety net. Persons lacking language skills, education, and training are overrepresented in farm and domestic work, occupations in which employers do not generally pay payroll taxes for Social Security. Those who had been employed in very low paying jobs or who have had insufficient work time credited to them, as

TABLE 5.4
TOTAL INCOME BY RACE, HISPANIC ORIGIN, AND SOCIAL SECURITY BENEFICIARY STATUS: PERCENTAGE DISTRIBUTION OF HOUSEHOLDS CONSISTING OF THOSE AGED 65 OR OLDER, 1994

	Beneficiaries[1]			Nonbeneficiaries		
	White	Black	Hispanic origin[2]	White	Black	Hispanic origin
Number (in thousands)	19,532	1,883	922	1,629	287	248
Total percent	100	100	100	100	100	100
Income						
Up to $6,000	7.1	20.2	15.4	39.0	52.8	65.6
$6,000-$11,999	27.5	44.6	44.6	14.2	10.8	16.8
$12,000-$29,999	42.9	28.1	32.6	20.4	23.6	11.9
$30,000-$59,999	16.5	5.5	6.2	15.5	6.5	2.9
$60,000-$74,999	2.1	0.6	0.4	2.8	2.0	0.3
$75,000-$99,999	1.9	0.8	0.5	2.4	2.6	1.4
$100,000 or more	1.9	0.3	0.3	5.6	1.8	1.0
Median income	16,214	9,030	9,788	9,998	5,600	5,197

[1] Social Security beneficiaries may be receiving retired-worker benefits, dependents' or survivors' benefits, disability benefits, transitional insurance, or special age-72 benefits.
[2] Persons of Hispanic origin may be of any race.

Source: Susan Grad, "Income of the Population 55 or Older," Publication no. 13-11871, Social Security Administration, January 1996, Table 3.4.

well as older immigrants who lack an adequate earning record in the United States, do not qualify at all. Many people who are eligible are not aware of the program or do not realize that they can apply, and pride or cultural taboos against accepting what is perceived to be "charity" prevent some retirees from receiving benefits. Still others never become U.S. citizens because they are unaware of their eligibility. For example, many Hispanics are still aliens despite the Immigration Reform and Control Act of 1986, which enabled undocumented residents to request citizenship.[21]

HEALTH CARE

Financial and social conditions are involved in the level of health care received by the elderly. The link between economic status and poor health consists of such correlates of poverty as deficits in nutrition and housing, excessive occupational exposures to hazards in past or present work life, and job insecurity. Additionally, problems of access to health care, based on personal suspicion of discrimination in treatment, transportation and linguistic barriers, dearth of neighborhood providers, lack of institutional and program outreach, and professional biases all play a role. Minorities tend to have limited insurance coverage, and their financial cushion to deal with medical emergencies is often very thin. Specific program features, such as Medicare's lack of prescription drug coverage and restrictions on preventive care, impose heavy burdens on minorities and women. In addition, first-generation immigrants are at a disadvantage upon reaching sixty-five, for fewer elderly among foreign-born persons of Asian or Hispanic origin are covered by Medicare than among native-born Americans of similar origin.[22]

Statistics show that African Americans are notably underserved with regard to modern health services. Those sixty-five years old and over report a significantly higher rate of unsatisfactory health than whites in the same age bracket (see Table 5.6, page 113). Preventive care is strikingly uncommon in this population. Influenza immunization rates are 40 percent lower for blacks than for whites, and the mammography rate for elderly African-American females is 50 percent lower than for whites. Visits to physicians are less common for blacks, and they are more likely to use outpatient clinics. A study comparing care in South Central Los Angeles, an area with a concentration of African-American and low-income residents, with the rest of Los Angeles County found that the South Central district

TABLE 5.5
INCOME SOURCES BY RACE, HISPANIC ORIGIN, AND SOCIAL SECURITY BENEFICIARY STATUS: PERCENTAGE DISTRIBUTION OF HOUSEHOLDS CONSISTING OF THOSE AGED 65 OR OLDER WITH INCOME FROM SPECIFIED SOURCES, 1994

	WHITE		BLACK		HISPANIC ORIGIN[2]	
	BENEFICIARIES	NONBENEFICIARIES	BENEFICIARIES	NONBENEFICIARIES	BENEFICIARIES	NONBENEFICIARIES
Number (in thousands)	19,532	1,629	1,883	287	922	248
Source of Income						
Percentage of units with:						
Earnings	20	36	17	27	17	22
Retirement benefits	100	29	100	24	100	8
Social Security	100	-	100	-	100	-
Benefits other than Social Security[1]	46	29	28	24	24	8
Other public pensions	15	20	11	16	6	4
Railroad retirement	1	8	0	2	0	2
Government employee pensions	14	13	11	14	6	3
Private pensions or annuities	34	11	19	9	19	4
Income from assets	72	55	35	26	38	15
Veterans' benefits	5	3	4	3	4	0
Public assistance	4	16	15	31	19	41

[1] Social Security beneficiaries may be receiving retired-worker benefits, dependents' or survivors' benefits, disability benefits, transitional insurance, or special age-72 benefits.

[2] Persons of Hispanic origin may be of any race.

Source: Susan Grad, "Income of the Population 55 or Older," Publication no. 13-11871, Social Security Administration, January 1996, Table I.4.

had significantly fewer special procedures for circulatory disease (coronary angioplasties, bypass surgery, and carotid endarterectomy) even after poverty is taken into account. This is believed to be the result of fewer physicians and hospital beds in the area.[23]

At age sixty-five whites have a higher life expectancy (using 1991 data) than African Americans. Women outlive men, but the racial difference is greater than the sex difference. Of the four groupings by gender and black versus white, African-American males have the lowest average number of years of life after sixty-five. This differential has been associated with several increased risk factors, including life-style (alcohol, smoking, and nutrition), low socioeconomic status that results in limited access to health services and lack of health insurance, less adherence to good health practices and preventive care owing to low educational levels and despair, and greater likelihood of occupational hazards and environmental exposure.

For the elderly in particular, an important indicator of chronic health problems is limitations in activities that are vital to independent living. Two major types of limitations are those involving basic daily care or "personal" care—activities such as eating, bathing, dressing, or getting around the house—and necessary chores such as shopping, cooking, and using the telephone that are referred to as "routine" care. (These are equivalent to the terms "activities of daily living" and "instrumental activities of daily living.") Blacks aged seventy and over, both male and female, have a higher prevalence of limitations in personal care and routine care compared with whites: 15.6 percent of black females have limitations in personal care compared with 8.6 percent of white females, while 10.7 percent of black males have such limitations compared with 6.7 percent of white males (see Table 5.7, page 114).

While difficulties in old age may have deep roots in earlier life, today's society can do a great deal to correct or limit the damage thus caused. Additionally, policies that will guarantee access to the services needed to deal with health problems and risks that arise in later years of life should not be weakened. A trend toward deregulation plunges too many older clients into a complex market where consumers are often at a disadvantage, and where the self-interest of providers and insurers may lead to service restrictions that are not compatible with timely and optimal care.

Medicare has been the major national program of health care financing for the elderly since its enactment in 1965. Data by race from Medicare are vital to tracking what is happening to elderly African Americans in their encounters with the health care system.

TABLE 5.6
RESPONDENT-ASSESSED HEALTH STATUS BY
RACE, SEX, AND AGE, 1992

RACE, SEX, AGE	RESPONDENT-ASSESSED HEALTH STATUS (PERCENTAGES)					N (IN THOUSANDS) (=100%)
	EXCELLENT	VERY GOOD	GOOD	FAIR	POOR	
65–74 YEARS						
White males	18.3	24.2	32.0	17.5	8.1	7,375
White females	17.3	24.6	35.2	16.8	6.2	9,011
Black males	12.1	17.6	27.9	29.0	13.4	711
Black females	8.6	15.5	34.1	26.3	15.5	932
75–84 YEARS						
White males	15.3	21.3	31.5	20.5	11.4	3,493
White females	14.3	22.3	32.5	21.9	9.0	5,321
Black males	10.9[1]	9.6[1]	33.0	25.3	21.3	286
Black females	6.3[1]	16.6	29.4	25.1	22.6	451
85 YEARS AND OVER						
White males	11.6	19.9	32.9	21.8	13.9	687
White females	3.4	9.0	33.1	23.0	10.6	648
Black males[1]	–	–	–	–	–	–
Black females[1]	–	–	–	–	–	–
65 YEARS AND OVER						
White males	17.0	23.1	31.9	18.6	9.5	11,559
White females	15.9	23.4	34.1	9.2	7.5	15,980
Black males	11.2	15.2	29.8	27.9	15.9	1,064
Black females	8.0	15.0	32.1	26.1	18.8	1,558

[1] Figure does not meet standard of reliability or precision.

Source: Robin A. Cohen and Joan F. Van Nostrand, "Trends in the Health of Older Americans: United States, 1994," National Center for Health Statistics, *Vital and Health Statistics* 3, no. 30 (April 1995), Chapter 2, Table 1, using data from National Health Interview Survey.

TABLE 5.7
**PERCENTAGE OF PERSONS AGED 70 AND OVER WITH
LIMITATIONS IN SELECTED TYPES OF ACTIVITIES AS A RESULT OF
CHRONIC CONDITIONS, BY RACE AND SEX, 1992**

Type of Limitation	White		Black	
	Male	Female	Male	Female
Personal care	6.7	8.6	10.7	15.6
Routine care[1]	8.8	14.2	10.9	18.1
Other activities[2]	22.9	16.9	23.6	15.4
Not limited[3]	61.6	60.3	54.8	50.9

[1] Excludes those who need help with personal care
[2] Excludes those who need help with personal care or routine care
[3] Includes persons of unknown limitation status

Source: Robin A. Cohen and Joan F. Van Nostrand, "Trends in the Health of Older Americans: United States, 1994," National Center for Health Statistics, *Vital and Health Statistics* 3, no. 30 (April 1995), Chapter 2, Table 3, using data from the National Health Interview Survey.

The nonwhite elderly population has fewer persons served under Medicare than does the population of white elderly. However, payments per person enrolled are higher for nonwhites.[24] This is believed to be the case because a statistically significant, lower percentage of African Americans avail themselves of preventive care and office treatment of acute disease or management of chronic disease, and a higher proportion wait until they require hospitalization. Medicare does not cover long-term care services, and in part as a result the disabled African-American elderly are a population especially at risk for poor health.

Lack of preventive and early care constitutes a major risk factor for poor health among African Americans. Not surprisingly, certain surgical procedures are performed at an abnormally high rate on African-American patients. Bilateral orchiectomy, which is primarily recommended in cases of metastatic prostate cancer, has an occurrence rate 2.2 times higher in African-American males than in whites. This is far out of proportion to the prevalence of prostate cancer in the two groups but precisely consistent with the higher rate of the disease's prevalence at its advanced stage among blacks (2.2 times the rate for whites). Findings like this are evidence of the serious consequences of the deferral of treatment and point to the need for greater access to health care providers among high-risk populations.

Adult-onset diabetes is one of the ten leading causes of death for both African Americans and whites who are sixty-five or older,[25] but it is much more common among nonwhite minorities. There is also a higher rate for minorities of serious complications and deaths from complications related to diabetes.[26] Among African Americans with diabetes as the principal diagnosis, amputations of all or part of a lower limb are 3.6 times as frequent as among whites. This is twice as high as the prevalence of diabetes in the two racial groups would predict. Since control of the progression of diabetes is dependent on good medical care and cooperation between physician and patient, it would seem that this situation could be improved through community education and good public health management.

For the general population, private health insurance is a major determinant of access to care. As an example, recent research has confirmed that insured persons are more likely to take advantage of cancer screening services.[27] For those under sixty-five (and not disabled), employer-based insurance is the main ticket to access. It is not likely that those without coverage while on the job will be able to afford private coverage as a supplement to Medicare after age sixty-five. Medicare meets only part of the cost of covered health services. Since this limits the ability to pay for care in retirement, the rate of coverage for minorities on the job can serve as an early indicator of whether there is likely to be a problem with access to care. This is important because, while Medicaid also helps those elderly of limited means who are eligible for it, the care is frequently not equivalent to what the insured elderly receive, and the means test requirement for Medicaid puts obstacles in the way of access.

Culture plays a role as well. For instance, some Hispanics are unfamiliar with the concept of health insurance. Further, in interviews conducted by the Health and Retirement Survey with individuals of preretirement age, Hispanics were the least likely to report that their retirement plan included health care. The absence of coverage occurs most frequently in households headed by Hispanic women, whose earning capacity may be limited by circumstances already discussed.

Elderly members of minority groups who live in urban areas tend to have better access to services because rural areas are more likely to be underserved. Thus, Native Americans may have difficulty obtaining health care unless they can reach a public hospital. Both urban and rural elderly poor, however, suffer from the limited availability of affordable transportation with which to travel to and from medical providers.

CONCLUSION

Protection of the quality of life of women and minorities in old age must start early on. Generally, measures that are helpful to low-income groups will be beneficial to women and minorities. The workplace is a key venue for such efforts. Access to steady employment at decent wages can be strengthened by effective equal opportunity programs, investment in education, and support of child care and elder care that lightens the burden on working-age adults. Basic protection of immigrants and others against peonage and other illegal exploitation in the workplace should be guaranteed, while upward movement can be encouraged by training individuals for places on career ladders and by helping them meet educational requirements for credentialed occupations. A good place to target affirmative action efforts is fast-growing industries because their existing employees probably would not be displaced in the process.[28]

These measures should ideally be founded on a national commitment to full employment. The notion that joblessness is natural or that its distressful effects should be tolerated for the sake of deficit reduction ought to be broadly rejected.

A critical part of the early-life approach is universalizing the access of working-age adults to health insurance, freeing them from dependence on employers' willingness to sponsor it. Financial coverage, to be effective, should be complemented by policies to ensure an infrastructure of health facilities in minority neighborhoods, so that service use appropriate to each age and either gender will be up to the standards of the larger community.

It is not clear that all individuals and groups can successfully save for old age, given income constraints and the inevitability of adversity for some. But the process of making prudent preparations can be encouraged through financial education of foreign-born, undereducated, or inexperienced members of the population, who may not understand compound interest, American financial instruments and markets, or how to select reliable channels of saving. Since housing is a major vehicle of personal saving in the United States, minorities should receive governmental assistance in obtaining equal access to mortgages and in eliminating the persistent discrimination in the housing and mortgage markets that constrains choice and contributes to poor housing, especially for low-income groups.[29] Tax incentives for retirement saving should be tailored to the needs of those earning modest wages as well as those with middle-range and upper incomes.

Early-life measures will ultimately benefit the elderly, but only policies directed at the needs of today's older population can advance the welfare of women and minorities who have already reached sixty-five or will soon do so. When elders encounter acute medical conditions, continuous care needs, loss of income sources, and fraying of the personal networks that supply material help and emotional and informational support, their personal resources are stressed despite all their earlier planning. All, no matter when they reach senior citizen status, need security against such events.

Given the high costs of medical care and the power of well-considered and appropriate care to influence the course of an older person's life, the system for financing and delivering health care presents many opportunities to better the outlook for women and minorities. At the same time, the workings of the health care system create potential hurdles to receiving the right care at the right time. Incentives that motivate private, entrepreneurial players and the cost-cutting objectives of public sector managers are largely responsible for this. Thus, strict rules on advance authorization of certain services, combined with slow administrative processing, may amount to claim denial and leave patients stranded. Financial failure of HMOs, a calamity that can leave thousands of patients without orderly access to care, has emerged as a significant risk to the elderly. Protections against mismanagement should be strengthened.

These conflicting possibilities are manifested in provisions of the Balanced Budget Act of 1997 that modify Medicare and readjust its relation to the private sector. On the positive side, older women gain by Medicare coverage of more frequent mammography and of a bone density test for osteoporosis. Regular mammography can reduce the risk of death from breast cancer in women fifty and older—a risk that is disproportionately high among racial and ethnic minorities.[30] The improved coverage of diabetes management services in the Balanced Budget Act will help correct the depressingly poor outcomes for older minority patients with diabetes described earlier.

The same law, however, has financial provisions that can work against the needs of low-income beneficiaries. As noted by Marilyn Moon and her colleagues:[31]

◆   Hospitals with a disproportionate share of low-income clients will face new limits on the growth of payments by Medicare.

◆   The Part B premium increase in the legislation severely burdens a
    low-income enrollee: an older person with a $10,000 income will
    have to pay 9.4 percent of income for Part B by 2007. While some
    financial aid toward the premium cost is to be provided for low-
    income enrollees, it will fall far short of shielding all Medicare-eligi-
    ble individuals from hardship.

◆   Some new, private plan options permitted by the Balanced Budget
    Amendment, such as medical savings accounts, have fewer consumer
    protections than current plans, while other options open the door to
    "adverse selection," or the attraction of only healthier and wealthier
    enrollees. Costs to Medicare may increase as a result, making the
    benefits for those in less favored risk groups more vulnerable to bud-
    get cuts. If an enhanced benefit package is offered to those who can
    afford it, physicians have an incentive to concentrate on their upper-
    income patients.

The expectation that managed care through market-based HMOs
heavily supported by Medicare would be the solution to Medicare's cost
problems without jeopardizing the flow of needed services has not been
met. While premiums started low as these plans sought to gain market
share, many HMOs have raised them or reduced benefits, especially for
prescription drugs. Medicare HMOs have withdrawn from certain markets after changes in federal reimbursement guidelines. Meanwhile, with
multiple options, retirees are not well prepared to make choices of plans,
and relatively few employers are helping to educate their retiree groups.[32]

These effects should be carefully monitored and corrective legislation
should be introduced as needed. For instance, the excessive number of
insurance options permitted by the Balanced Budget Amendment especially affects women and minorities—women because they were traditionally expected to show passivity and compliance, ethnic minorities because
of language difficulties and unfamiliarity with the features of American
health care. The right to appeal only after a window of opportunity for
bettering health has been closed is of little value to any patient. The government should increase the market power of vulnerable groups by ensur-
ing that information about alternative options for care plus assistance in
finding appropriate care are provided to those least able to navigate the
scientific and administrative complexities of the health care system. Patient
rights legislation should be expanded, and the ombudsman concept should
be put into practice.

The policies and practices of service providers that are a deterrent to care seeking by minority group members should be shaken up. Outreach workers and bilingual staffs in health and social service organizations create a more receptive situation and, by facilitating communication, foster prompt and appropriate care. Medical and nursing schools should maintain courses on geriatrics and the care of female and ethnic minority patients, and health care agencies need to have in-service workshops to improve delivery of service in a fashion that is sensitive to culture, gender, and immigrant status. The cultural difference that exists when physicians come from an ethnic majority and patients do not is one of the great barriers to a relationship based on understanding and a successful care process. Representation of varied backgrounds in medicine is strengthened by programs such as that of the National Health Service Corps scholarships, which embody the principle of assisting all those willing to serve in medically deprived areas. Such programs should be preserved and expanded. New York State has a loan forgiveness program conditional on postgraduate service in a hospital in underserved areas; states that do not offer such aid now could consider doing so, especially those with large ethnic minority populations.[33]

In addition, preprofessional education of minorities, making possible a more representative pool of medical school applicants, should be strengthened. The percentages of African Americans and Hispanics with college degrees remain well below that for whites; the situation is similar for the percentages with professional degrees.[34]

While debates about Medicare policy continue, little has been done to provide security against long-term care needs. Dependence of elderly patients on family caregiving often involves elderly spouses whose capacity to perform is limited. Informal care has been a tradition in many cultures, but the burdens, most frequently borne by women, should be lightened by respite programs, assistive devices, insured home care, and other social resources.

Groups at high risk for poverty can best be protected by repulsing direct and indirect attacks on economic security programs. The principle of adjusting benefits for cost-of-living changes ought to be kept. Proposals to revise the consumer price index should consider that there are declines offsetting the claimed increases in the quality of goods and services. Older customers often prefer the simpler products they were used to before more complex models displaced them. The consumer expenditure survey used formerly to measure the cost of a minimum budget for seniors should be revived but adapted to the prevailing diversity of marital status and living arrangements. For the purpose of Social Security benefit adjustment, items that become necessities as age advances should be part of the market basket that is priced.

   Inadequate benefit levels depress the incentive to apply for public aid—there are many who are eligible but do not apply[35]—and leave some of those who are approved in serious need. As the age for full retiree benefits under Social Security is raised, protections against poverty for involuntary part-timers and the unemployed should be legislated. Preventing cutbacks in Medicaid and Medicare is important for economic security as well as health security.

   Universal entitlement to security in dealing with economic risks, sustaining purchasing power, and protecting health over the course of life is a fundamental legacy of our democratic society and a unifying influence. Groups with special circumstances and needs receive great value from programs that aim to benefit all and to which everyone is expected to contribute according to ability to pay. The recognition of the special difficulties facing women and minorities should be a stimulus and a reminder to make sure that all have entry into and equal treatment in the core programs that protect against risk and guarantee opportunity. This means investigating the likely effects on vulnerable groups when existing programs are revised and especially when limitations are proposed. In addition, active representation of these groups at the levels of program operation, service delivery, and formal monitoring are essential in a society of diverse composition and democratic intent.

6

SAVING, GROWTH, AND SOCIAL SECURITY:
FIGHTING OUR CHILDREN OVER SHARES OF THE FUTURE ECONOMIC PIE?

James H. Schulz

Despite the repeated predictions of various social commentators, there is no intergenerational conflict in the United States today. The empirical evidence to the contrary is considerable and conclusive.[1]

But what about the future? With the American population aging and the retirement of the baby-boom generation not many years away, some people argue that intergenerational conflict is inevitable.[2] The truth is, however, that there is no general agreement on this question, only controversy.

The literature on socioeconomic effects of population aging is now quite large. Almost all of it starts with projecting into the next century the results of current demographic trends and pointing out the impact that this may have (or "is going to have") on the intergenerational question. This literature is dominated by dire prophecies that are now familiar to almost everyone:

◆   Each future worker will have to support too many retired people.

◆   Social Security will go bankrupt and will not be there when younger workers retire.

This chapter was originally released as a Century Foundation white paper in 1998.

♦   The *entire* federal budget will ultimately have to go to pay for entitlements.

♦   Older people are being luxuriously supported at the expense of our children.

♦   Population aging will destroy our nation's global competitiveness, perpetuating the curse of low growth and a shrinking economic pie.

Given the apocalyptic nature of these predictions, a visitor from Mars would be likely to dismiss them and search for more balanced discussions. But the reader knows that these predictions cannot be dismissed; today, they represent the accepted opinion of the bulk of the American population.

For decades now there has been waged a kind of holy war designed to "wake up" the American public to the supposed dangers resulting from the aging of America's population. Driving this war is the goal of turning Americans against one of the nation's most popular programs—Social Security. However, this war is not so much about unsustainable Social Security and Medicare or about current budget deficits. Rather, it is really about the age-old questions associated with the appropriate distribution of income in the United States—between the rich and poor, whites and nonwhites, and the strong and the weak.[3] And it is also about a medical care system with soaring costs, a lack of agreement about how these costs are to be paid, and the uneven and inequitable protection provided to individuals against the costs of major illnesses.

The current, warlike campaign against "entitlements" promotes an intergenerational conflict that does not yet exist and undermines the already tenuous sense of community and social solidarity that exists nationally. That is, it encourages long-term confrontation between age groups over the distribution of the nation's output.

"CONSUMING OUR CHILDREN" AND OTHER SUCH HORRORS

In an article entitled "Consuming Our Children?" Subrata Chakravarty and Katherine Weisman argue: "Many young people complain that they can't live as well as their parents did. They may well be right. We are witnessing nothing less than a massive transfer of income and wealth from the younger generations to the older."[4] This theme has been repeated over and over again—starting with the unsubstantiated assertion made by eminent demographer Samuel H. Preston in 1984 that the elderly were responsible for the deteriorating social and economic situation of children in the United States.[5]

The "consuming our children" theme, however, is only one aspect of the intergenerational conflict "horrors" many people write about. Another issue concerns whether the needs of a growing aged population threaten the integrity of the political system. The apocalyptic proclamations go back at least two decades. In 1978 economic journalist Robert J. Samuelson got politicians' attention by publicly attacking the elderly in the *Washington Post*. Up to that time older people were viewed by almost everyone in America as the most deserving of the poor. But Samuelson argued that the situation had changed and that there was now a "withering freedom to govern" resulting from the "soaring costs [of programs] for elderly" persons:

> The aged have handcuffed [President] Jimmy Carter. They will probably do the same for his successors well into the next century. Increasingly, invisible forces of population change will limit the freedom to govern.
>
> Put simply, the slow increase in the aged population, combined with the massive rise in assistance already promised the elderly, means that neither the president nor the Congress can afford to provide much new spending for anything else—unless they want to raise taxes or run permanently large budget deficits.
>
> . . . The seeds of conflict are obvious enough: between educators and doctors, as well as between young and old. In short, population change—slowly and almost invisibly—is pushing Congress and the bureaucracy around with a power that has few rivals.[6]

Samuelson's article—if written today—would accurately summarize the prevailing fears. His once-deviant view is now the dominant view. What has changed since he began writing about the topic is, first, the huge federal deficits generated in the Reagan and Bush years (frequently blamed on the elderly). Next, there is increased attention to the problems arising when the baby-boom generation retires. And, finally, we see occurring the most vicious attacks on Social Security since its creation in the 1930s.

Criticism of the elderly reached new heights when former governor of Colorado, Richard D. Lamm, in an unprecedented and almost unbelievable act, mounted a bid for the presidency in 1996 with a campaign based almost solely on attacking the elderly. He claimed that older people were making unreasonable economic demands—demands that represented a serious drain on the nation, now and especially in the years to come.

The calamitous predictions by the prophets of doom have fallen on receptive ears because these people argue that the survival of some of our most important social and economic ideals is at stake. They maintain that population aging will seriously undermine our efforts to compete in the new global marketplace—threatening future economic growth and, hence, the "American dream" that each generation will have a standard of living better than its predecessor. In fact, as noted above, they anticipate that we will end up "consuming" our own children in a sense, even as there is a progressive immiserization of future generations. And, as if that were not enough, they predict that one of America's most popular institutions, Social Security, is unsustainable and will become a "bad deal" for future generations—if it survives at all.

No wonder these prophets of doom have gotten widespread attention. Who can ignore, for example, the recent statement of the well-known economist Lester Thurow: "A new class of people is being created. . . . It [the elderly class] is a revolutionary class, one that is bringing down the social welfare state, destroying government finances, altering the distribution of purchasing power and threatening the investments that all societies need to make to have a successful future."[7] Notwithstanding, this chapter will make the case that these dire predictions should not be taken seriously, that they are based on simplistic and erroneous demographic analyses, and that, to the extent economics is considered, the analysis is equally simplistic and seriously deficient.

VOODOO DEMOGRAPHY

It is now commonplace to read about "dependency ratio" statistics. Almost every prediction of demographic doom starts with one basic statistic of growing dependency: in the year 2030, given current Social Security law, there will be only 2.0 workers per Social Security recipient—in contrast to the current level of 3.3 workers per recipient.[8] This is often called the aged dependency ratio, measuring the relationship between old-age Social Security recipients and those workers paying Social Security taxes. The truth is that aged dependency ratios are one-sided and very misleading. As will be explained shortly, the correct way to look at this issue is to compare the number of workers to the number of dependents of all ages (nonworkers), and then to factor in the varying costs of supporting different groups of dependents and the rising level of incomes as a result of economic growth. On this measure, there is no problem of the sort suggested by the aged dependency ratio.

In almost all industrial countries, the "total dependency ratio" (taking into account both young and old dependents) is actually quite low, much lower than in the past and much lower than in developing nations today.[9] An even better measure to use, however, is one whose ratios take into account who is actually in the labor force for all age cohorts. Projections of the "labor force dependency ratio" (measuring those who are not in the labor force against those who are) indicate that for all ages this figure is expected to decline until around the year 2010 and that it will not surpass the high levels reached around 1960. As Figure 6.1 shows, looking at people working and not working in all age groups (children, youths, middle-aged, and the aged), increases in the numbers of aged not working are counterbalanced by declines in dependency in the other age groups. In Figure 6.1, the total labor force dependency ratio is set to decline from

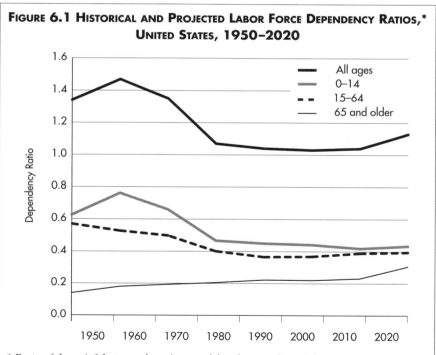

FIGURE 6.1 HISTORICAL AND PROJECTED LABOR FORCE DEPENDENCY RATIOS,* UNITED STATES, 1950–2020

* Ratio of those (of designated ages) not in labor force to those (of any age) in labor force

Source: James H. Schulz, Allan Borowski, and William H. Crown, *Economics of Population Aging: The "Graying" of Australia, Japan, and the United States* (Westport, Conn.: Auburn House, 1991).

about 1.5 in 1960 to about 1.0 in 2010. After 2010, the total ratio is strongly influenced by the retiring baby-boom cohort and rises slightly to 1.1. After that, it levels off.

There have been all sorts of demographic statistics presented in the aging discussions to date. Most of them are worthless in assessing the economic impact of an aging society. Population analysis without economics is a kind of voodoo demographics with regard to the issues in question.[10] The parents of the "baby boomers" registered a per capita GDP of $12,195 in 1964. Assuming less than 2 percent annual growth, the retired boomers and their children will enjoy in the year 2030 a per capita income (inflation adjusted) that is almost three times as large ($35,659).[11]

Analyzing the impact of population changes on the economy is a far more difficult challenge than simply presenting demographic dependency ratios. So there may be a generally offsetting decline in the number of children as the number of older people increases (see Figure 6.1): What does that mean in economic terms? Is the amount of the economic resources consumed in a year the same for babies and old people? For preschoolers? For teenagers? For college students? For mothers at home with their children? Obviously not.

Very little research has been done on this question of the varying costs of supporting different groups of dependents. In one of the few economic studies to date, Allan Borowski, William Crown, and the author have statistically weighted the demographic data shown in Figure 6.1 to reflect the "private support costs" associated with different age groups of nonworking persons. We also looked at the potential effect of future economic growth. Based on this extension of the demographic statistics to incorporate economic differences, we concluded, first, "that the economic impact of demographic aging is not as bad as those doomsayers who use simplistic dependency ratios would have us believe. Second, as in other areas of social policy, relatively small increases in economic growth rates have the potential to substantially moderate the ill effects of other factors that have a negative impact."[12] In fact, our research concluded that the overall "support burden" pertaining to nonworking individuals could be less in the years 2030–50 than it was during 1950–70, assuming a relatively high rate of economic growth.[13]

Analyzing economic data over the past one hundred years for the United States and ten European countries, Richard A. Easterlin (one of the nation's top experts on population economics) also finds little support for predictions that population aging will have a negative impact on economic growth and the welfare of future generations.[14] He finds a generally consistent inverse relationship between trends in economic growth and population growth—economic growth rising while population growth falls. As he points out, this "is just the opposite of what one would have expected if declining population growth were exerting a serious drag on the economy." Moreover, based on the historical data, "one would be hard put to argue that dependency had much to do with the dramatic post-1973 drop in economic growth rates, and, not surprisingly, it is never mentioned in scholarly attempts to explain this decline."

SAVING AND POPULATION AGING*

Easterlin points out that economists have paid relatively little heed in the past to demography in explaining changes in economic growth rates.[15] Instead, they have given a lot of attention to the role played by another contributor to the economic growth process—saving. If saving is reduced by population aging, then economic growth *might* be affected.

The potential impact of demographic aging on saving and growth has been a major issue in the debate over Social Security for many decades. Contemporary calls for privatization of Social Security are motivated in part by a desire to ensure that retirement pension programs do nothing to diminish saving and growth. Former associate Social Security commissioner Lawrence Thompson argues that the historical fact that public pensions have not been as likely as private ones to accumulate assets through saving ". . . is perhaps the most important fault line in the current world-wide debate over the costs of an aging society and the future of social security."[16]

The dialogue on this subject began in earnest with a paper published in 1974 by economist Martin Feldstein. Feldstein argued that historical data indicated that America's Social Security system depressed national saving by providing people with retirement income through collective pensions, encouraging individuals to reduce their private saving. Feldstein's empirical analysis found a sizable reduction in personal saving over the early years of the program. A big but inconclusive debate followed. Two

---

* As an economist myself, I am especially annoyed (and puzzled) by the arguments many economists use, almost by rote, to explain the supposed impact of Social Security on our national rate of savings. Therefore, this section of the chapter goes into some detail to explain and evaluate the prevailing literature, especially since the literature to date has been mysteriously deficient in articulating the limitations of past analyses.

Social Security Administration economists, Dean Leimer and Selig Lesnoy, found, for example, errors in Feldstein's calculations, reporting only small negative (and even some positive) savings effects when the errors were corrected.[17] In general, the empirical studies to date on this question have been inconclusive.[18]

Another way that demographic aging could reduce aggregate saving is if there turns out to be a general pattern of behavior among individuals, when they are old, to save less and consume more. Economists have long theorized that people would accumulate savings for old age and then spend down most or all those savings before the end of life (the "life-cycle hypothesis"). If true, the aging of a population should be associated with a reduction in aggregate saving (all other things held constant). Once again, though, the empirical evidence is very mixed. Many studies show that "savers" continue to save for most or all of their retirement years, but a few researchers find the opposite. The 1997 annual report of the U.S. Council of Economic Advisers concludes that "economists have been at a loss to explain much of the behavior of personal savings during the 1980s."[19]

But the lack of "hard evidence" and reasonable certainty with regard to the impact of population aging on saving has not stopped some advocates of privatization. They argue that Social Security is a big part of the explanation for America's currently low saving rates and part of the reason why economic growth rates have not been higher. Those voicing grave concern and dire predictions about population aging and entitlements single out one possibility (among many) as the dominant—seemingly sole—determinant of our economic future, the saving rate. For example, in a recent speech on the economic impact of an aging society, former chairman of the Federal Reserve System Paul A. Volcker focused almost exclusively on saving: "If the huge Boomer generation is encouraged to save more, the result will be a favorable and direct effect on the U.S. economy in the new century. An increase in personal savings rates beyond our historical level of four percent will favorably affect our economy."[20] Similarly, Senator Bob Kerrey and former senator John C. Danforth, in the interim report of the Bipartisan Commission on Entitlement and Tax Reform, focused on saving: "To ensure the level of private investment necessary for long-term economic growth and prosperity, national savings must be raised substantially."[21] And the president's Council of Economic Advisers in its 1997 report states categorically that "the nation needs to raise its overall rate of saving to improve long-term economic growth."[22]

The Simplistic Notion that Saving Determines Growth

Why is saving so important for growth? Here is the way eminent economist James M. Buchanan explains the growth process to noneconomists:

> The act of saving allows for a release of resources into the production of capital rather than consumer goods. This increase in capital inputs into the market operates in essentially the same fashion as an increase in the supply of labor inputs. The increase in capital expands the size of the economy and this, in turn, allows for an increased exploitation of the division and specialization of resources. The economic value of output per unit of input expands, and *this result ensures that all persons in the economic nexus, whether they be workers, savers, or consumers, are made better off and on their own terms.*[23] [emphasis added]

Buchanan's certainty of favorable results from saving is not shared by economists who specialize in this subject matter. The literature on saving, investment, and growth is extensive, complicated, sophisticated, highly controversial, and generally inconclusive. But one would never know that from reading the savings policy prescriptions of most economists today. The complexities and ambiguities of economic theory and empiricism in this area are generally ignored.

Economists today are generally unanimous in pointing to the need to increase saving in order to promote economic growth in the United States. The emphasis given by many economists to saving results in part from a long tradition in economics. Both traditional neoclassical growth theory and more recent growth theory focus on the role of saving. Economist Robert A. Blecker points out in a recent review article: "Since the late 1970s, mainstream macroeconomics has been dominated by a conservative policy consensus, which emphasizes raising national saving rates and avoiding government intervention in financial or labor markets."[24]

Thus, it is not surprising to find great concern about Social Security among those economists who see it as a major government program that reduces the aggregate saving needed for growth. For example, economist Edward M. Gramlich, the chair of the most recent Social Security Advisory Council, writes:

> In the end the most profound impact of Social Security on the economy, for good or ill, is its impact on national saving and investment. In the long run the most important policy-controlled determinant of a

country's living standards is its national saving ratio, according to neo-classical growth models of the sort that were developed by Robert Solow. . . . The United States now saves an extraordinarily low share of its national output. The disappointing aspect of this low national sav-ing is that as long as it persists, living standards are not likely to rise very rapidly in the future.[25]

As articulated by Gramlich, low saving translates into slow growth and lower living standards. Note that there are no ifs, ands, or buts in Gramlich's statement.

However, the point is not so much what Gramlich thinks; more important is that his opinion is highly representative of the current poli-cy prescriptions of many other economists. For example, Martin Feldstein, in an article promoting privatization of Social Security, asserts: "There is, however, no doubt that the net effect of the transition from the PAYGO [pay as you go] system to the prefunded PRA [Personal Retirement Accounts] system would be a rise in national saving and therefore a larg-er capital stock and a higher level of real national income."[26] This and similar views of various economists seriously distort the discussion about population aging and economic growth. As will be shown below, such a reductionist articulation of the sources of economic growth ignores decades of research and debate since Solow's insightful but seriously deficient early modeling efforts. There are many important determinants of the rate of growth of a nation's economy.[27] To imply that saving is the only one, or that it is the most important one, is just bad economics.

Why do most economists think saving is so important? The usual answer given is that saving is necessary if there is to be investment by busi-nesses in new factories and equipment. Saving is defined as the amount of current income that is not spent (not consumed) on finished goods and ser-vices over some specified time period. The economic resources of a nation (its land, labor, and capital) are limited and can be used to produce goods that are consumed and used up or, alternatively, to produce goods that can be used to produce greater quantities of goods in the future ("capital goods"). Saving is necessary to generate the wherewithal for investment, and investment potentially results in new productive capacity that can be the basis for economic growth in future years. So from a growth perspective, saving is a good thing. Clearly it is better than no saving or low saving.

But the definitional relationship that "saving always equals invest-ment always equals growth" is too simplistic to base decisionmaking on. This view of saving is a far cry from the real world. Recent research sug-gests that increasing private saving, other things being equal, does little to raise private investment. In fact, econometric analysis by David Gordon supports the view of a sizable minority of economists that investment generates saving, not vice versa.[28]

First of all, increased saving makes investment possible, but the amount and nature of the investment that actually occurs depends on a wide variety of conditions. For example, the United Kingdom, with the highest level of funded occupational pensions in Europe and more than £10 billion ($16.6 billion) in "personal saving" accounts, has not seen any appreciable increase in its recent investment rates. Nor has it achieved a higher rate of growth than European countries, such as Germany, that rely very heavily on pay-as-you-go social security pensions.[29]

Second, as Gordon points out, "saving fails to generate investment in part because increased personal saving does not appear to alter the financial constraints (credit availability) affecting investment."[30]

Third, research indicates that profitability should be regarded as a significant influence on how much actual investment occurs—along with demand, demand and profit expectations, and the relative costs of capital to labor.[31]

Fourth, there is not just one source (saving) or two (saving and investment) that are the key determinants of growth. While saving and investment are necessary, they are not sufficient to ensure that the rate of growth will be adequate to achieve any specified set of goals. There are many other factors that are as important—or perhaps more important, such as technology, know-how, and entrepreneurial drive. All economists know this, which makes one wonder why so many have chosen to ignore the other wellsprings of growth when the question of population aging comes up. As Richard Nelson remarks, "the key intellectual challenge to formal growth theory . . . lies in learning how to formally model entities that are not easily reduced to a set of numbers, such as the character of a nation's education or financial system or the prevalent philosophy of management."[32]

CREDIT CARDS AND SAVING

Before looking more closely at the other influences on growth, it is important to make clear the relatively minor role aging policies actually play in determining aggregate saving. If one were to ask people on the street what are the major considerations that influence how much they save, it is not likely that they would say much about the amount they expect to get in retirement from public and private pensions. Nor are they likely to mention the single most important source of personal saving for the majority of people —accumulation of home equity through their mortgage payments; most do not think of that as saving. Instead, people are more likely to talk about the high cost of living and the difficulties they have just "making ends meet."

In her article "The Joy of Consumption," Jane Katz points out that rising incomes do not slow our desire to spend. For most people, consumption is no longer about buying necessities. Instead, it is in large part a social phenomenon. "In a market economy, we must buy the things we need to take our place in the community."[33] As Katz notes, rising incomes do not relieve the pressures on the middle class to keep up; moreover, they probably place extra burdens on the poor to avoid the stigma of falling behind in what has been called "conspicuous consumption."

Everyone in the United States is aware of how easy it is for most individuals to borrow money to finance consumption—for stereos, televisions, vacations, automobiles, meals, and almost anything else that their fancy desires. The credit revolution in the United States is one of the most important developments of the postwar period. The expansion of revolving credit has been dramatic, with much of the growth going to credit cards. Over the past two decades, the bank credit card share of revolving credit has risen from less than half to more than two-thirds.[34]

Of course, most readers will not be surprised—since they carry around an average of three to four credit cards and receive offers of new cards every month. Credit providers have gone to extreme lengths to push people into debt. One recent letter printed by USA Today was from a parent reporting that her college student daughter had five credit cards—amassing a "tremendous amount of debt." Yet the only job the daughter ever held was working part time in a pizza shop. "I recently bought some books at my local college bookstore. The clerk put my books in the bag along with several credit card applications. Who wouldn't be tempted?"[35]

The credit card boom is, for many people, a wonderful source of credit at a cost that is high but usually lower than the costs involved in getting money from banks, "money stores," and other more traditional alternatives.[36] But using credit "to spend" is the opposite of saving; credit (when used) leads to debt.[37] Is it not reasonable to think that low saving rates in the United States are in part a result of easier credit in our consumption-oriented society—with its conspicuous consumption, television, radio, and print media advertising, and newfound ways of "buying now and paying later"? As Figure 6.2 indicates, rapid growth in consumer debt started around 1982—about the same time as personal saving rates began their sharp decline.

FIGURE 6.2 CONSUMER DEBT,* 1974–1994

* Ratio of debt to disposable household income

Source: Based on *Economic Report of the President, 1995* (Washington, D.C.: U.S. Government Printing Office, 1995), Chart 2–3.

Is the credit boom merely a new way to finance consumption, or is it a new contributor to rising net consumption and lower personal saving? Looking to the economic literature for an informed opinion on the credit card phenomenon would result only in disappointment. A search of books and articles over a twenty-eight-year period found 4,395 citations mentioning "saving" and 213 articles mentioning "saving and Social Security." In contrast, there were 36 citations on credit cards and only one that looks at "saving and credit cards."[38]

One rarely hears prominent policymakers (or economists) worry about the impact of rising consumer debt on saving or talk about ways to stop the rise. Yet consumer debt continues to climb. The Consumer Federation estimates that, on average, households that carry a credit card balance have more than $7,000 in card debt; this results in households paying an average payment of more than $1,000 each year in card interest and fees.[39] (That is double the amount in 1990.) Figure 6.3 (see page 134) shows household debt payments as a percent of disposable personal income—rising from a little more than 15 percent in early 1994 to 17

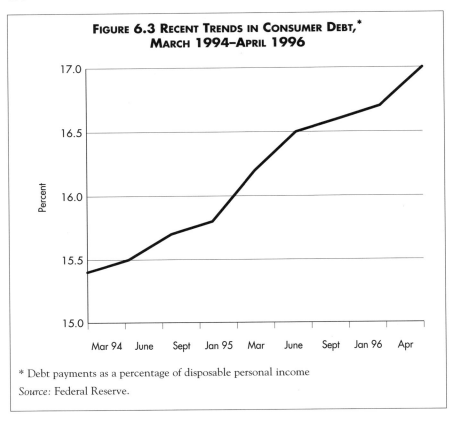

FIGURE 6.3 RECENT TRENDS IN CONSUMER DEBT,*
MARCH 1994–APRIL 1996

* Debt payments as a percentage of disposable personal income

Source: Federal Reserve.

percent in early 1996. "Nearly 1 in every 3 families whose household income is below $10,000 now has credit-card obligations that exceed 40 percent of its income. . . ."[40]

Harvard economist James Medoff and financial consultant Andrew Harless argue that, "at present, the United States is locked in a situation in which Americans borrow (instead of save) to make up the difference between their expectations and the disappointing reality of slow growth."[41] In a frantic race to keep up, families often take on more debt than they can handle. Figure 6.4 shows the rising rate of bankruptcy filings in recent years.[42]

PERSONAL VERSUS BUSINESS SAVING

Historically, the amount of net personal saving (new saving minus new debt) by all households in the United States has been roughly equal to the amount of investment that goes into owner-occupied housing. That

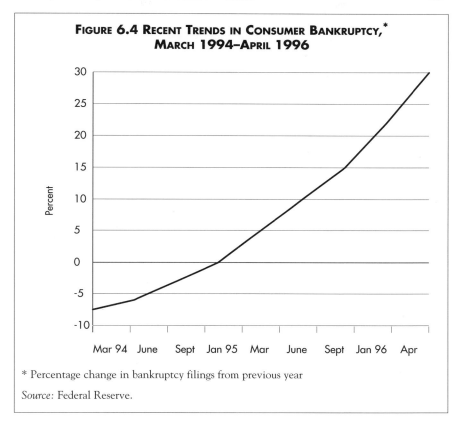

FIGURE 6.4 RECENT TRENDS IN CONSUMER BANKRUPTCY, *
MARCH 1994–APRIL 1996

* Percentage change in bankruptcy filings from previous year

Source: Federal Reserve.

is, the magnitude of household saving has been just enough to allow for the replenishing and expansion of our housing stock. If that is true, where does the saving come from that allows businesses to invest in new plant and equipment?

Capital markets are rapidly becoming global. The savings of individuals in the United States can now be pooled with the savings of millions of others around the world. The fact that financial capital can now move easily and quickly across national borders in search of "the best returns" further changes the basic nature of the traditional interaction between saving and investment. At the same time, it creates new social problems as producers generate goods and services using globally dispersed resources, often leaving local communities to decay and local labor pools unemployed.

In the historically important growth sector of corporate production, the overwhelming majority of saving needed to facilitate new investment comes from savings generated internally by the corporations themselves in the form of retained earnings and depreciation allowances.[43] In 1994, gross business saving exceeded $800 billion, more than four times aggregate personal saving in the same year.

WHAT ROLE FOR SAVING?

The point is not that saving has an unimportant role to play in growth, or that policies to encourage such saving are inappropriate. Rather, the prior discussion seeks to place the issue of population aging and saving in proper perspective. As a World Bank report puts it, "Funded [pension] plans have the potential to increase household saving and productive capital formation, whereas pay-as-you-go plans do not. But this potential may not be realized . . ." unless conditions are right.[44]

Instead of qualified statements similar to the World Bank's, readers frequently are confronted with pronouncements that make it seem that the impact of population aging and Social Security on saving is the most, or one of the most, important considerations in evaluating policy options relating to growth. As just pointed out, though, saving is done by many sectors of the economy and for a variety of reasons. The significance of population aging and Social Security for the level of saving rates is certainly small in relation to that of many other determinants. As the late Arthur Okun, an eminent macroeconomist, once said, "The specter of depressed saving is not only empirically implausible but logically fake. . . . The nation can have the level of saving and investment it wants with more or less income redistribution, so long as it is willing to twist some other dials."[45]

If it is a matter of twisting some dials, why don't we just do it? A large part of the answer is that those dials are marked "Social Security," "taxation," "interest rates," "credit availability," and other highly politically sensitive issues.

ALLEVIATING THE STRAINS OF POPULATION AGING: MAKING THE PIE BIGGER

Even if Social Security reduces saving (and there is no proof that it does), people worried about future growth and the "economic pie" available to share should look elsewhere for factors determining the outcome. For example, one of the giants of economics, Alfred Marshall, once wrote: "Knowledge is the most powerful engine of production; it enables us to subdue nature and satisfy our wants."[46] His statement reminds us that the job of dealing with any economic strain arising from the baby boom and population aging does not rest solely on increasing saving.[47]

All one has to do is look around at businesses that succeed and fail to see that saving is only one of many important sources of growth. Twenty-five years ago America was the leader in tire production around the world, and Akron, Ohio, was the tire capital—with four of the five biggest tire companies in the country located there. As the *Economist* pointed out recently, "Now only one of those firms, Goodyear, remains both American and a market leader. Akron was undermined by Americans' enthusiasm for longer-lasting radial tyres after the 1973 oil shock. The problem was not that Akron's firms did not know how to make radial tyres; the technology was decades old. What they were unable to do was adjust their business model, which relied on short-lived tyres."[48]

The American tire industry did not decline because of a lack of available saving; these companies were huge and had been profitable, with lots of retained earnings. What was missing was the right combination of entrepreneurial spirit, risk taking, and successful managerial skills.

The *Economist* description of businesses currently thriving in the Silicon Valley makes for a striking contrast with the American tire industry.

> To an unusual degree Silicon Valley's economy relies on what Joseph Schumpeter, an Austrian economist, called "creative destruction." Some modern writers have rechristened the phenomenon "flexible recycling," but the basic idea is the same: old companies die and new ones emerge, allowing capital, ideas, and people to be reallocated. An essential ingredient in this is the presence of entrepreneurs, and a culture that attracts them.
>
> Research has increasingly concentrated on clusters . . . where there is "something in the air" that encourages risk-taking. This suggests that culture, irritatingly vague though it may sound, is more important to Silicon Valley's success than economic or technological factors.[49]

And, as the *Economist* acknowledges, venture capital has been pouring into Silicon Valley. Low saving rates have not been a problem.

The early neoclassical growth models referred to by Gramlich are based on a primitive, unsophisticated view of business organizations, technological change, and innovation. Over the years, Richard Nelson, among others, has pointed out the complexities of growth and the key role played by parameters other than saving. Many economists' models treat businesses like machines, ignoring empirical research clearly documenting the fact that businesses are social systems that are often resistant or unresponsive to executive commands.[50] Thus, "management style," for example, can make a big difference in the success or failure of a firm.

What about knowledge—the education of the work force and the development of a scientific base for facilitating and stimulating the use of new technologies? As Marshall and many other economists have indicated, it is vitally important to spend sufficient societal resources on human capital.[51] "All over the world it is taken for granted that educational achievement and economic success are closely linked—that the struggle to raise a nation's living standards is fought first and foremost in the classroom."[52]

Investment in intangible and human capital, excluded from conventional measures of saving and investment, far exceeds in magnitude (and very likely in importance) the private saving in tangible capital.[53] Starting with the Morrill Land Grant College Act of 1862, the United States has been a world leader in government support for education and research. "As early as 1890," Theodore Schultz writes, "the ratio of university students per 1,000 primary students in America was two to three times that of any other country, and this gap was maintained and increased through the period of American industrial ascendancy."[54]

Knowledge, education, technological change, and entrepreneurship together form a powerful engine for economic growth. The Austrian School of economists (such as Joseph Schumpeter, Ludwig von Mises, and Friedrich Hayek) recognized this. This tradition continues among economists in Austria today, with a strong emphasis on the role of knowledge and discovery (what the Austrians call "entrepreneurial discovery").[55] Except for the work of a few economists (like Nelson, Schultz, and Herbert Gintis), this focus is sorely missing from American mainstream economics.

Again, it is not that economists in the United States have ignored the role of technology, risk taking, and entrepreneurship. Rather it is that the importance of these things is almost always missing from, or downplayed in, most policy discussions about issues related to economic growth and, in our case, the specific issues related to population aging and Social Security.

The discussion in this chapter has only skimmed the surface of what is important to promoting economic expansion. The list of potential sources of growth is very long.[56] If increased saving were the only requirement for growth, there would be many fewer underdeveloped countries in the world today. Ask the former leaders of the USSR, or the current leaders of Russia, why Moscow's planned economy, with lots of forced saving, ended up as a disaster.

Not only is most of "the burden of the elderly" literature overly simplistic but it also encourages people to look for solutions in the wrong places. Increasing economic growth rates is a very complex task and one still not well understood. Yet, good public policy requires recognizing those complexities and articulating them to the general public. Today, as ever, the most important determinants of the future economic welfare of people of all ages are those already alluded to that influence the rate of growth: technological change, entrepreneurial initiatives and risk taking, managerial skills, government provision of infrastructure, saving, investment in human and business capital, labor force participation levels, and so on. The debate over how best to make an economic system grow is not primarily an aging (or Social Security) discussion. In fact, Social Security and the aging of populations have relatively little to do with the outcome.

Economist Richard Disney, who recently undertook a comprehensive and careful review of the relevant economic literature, concludes that "there is no 'crisis of aging.' Although many countries now exhibit dramatic demographic transitions, talk of a 'crisis of aging' is overblown. . . . [T]here is no evidence of adverse effects of aging on aggregate productivity. Microeconomic and macroeconomic studies have failed to uncover any convincing evidence that differences in demographic structure between countries and over time are a major factor in determining productivity levels."[57]

Michael Cichon of the International Labor Office, using a simulation that models the demographic and economic characteristics of OECD countries, reaches similar conclusions: "There is no old-age crisis, but there certainly is an employment and public policy challenge. Those who stare at the changing pattern of the 'population tree' and conclude quickly and with a dose of Populist bravado that the present social protection has to be changed radically, are simply barking up the wrong tree." [58]

THE ENTITLEMENT MYTH:
AND CHICKEN LITTLE SAID, "THE SKY IS FALLING"

Social Security disbursements are a direct cause of our [current] federal deficit.[59]

—Peter G. Peterson

To ensure that today's debt and spending commitments do not unfairly burden America's children, the government must act now. A bipartisan coalition of Congress, led by the President, must resolve the long-term imbalance between the government's entitlement promises and the funds it will have available to pay for them.[60]

—Report of the Bipartisan Commission
on Entitlement and Tax Reform

Great myths persist with regard to deficit spending and the current state of entitlement funding.[61] These two quotes serve as a reminder of the importance of distinguishing between the short-term and long-term dimensions of the federal government's budget deficit predicament. The general view is that Social Security entitlements cause many serious problems in both the short and long run. The truth is that Social Security entitlements cause almost no problems in the short run and a few in the long run. Social Security and Medicare have *not* been responsible for the recent federal deficit. To understand this, look first at Table 6.1, which summarizes the federal budget for 1993. At $461 billion, Social Security and Medicare combined are the largest entry in the table. The total budget deficit for 1993 was $255 billion. Since Social Security and Medicare represent 33 percent of total expenditures, these programs look like they might be major contributors to the deficit.

But now look at Table 6.2 (page 142). This table splits the federal budget into two classes, one for Social Security and Medicare and the other for all other expenditures. Budget I (the non-Social Security budget) has a deficit of $307 billion. That is, the tax revenues were insufficient to pay for these expenditures (defense, interest payments, running the government, etc.), or the expenditures were too high. In contrast, Budget II (the Social Security budget) generates a surplus of $51 billion. Thus, the overall deficit in Table 6.1 ($255 billion) is lower than the $307 billion deficit in Budget I solely because the Social Security surplus is factored in with the much higher deficit for the non-Social Security part of the federal budget.

Social Security was included in the federal budget for the first time in 1969. The surpluses generated during the 1960s and 1970s had the effect of helping to balance the budget. In fact, when the accounting procedure was introduced in 1969, the Social Security surplus from that year permitted President Johnson to take credit for sending a "balanced budget" to Congress instead of one with a deficit. In the 1970s and 1980s, when Social Security sometimes ran a deficit, some government officials tried to blame the very much larger *total* federal deficit (see Figure 6.5, page 143) on "out-of-control" nondiscretionary programs like Social Security. Currently, Social Security is generating surpluses, as it has throughout most of its history. Operating on a self-financing and partial funding basis (with current benefits mostly dependent on current taxes), Social Security taxes and expenditures must be kept in close balance. Unlike other federal programs, there is no possibility that Social Security will generate large deficits over long periods of time.

TABLE 6.1 FEDERAL BUDGET, 1993

TYPE OF EXPENDITURE	AMOUNT ($BILLIONS)	PERCENTAGE OF TOTAL
Net interest	199	14
National defense	291	
Medicaid, public health, medical research	99	42
Public assistance (+ SSI, food stamps)	207	
Subtotal	796	
Everything else except Social Security: Internal affairs, science and space, energy, natural resources and environment, agriculture, transportation, education and training and social services, veterans, legal, general government	152	11
Subtotal	948	
Social Security and Medicare	461	33
Subtotal	1,409	100
Total Receipts	1,154	
Deficit	-255	

Sources: *Economic Report of the President, 1995* (Washington, D.C.: U.S. Government Printing Office, 1995); Social Security Administration, *Annual Statistical Supplement* (Washington, D.C.: U.S. Government Printing Office, 1994).

If Social Security is not the source of the deficit, what is? As a result of the major cuts in tax rates (and the indexing of ceilings to prevent inflation pushing taxpayers into higher tax brackets)[62] legislated during the Reagan years, the flow of revenues to the government has been drastically curtailed. This action coincided with a dramatic increase in defense expenditures during the 1980s (see Figure 6.6, page 144). While defense expenditures have declined in recent years, the defense spending legacy of

TABLE 6.2 SPLIT FEDERAL BUDGET, 1993

TYPE OF EXPENDITURE	AMOUNT ($BILLIONS)	PERCENTAGE OF TOTAL
BUDGET I		
Net interest	199	21
National defense	291	30
Medicaid, public health, medical research	99	10
Public assistance (+ SSI, food stamps)	207	22
Subtotal	796	
Everything else except Social Security: Internal affairs, science and space, energy, natural resources and environment, agriculture, transportation, education and training and social services, veterans, legal, general government	152	16
Total Expenditures	948	100*
Total Receipts	641	
Deficit	-307	
BUDGET II		
Social Security Totals: OASDHI** Receipts	512	
OASDHI Expenditures	461	33
Surplus	+51	
Deficit	-256	

*   Does not add to 100 percent due to rounding.

** OASDHI (Old-Age, Survivors, Disability, and Health Insurance programs)

Sources: Economic Report of the President, 1995 (Washington, D.C.: U.S. Government Printing Office, 1995); Social Security Administration, *Annual Statistical Supplement, 1994* (Washington, D.C.: U.S. Government Printing Office, 1994).

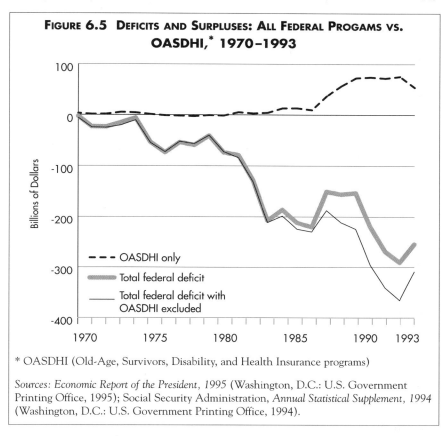

FIGURE 6.5 DEFICITS AND SURPLUSES: ALL FEDERAL PROGAMS VS. OASDHI,* 1970–1993

Billions of Dollars

- - - OASDHI only

━━━ Total federal deficit

──── Total federal deficit with OASDHI excluded

* OASDHI (Old-Age, Survivors, Disability, and Health Insurance programs)

Sources: Economic Report of the President, 1995 (Washington, D.C.: U.S. Government Printing Office, 1995); Social Security Administration, *Annual Statistical Supplement, 1994* (Washington, D.C.: U.S. Government Printing Office, 1994).

the Reagan-Bush years—the interest on the huge deficits generated during the 1980s—remains to be paid for years to come. Interest payments currently represent about one-fifth of the non-Social Security budget (see Table 6.2).

In the long term, however, the Social Security surpluses will end, and the reserves of the Social Security trust funds will decline rapidly (see Figure 6.7, page 145). That is why there is unanimous agreement among policymakers that changes will have to be made in the policies governing the Old-Age, Survivors, and Disability Insurance (OASDI) programs. The controversy is over the type and magnitude of the changes to be introduced.[63]

There can be no doubt that ultimately the OASDI "entitlement issue" will be resolved. Numerous proposals currently are on the table for dealing with the future shortfall. Contrary to the Chicken Little cries from some writers ("The sky is falling!"), there should be little concern that Social Security will be given a firm financial footing.

FIGURE 6.6 DEFENSE EXPENDITURES, 1970–1996

Source: Economic Report of the President, 1996 (Washington, D.C.: U.S. Government Printing Office, 1996).

But the resolution of issues related to the health care system will not be as easy. Figure 6.8 (see page 146) shows, for example, that the projected big growth in future entitlement expenditures comes not from OASDI but from Medicare. When President Clinton first took office, he identified government expenditures on medical services as a "budget killer." He tried comprehensively to reform the nation's approach to health care financing but met with strong resistance. In his second term, a somewhat chastened Clinton and Congress continued to struggle with these costs, but only incremental changes were discussed. In the absence of basic reform, there seemed to be little choice but to shift more of the costs onto private parties—especially service providers and the elderly themselves.

The medical cost issue will continue to be of much greater concern. Our health delivery system is currently undergoing dramatic structural shifts, with the final outcome and implications quite uncertain. Many experts, however, expect the costs of various services to keep rising over the long run.

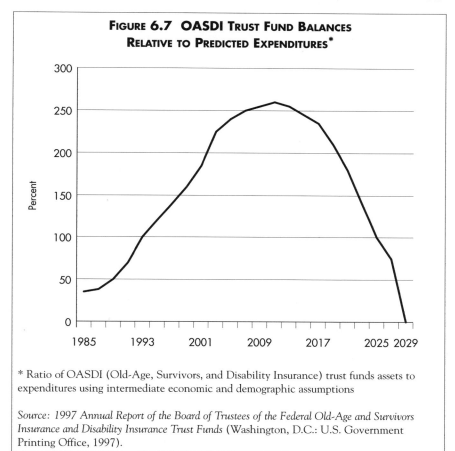

FIGURE 6.7 OASDI TRUST FUND BALANCES
RELATIVE TO PREDICTED EXPENDITURES*

* Ratio of OASDI (Old-Age, Survivors, and Disability Insurance) trust funds assets to expenditures using intermediate economic and demographic assumptions

Source: 1997 Annual Report of the Board of Trustees of the Federal Old-Age and Survivors Insurance and Disability Insurance Trust Funds (Washington, D.C.: U.S. Government Printing Office, 1997).

But that is not the focus of the current discussion. Paradoxically, much of the talk about *radical reform* has concentrated on pension reform—not on the bigger problem of national health care costs.

A variety of schemes have been proposed to privatize part or all of the mandatory public pension program in the United States. Why? For reasons discussed earlier in this chapter, proponents see public pension reform as a way to deal with the deficit, to promote more saving, and hence to promote economic growth.[64] Reform also is being pushed by those who are hostile to most government programs because of the supposed cost to individual liberty. Finally, a large number of players in the private sector investment industry are understandably anxious to increase their business by managing more of the public's retirement monies.

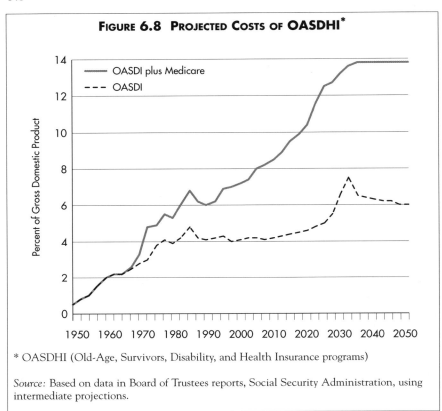

FIGURE 6.8 PROJECTED COSTS OF OASDHI*

* OASDHI (Old-Age, Survivors, Disability, and Health Insurance programs)

Source: Based on data in Board of Trustees reports, Social Security Administration, using intermediate projections.

NOT GENERATIONAL CONFLICT BUT CONFLICT BETWEEN RICH AND POOR

Barely 10 percent of the federal budget goes to what people normally think governments do: laws, roads, natural resources, education, agriculture, transportation, general government services, and so forth. Figure 6.9 shows the trend of federal spending divided into three broad categories: redistributive payments (transfers), expenditures on military goods and services, and expenditures on all other goods and services. The redistributive payments presented here are different from the usual numbers, including not just transfer payments to individuals but also redistribution of income through debt interest payments, grants to state and local governments, and subsidy payments. The data indicate that throughout the whole postwar period only about 10 percent of the activity of the federal

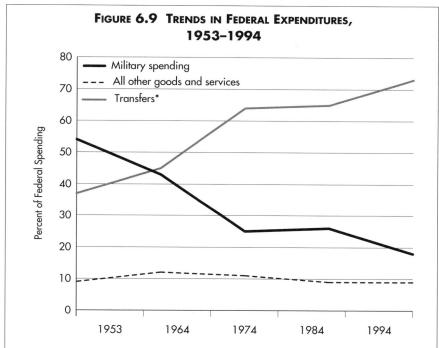

**FIGURE 6.9 TRENDS IN FEDERAL EXPENDITURES,
1953–1994**

Key:
— Military spending
- - - All other goods and services
— Transfers*

(y-axis: Percent of Federal Spending, 0 to 80)
(x-axis: 1953, 1964, 1974, 1984, 1994)

* Transfers are defined as transfers to individuals and the rest of the world plus grants-in-aid to state and local governments plus net interest plus subsidies.

Sources: Data for 1953–82 from W. C. Peterson, "The U.S. 'Welfare State' and the Conservative Counterrevolution," *Journal of Economic Issues* 19, no. 3 (September 1985). Data for 1984–94 from the *Economic Report of the President*, various years.

government (as measured by spending) has gone to the purchase of non-military goods and services. The other 90 percent has been used, first, to redistribute income and, second, to fund the defense establishment.

Thus, for the past half-century or more, the issue of redistributing income has been a major activity of the federal government. Moderation or elimination of poverty has been one of its primary goals, especially dealing with the poverty that arises in old age as a result of individuals' inability or unwillingness to save for retirement.

However, according to Andrew Glyn, in recent years there has been a profound shift in industrialized countries with regard to economic goals and policies—including the philosophy of income distribution.[65] According to the new, conservative orthodoxy, ". . . the equalitarian trends represented in government welfare spending had to be halted, if not reversed. This lurch in the stance of policy making throughout the capitalist world represented at bottom an attempt to claw back from workers some of the gains that the long period of high employment [during much of the 1950s and 1960s] had brought them in terms of wages, working conditions, and welfare."

In the 1980s and 1990s, with all the exaggerated concern about saving rates and budget deficits, there has been a tendency to view the redistribution of income each year through these transfer programs—especially Social Security—as a disincentive to household saving and financial prudence and as a prime culprit in the federal government's difficulties with balancing its books. At the same time, advocates of greater private saving have largely ignored the growing inequality of recent decades.

Many observers have forgotten the basic reasons for the various government programs redistributing income. Social insurance programs were first developed in the depression decade of the 1930s. But their mission is just as relevant today as it was then. Social Security is not just for helping people deal with the problems arising from big depressions (which we hope are gone forever).[66] On a more fundamental level, the need grows out of the labor-related problems (downsizing, early retirement, unemployment) arising from the successful and "efficient" operation of a market economy.[67]

Economic development holds great potential for many nations and has, in itself, decreased absolute poverty in many countries of the world. The problem with the use of market mechanisms to promote growth is the uncertainty they can bring to bear on people's livelihood and welfare—especially with regard to employment. Social Security has been a formidable resource over the years in helping market economies to thrive by "buffering" changing employment needs.[68]

With market incentives that promote efficiency, innovation, and growth also come shifting demand for products, layoffs, early retirement incentives, unemployment, inequality, bankruptcy, community decay, and social disruption. The creation of Social Security and other pensions should be seen as one of society's ways of dealing with the growing problems individuals have in finding work as they age. But, more important, these programs and initiatives should be seen in the context of ever-changing employment needs and the chronic unemployment characterizing market economies. In the words of Dan Jacobson, "more and more governments and unions have . . . come to recognize that adopting employment buffering strategies or developing worker-oriented adjustments and job-replacement strategies are a vital and, indeed, expedient element in human resource policies."[69]

Social Security offers economic protection to middle- and low-income workers that cannot be provided for efficiently and effectively through private means. The case for a program like this that deals with social inequity and insecurity has never been stronger.

Evolving Social Security benefits and early retirement policies in the United States also reflect in a significant way changing economic attitudes about labor force needs and the changing macroeconomic situation. The "early retirement" phenomenon witnessed over recent decades should be viewed as part of an uncoordinated market solution to the stagflation of the 1970s, the high unemployment during the years following the OPEC oil crisis, and, more recently, the new demands of global competition and economic interdependency. Public and private pensions have been a major part of that solution.

It is important to see through the smoke screen of rhetoric about unsustainable dependency ratios (what I refer to as "voodoo demographics"), low saving causing low growth, entitlements "consuming our children," and the proliferating tales of "greedy geezers." Remember that the focus of discussions about national economic security should really be on issues such as maintaining low unemployment, cultivating the sources of growth (not just saving), and achieving a more equitable income distribution—issues that go back many years before the "Social Security debate." The debate about intergenerational redistribution and providing for people in old age can be (and should be) carried on in a totally different way from the scapegoating displayed so frequently in American society today.

7

ARE AMERICANS SAVING ENOUGH FOR RETIREMENT?

William G. Gale

T he baby-boom generation—the roughly 76 million people born between 1946 and 1964—has had a major influence on American society for five decades. From jamming the nation's schools in the 1950s and 1960s to crowding labor and housing markets in the 1970s and 1980s, boomers have reshaped economic patterns and institutions at each stage of their lives. Now that the leading edge of the generation has turned fifty, the impending collision between the boomers and the nation's retirement system is naturally catching the eye of policymakers and the boomers themselves.

Retirement income security in the United States has traditionally been based on the so-called three-legged stool: Social Security, private pensions, and additional household saving. The system has served the elderly well: the poverty rate among elderly households fell from 35 percent in 1959 to 11 percent in 1995.

But problems loom in the future. Partly because of the demographic bulge created by the baby boomers, Social Security faces a long-term imbalance. The solution, even if it involves privatization, must in some way cut benefits or raise taxes.[1] Thus, the future economic status of the elderly hinges critically on the adequacy of private saving and private pensions.

This chapter was originally released as a Century Foundation white paper in 1998.

The private pension system has changed dramatically in nature, shifting away from traditional defined benefit plans to defined contribution plans, which provide workers with much more discretion over participation, contribution, and investment decisions. Naturally, this invites questions about the future ability of pensions to help finance retirement.

The personal saving rate has remained low for more than a decade, and net personal saving other than pensions has virtually disappeared over the past ten years.[2] A significant proportion of people currently reaching retirement age have low levels of financial assets.[3] A large proportion of younger households may also be saving too little to finance their retirement.[4]

People who do not provide for themselves now may be more likely to put pressure on public assistance programs in the future. In addition, a number of trends—including increased life expectancy, earlier retirement age, escalating health care costs, likely reductions in Social Security, and the longer-term deterioration of family networks—will make retirement preparation more difficult in coming years.

These developments would be enough to raise concern about retirement preparation under the best of circumstances. But the prospect of a huge generation edging unprepared toward retirement raises particular concerns about the living standards of the baby boomers in old age, the concomitant pressure on government policies, and the stability of the nation's retirement system.

SOME CONCEPTUAL ISSUES

Whether Americans are saving adequately for retirement depends in part on a number of definitional and conceptual issues. First and foremost, what is meant by "adequate?" One definition of adequate retirement wealth is to have enough resources to maintain preretirement living standards. A common rule of thumb, often used by financial planners, is that retirees should be able to accomplish this goal by replacing 60 to 80 percent of preretirement income.[5] Retiree households can maintain the same standard of living with less income than when working because they typically have more leisure time, smaller family size, and lower work related expenses. Their taxes are lower, both because they escape payroll taxes and because the income tax is progressive. And most have already paid off their mortgages and debts relating to other durable goods. On the other hand, older households may face higher and more uncertain medical expenses, even though they are covered by Medicare.

Maintaining living standards, though, raises some important conceptual problems. For example, retired people have much more leisure time and so literally can substitute time (leisure) for money (consumption expenditure) in maintaining living standards. Understanding the rate at which households make this trade-off is a difficult task. Also, what does it mean to maintain standards of living when health is declining as people age? If the definition is that retirees are restored to the health status they enjoyed as twenty-two-year-olds, clearly enormous expenses would be required, and virtually no one could be said to have "enough" to maintain living standards by that definition. Implicitly, people probably have in mind some age-appropriate health status as a benchmark, but what that benchmark is may vary dramatically across the spectrum of retirees.

In part, the right definition of "enough" depends on why the question is being asked. For example, from a policy perspective, it may be sufficient if boomers maintain, say, 90 percent of their living standards. If that level were achieved, people might decide that there were more pressing uses of limited public resources.

Depending on why the question is asked, other plausible definitions of saving "enough" include having enough resources to stay out of poverty, keeping income above 150 percent of the poverty line, and so forth. There is no hard and fast definition that will satisfy all purposes. Moreover, any measure of what it means to save enough may vary across households in relation to their risk aversion, health status, expectations, preferences for saving, income uncertainty, family size, and other factors.

A second issue is which assets or income sources to include in any measure of how well baby boomers are preparing for retirement. There is near universal agreement that financial assets targeted to retirement, Social Security, and pensions should be included. There are disagreements about whether housing wealth, other assets, labor income earned in "retirement," inheritances, or government benefits should count. As before, to some extent the decision whether to include a certain form of income hinges on what question is being asked.

Some studies focus only on how much retirees are putting aside in personal saving for retirement. There, the outlook appears bleak. James Poterba, Steven Venti, and David Wise found that, in 1991, the median household headed by a sixty-five- to sixty-nine-year-old had financial assets of only $14,000.[6] But expanding the measure to include other assets paints quite a different picture: adding in Social Security, pensions, housing, and other wealth, median wealth was about $270,000.

A third issue—crucial but as yet little explored—is that concerning which baby boomers are not providing adequately for retirement and how big the gap is between what they have and what they should have. Some boomers are doing extremely well, others quite poorly. Summary averages for an entire generation may not be useful as descriptions of the problem or as suggestions for policy.

PREVIOUS RESEARCH

The Congressional Budget Office (1993) recently compared households aged twenty-five to forty-four in 1989 (roughly the boomer cohort) with households the same age in 1962. Boomer households, it turned out, had more real income and a higher ratio of wealth to income than the previous generation. Though this finding initially seems optimistic, in fact the CBO study implies that baby boomers are going to do well in retirement only if the current generation of elderly is thought to be doing well, if the retirement needs of the two generations are the same, if the experience from middle age to retirement is the same for both generations, and if boomers will be satisfied to do as well in retirement as today's retirees.

None of these conditions is guaranteed. First, although the current generation of elderly are generally thought to be doing well in retirement, some 18 percent were living below 125 percent of the poverty line in 1995. Second, retirement needs may be higher for boomers because they will live longer than the previous generation and will likely face higher health costs.

Third, whether the boomers will have a similar experience from middle age to retirement is an open question. The previous generation prospered from the growth of real Social Security benefits in the 1970s. They also benefited from the inflation that caused a dramatic increase in house values in the 1970s and reduced the real value of mortgage debt. However, if housing is not to be included in the wealth measures of adequacy, as many would argue it should not be, then it is unclear why an increase in housing values should be thought of as having helped the previous generation.

Other "onetime" events favor the boomers. First, the stock market fell in real terms in the 1970s, but the S&P 500 has risen by more than 500 percent since 1982. Second, more female boomers are working, and those that do earn more than women in the previous generation. This will raise their pension coverage and benefits. It also implies that boomers will have a bigger drop in work-related expenses in retirement. Third, pension coverage and pension tenure, including 401(k)s, may be higher for male boomers as well because of the maturing of the pension system. Fourth, boomers are having fewer children than their parents did, reducing their living expenses during working years. Fifth, lifetime earnings may peak later for boomers than for the previous generation because boomers are more likely to be in white-collar jobs than in jobs that emphasize physical effort. This means that at any given age, relative to the previous generation, boomers have a greater proportion of their lifetime income (from which to save) ahead of them and will be more likely to be able to work longer if they wish.

Finally, doing as well as the previous generation may not be considered a satisfactory accomplishment either on personal grounds or as a policy goal. For example, living standards tend to rise over time as productivity growth makes workers more efficient. Thus, telling a thirty-five-year-old worker that he or she has the same living standard now as a thirty-five-year-old worker did thirty years ago is not likely to elicit much cheer. A more plausible measure of what constitutes adequate saving is to compare the living standard of boomers in retirement to the one boomers enjoyed during their working years. For all of these reasons, how to interpret the CBO's result is unclear, even if the result itself is unambiguous.

The most comprehensive study of these issues was undertaken by Stanford professor Douglas Bernheim in conjunction with Merrill Lynch. Bernheim developed an elaborate computer model that simulates households' optimal saving and consumption choices over time as a function of family size, earning patterns, age, Social Security, pensions, and other characteristics.[7] He then compared households' actual saving with what the simulations suggested they should be saving. His primary finding, summarized in a "baby boomer retirement index," is that boomers as a whole are saving only about one-third of what they should be to maintain preretirement living standards.

While this finding has generated substantial attention, it is not well understood. The index does not measure the adequacy of saving by the ratio of total retirement resources (Social Security, pensions, and other assets) to total retirement needs (the wealth necessary on the eve of retirement to maintain preretirement living standards). Instead, it examines the ratio of one type of "other assets" to the portion of total needs not covered by Social Security and pensions.

Table 7.1 (see page 156) helps explain how Bernheim's index is constructed. In case A, a hypothetical household (or group of households) needs to accumulate 100 units of wealth. It is on course to generate 61 in Social Security, 30 in pensions, and 3 in other assets.[8] Total retirement

TABLE 7.1 ALTERNATIVE MEASURES OF THE ADEQUACY OF RETIREMENT SAVING

CASE	SOCIAL SECURITY (1)	PENSION (2)	OTHER ASSETS (3)	TOTAL RETIREMENT RESOURCES (1) + (2) + (3)	NEEDS (4)	BOOMER INDEX (%) (3)/[(4) - (1) - (2)]	TOTAL RESOURCES INDEX (%) [(1) + (2) + (3)]/4
A	61	30	3	94	100	33	94
B	0	0	33	33	100	33	33
C	20	20	20	60	100	33	60
D	61	0	33	94	100	85	94
E	61	0	17	78	100	44	78
F	61	30	3	94	95	75	99
G	61	30	3	94	93	150	101

Definitions: *Total Retirement Resources* = Social Security + pensions + other assests.

Needs = accumulated wealth on the eve of retirement that keeps living standard in retirement equal to living standard in working years.

Boomer Index = (other assets) / (needs – Social Security – pensions).

Total Resources Index = (total retirement resources) / (needs).

Source: Author's calculations.

resources are therefore projected to be 94 percent of what is needed to maintain living standards. But, according to the boomer index, the household is saving only 33 percent (that is, 3/[100–61–30]) of what it needs.

Thus, one problem is that the level of the boomer index provides little information about the overall adequacy of retirement preparations. In particular, having the boomer index stand at one-third does not imply that, in the absence of changes in saving behavior, boomers will have living standards in retirement equal to one-third of their current living standard. It could mean that (as in case B), or it could mean retirement living standards will be 60 percent of current ones (case C), or 94 percent (case A), or even more than 99 percent (if Social Security and pension benefits were 99 and other saving were 0.33).

A second problem is that changes in the boomer index over time, or differences across groups, do not correspond to changes or differences in the adequacy of overall retirement saving. If, as in case D, the household in A rolls over its pension into an IRA, the boomer index rises dramatically though total retirement resources are unchanged. If, as in case E, household A rolls over half of its pension into other assets and spends the rest on a vacation, the household clearly is less prepared for retirement— its stock of total retirement resources falls—yet it obtains a higher boomer index than in case A.

A third problem is that the boomer index can be extremely sensitive to estimates of retirement needs. In case F, retirement needs are 5 percent lower than in A, but the boomer index rises from 33 percent to 75 percent. In case G, retirement needs are 7 percent lower than in A, and the boomer index rises to 150 percent.

Bernheim points out that biases in his model cause it to understate the retirement saving problem. The wealth measure, he notes, includes assets the household has earmarked for retirement as well as half of other nonhousing wealth. The model also assumes that there will be no cuts in future Social Security benefits or increases in Social Security taxes, and that life expectancy will not be extended.

But other factors cause the model to overstate the problem. Pension wealth is probably understated. Pension coverage is almost surely understated because any male not covered at the time of the survey, when the respondents are thirty-five to forty-five years old, is assumed never to be covered. Data from Current Population Surveys, however, suggest that pension coverage rates rise by 20 percent from age thirty-five to age fifty-five.[9] Pension benefits may also be understated: Bernheim uses an 18 percent replacement rate of earnings between ages sixty-one and sixty-three, based on data from the 1970s. Because the pension system grew rapidly from the 1940s to the 1970s, workers retiring in the 1970s likely had fewer years in the pension system and hence lower benefits than the boomers will upon retiring. Somewhat more recent data using the 1983 Survey of Consumer Finances suggest replacement rates of 25 to 30 percent and possibly higher.[10]

The basic model excludes all housing wealth; Bernheim's calculations show that including housing would raise the index to 70 percent. The model also excludes all inheritances. A substantial minority of boomers are expected to receive inheritances, typically estimated to be in the range of $10,000 to $30,000.[11] The model assumes that people will retire at age sixty-five, though the Social Security normal retirement age will be sixty-six for most boomers and sixty-seven for the youngest. It excludes all earnings after "retirement," though about 17 percent of the income of the elderly in 1988 came from working.[12] Some portion of this income is earned by people who "need" to work, but casual evidence suggests that a good number of people would like to continue working even if they do not need to. With partial retirement on the increase, boomers may work even more in their senior years, regardless of the adequacy of saving.

There is no allowance in the model for reductions in work-related expenses for those who do retire. This may be an especially important consideration for the growing number of two-earner families. Nor are there allowances for the fact that people eventually pay off their mortgage and hence can continue to consume the same amount of housing services but at greatly reduced cash cost. Data from the 1992 Survey of Consumer Finances indicate that 90 percent of baby boomers that owned homes had outstanding mortgages, compared to about 7 percent of homeowners aged seventy or higher. Similar qualifications apply to other durable goods—furniture, carpets, appliances, cars, clothes. The model used by Bernheim assumes that people rent these items and therefore have to pay for their use every year. In reality, people usually have purchased such items and so do not need to continue making payments after retirement.

Finally, the model also does not allow for any decline in living standards, though a small decline hardly seems like an important policy concern. This is important because, as noted, the boomer index can be extremely sensitive to small changes in assets or needs.

Whether these biases are larger or smaller than the countervailing ones observed by Bernheim is not obvious. Owing to the current uncertainty over the effects of these various influences on our perception of retirement security, measuring and identifying biases accurately is an important area for future study.

SOME NEW RESULTS

Despite the extant research, fundamental questions remain not only unanswered but also in some cases unasked: What proportion of households is saving adequately for retirement? How has the proportion changed over time? What are the characteristics of such households? Among those not saving adequately, how big is the problem?

I have developed preliminary estimates in response to these questions using data from the 1983, 1986, 1989, and 1992 Surveys of Consumer Finances. These are nationally representative household surveys undertaken by the Federal Reserve Board. The sample consists of married households where the husband is aged twenty-five to sixty-four and works at least twenty hours per week.

To determine whether a household is saving adequately requires comparing its actual wealth to a measure of its target wealth. The measures of actual wealth are taken from the surveys. Target wealth indicates how much a household needs to have accumulated, given certain characteristics, to be "on track" for saving enough for retirement. The characteristics that affect this calculation include age, earnings, education, and pension status. People that are older or have higher earnings need to have accumulated more wealth; those with pensions need to have accumulated less (nonpension) wealth than those without. Controlling for the other variables, those with higher levels of education need to have accumulated less than those with lower levels of education. The reason is that workers with higher levels of education tend to have earnings paths that rise more steeply with age and peak later in life. Thus, at a given age and level of earnings, a worker with more education would be expected on average to have more future income than a worker with less education.

To determine target wealth for each household, I use results from Douglas Bernheim and John Karl Scholz,[13] who calculated target wealth-to-earnings ratios as a function of household age, education, and pension status. This ratio can be multiplied by household earnings to determine each household's target wealth level. Because the figures from Bernheim and Scholz use Bernheim's model, the estimates presented here suffer from the same biases as discussed above.

Table 7.2 (see page 160) shows that in 1992, not counting housing equity, about 47 percent of all households—and 48 percent of baby boomers—were saving adequately. When half (or all) of housing equity is counted, the adequacy rate climbs to 61 percent (or 70 percent) for all households and about the same for baby boomers. All three measures have

TABLE 7.2 ADEQUACY RATES: Percentage of Households Deemed to Be Saving Adequately for Retirement

All Households in the Sample

	WEALTH DEFINITION		
Year	Narrow	Intermediate	Broad
1983	44.0%	65.7%	75.9%
1986	52.7	71.3	77.7
1989	43.3	63.0	71.5
1992	46.8	61.1	69.7

Baby Boomer Households

Year	Narrow	Intermediate	Broad
1989	47.7	66.7	72.8
1992	48.1	63.0	71.0

Sample: Married couple where the husband is aged 25–64 and works at least 20 hours per week.

Definitions: *Baby Boomer Households* = households where the husband was born between 1946 and 1964.

Narrow Wealth = Financial assets (checking and money market accounts, CDs and savings accounts, IRAs and Keoghs, mutual funds, stocks and bonds, trusts, cash value of life insurance, and employer-related thrift account balance) plus nonfinancial assets (business, other real estate, and other assets) minus total debt (lines of credit, credit card debt, other real estate debt, other debt).

Intermediate Wealth = Narrow Wealth plus 50 percent of housing equity.

Broad Wealth = Narrow Wealth plus 100 percent of housing equity.

Source: Author's calculations from the 1983, 1986, 1989, and 1992 Surveys of Consumer Finances.

fallen since 1986. This may be a little misleading, since the 1986 sample was a reinterview of selected respondents of the 1983 survey rather than a random cross section. However, in 1992 the intermediate and broad wealth measures were below their 1983 levels, which is more troubling.

In any given year, adequacy rates are prone to rise with education and income. Within the baby-boom generation, adequacy rates generally decline somewhat with age. This is consistent with a point made by Bernheim that the older boomers should be saving at a higher rate but do not appear to be doing so. Adequacy rates tend to be higher for boomers with pensions than for those without, either because pensions raise households' overall wealth or because people more oriented toward saving and thinking about retirement are also more likely to have jobs with pensions.

Interestingly, high adequacy rates do not necessarily require high levels of observed saving. For example, suppose annual retirement needs are 75 percent of final earnings. According to the Social Security Administration, Social Security benefits replace about 47 percent of final earnings for the average worker with thirty-five years of experience who earns $40,000 at retirement and has a nonworking spouse. With pensions typically replacing 25 to 30 percent of final earnings, a household with Social Security and a pension would not need much more saving to maintain adequate living standards, especially if at least one member of the household can work for a time in "retirement," expects to receive bequests, or expects to use housing equity to support retirement consumption.

Table 7.3 (see page 162) examines the difference between current target wealth and current actual wealth among households that are not saving adequately (ignoring all housing equity). For many such households the wealth shortfall is relatively small. The median inadequate saver has a shortfall of $22,000, or about six months of earnings—a problem that could be solved either by postponing retirement for six months or by accepting a relatively small reduction in retirement living standards. Even among sixty- to sixty-four-year-olds, the median inadequate saver could obtain a sound retirement by working for an additional two years.

Thus, the glass can be viewed as half full or half empty. When housing equity is ignored, the typical household seems to be either just barely saving enough or just missing the target. When housing is included, more than two-thirds of households appear to be above the minimum wealth they need, given age and other considerations. Roughly speaking, a third of the sample is doing well by any measure, a third is doing poorly by any measure, and the status of the middle third is ambiguous. Both of the following statements are true: up to two-thirds of the households in the sample are now saving at least as much as they should be; and two-thirds are "at risk" in that any deterioration in their situation could make it impossible for them to maintain their current living standards in retirement.

In short, two issues matter tremendously to any characterization of the problem: the heterogeneity of saving behavior across households and uncertainty concerning the right measures of wealth to use and the future

TABLE 7.3 ADEQUACY GAPS, BY AGE, 1992
Inadequate Savers, Using Narrow Wealth Measure

Age	GAP IN DOLLARS			GAP/ANNUAL EARNINGS		
	25%	50%	75%	25%	50%	75%
25–29	1,710	2,960	4,850	0.068	0.117	0.239
30–34	1,900	3,400	5,920	0.071	0.100	0.176
35–39	8,020	13,180	23,390	0.227	0.367	0.491
40–44	14,260	26,940	51,220	0.425	0.734	1.100
45–49	19,300	33,500	56,420	0.404	0.824	1.396
50–54	24,770	65,100	82,450	0.888	1.252	1.816
55–59	32,510	51,800	98,670	1.049	1.496	1.900
60–64	29,140	75,470	153,420	1.022	2.166	2.914
All Households	5,920	22,480	51,880	0.199	0.519	1.252
Baby Boomer Households	4,450	13,480	29,099	0.150	0.378	0.732

Sample: Married couples where husband is aged 25–64 and works at least 20
             hours per week for households saving inadequately.

Definitions: *Narrow Wealth* = Financial assets (checking and money market accounts,
             CDs and savings accounts, IRAs and Keoghs, mutual funds, stocks and
             bonds, trusts, cash value of life insurance and defined contribution pen-
             sion account balance) plus nonfinancial assets (business, other real estate,
             and other assets) minus total debt (lines of credit, credit card debt, other
             real estate debt, and other debt).

             Broad Wealth = Narrow Wealth plus 100 percent of housing equity.

             No College = Head's highest educational attainment less than or equal to
             15 years of schooling.

             College = Head's highest educational attainment greater than 15 years of
             schooling.

             Pension = Head covered by a defined benefit or defined contribution
             pension (not including 401[k]s).

             Gap = Target wealth level–actual wealth level.

Source: Author's calculations based on the 1992 Survey of Consumer Finances.

course of the boomers. The results examined here refer only to a sample of married couples where the husband works full time. Other married couples and singles are likely to be faring worse.

THE UNCERTAIN FUTURE

The uncertainty of forecasts about the adequacy of saving should be a predominant concern. There are several reasons why it is difficult to make projections with confidence. First, as a society, we have as yet little understanding of the dynamics of retirement. Only one or two generations have had lengthy retirements, and crucial aspects of retirement living standards—pensions, health care, asset markets, Social Security, life span, family living arrangements, retirement age—have changed rapidly over time. Two well-known recent phenomena—the anemic saving rate and the soaring stock market—send diametrically opposing messages about the status of retirement preparation in the United States.

Relatively long-term predictions are inherently fraught with error. Consider the difficulty of predicting, in 1982, the fate of people who were to retire fifteen years later. In 1982, the country had just finished a decade marked by high personal saving, two major oil shocks, several recessions, skyrocketing house prices fueled by inflation, high tax rates and interest rates, and a disastrous performance by stocks. Since then all of those economic parameters have reversed themselves: personal saving has plummeted, energy prices have similarly fallen sharply, house prices have stagnated as inflation, tax rates, and interest rates have fallen, and the stock market has increased many times over. The economy has suffered only one recession in the past fifteen years. In addition, health care costs rose dramatically, there was a major Social Security reform, and numerous tax changes influenced the treatment of retirement funds.

Of course, every generation has faced uncertainty with regard to its future. It is not obvious that the boomers' prospects are riskier than those faced by previous generations at similar stages in the life cycle or those to be faced by "generation X." It is, however, worth focusing on some of the major sources of uncertainty.

Retirement patterns. The "adequacy of saving" can be flipped around to become nothing more than an "age of retirement" issue. In the extreme, if people never retire, they do not need any retirement saving. More generally, working longer reduces the length of retirement and therefore, even if the extra earnings are not saved, raises the adequacy of retirement wealth preparations.

Average age at retirement, which fell throughout the twentieth century for men, may start rising regardless of the adequacy of saving. Many of today's jobs do not depend on "brawn" and can thus be done by older people. The normal Social Security retirement age will rise to sixty-six by 2008 and sixty-seven by 2025 even in the absence of further changes to the program.

There is also increasing evidence that people would prefer to reduce their hours worked gradually rather than abruptly. There are some obvious institutional problems here, but Christopher Ruhm finds evidence that only 36 percent of household heads retire immediately at the end of their career jobs and nearly half remain in the labor force for at least five additional years.[14] About 47 percent of workers eligible for a pension continue to work after leaving their career job. If people choose to continue to work even after "retirement," this will bolster the resources available to support living standards in retirement.

Life expectancy. A related uncertainty involves life expectancy. Expectations about remaining years of life for sixty-five-year-olds have risen significantly in the past two decades and are projected to grow further. From a retirement saving perspective, living longer means having to stretch resources over a longer period.

Home equity. Uncertainty regarding home equity is twofold. First, how will housing prices evolve? Both easing demographic pressures and the long-term reduction in tax rates in the 1980s may diminish the value of housing.[15] The second issue is the extent to which housing should be conceived as part of the wealth used to support living standards.[16] Excluding housing wealth is sometimes defended on the grounds that people do not like to move when they are old, but this is somewhat misleading. Households can extract equity without moving, via reverse mortgages.

Other reasons to include or exclude housing equity in wealth depend on the underlying purpose. For example, as a public policy concern, a retired couple that lives in a $300,000 house and has little cash or financial assets but refuses to dip into housing equity may not be considered to have very pressing needs.

In the 1970s, housing was a highly profitable investment, so people would naturally have put more money into housing rather than less. In the 1980s and 1990s, as housing has become a less attractive asset to hold for demographic and tax reasons, people may be more willing to extract equity from their houses. The elderly in the 1970s had lived through World War I, the Great Depression, and World War II and so may have had different attitudes toward the importance of maintaining a precautionary stock of wealth. Baby boomers, in contrast, have always been willing to countenance financing through housing equity. In fact, boomers have been among the major loan recipients in the booms in home equity lending in the 1980s and 1990s. The issue becomes whether the boomers, when they are elderly, will behave more like they did when they were young or more like today's elderly. Recent policy changes have eliminated the taxation of the first $500,000 of capital gains on a house. This may induce more retired people to sell their homes in the future and allow them to consume their housing wealth. The fact that the current generation of the elderly have not already done so may just indicate that they are doing quite well; that is, they have adequate saving from other sources.

The evolution of asset markets. Equity values cannot continue to grow at the rapid rates experienced in 1996 and 1997. And even if the boomers accumulate what seem to be sufficient retirement funds under standard rate-of-return assumptions, they will—loosely speaking—all want to cash in those funds at roughly the same time. That might mean massive sell-offs of securities that could depress asset values and reduce stock market returns. Conceivably, asset prices could fall sharply, but since equity markets are forward-looking, it may be more likely that they would remain stagnant for a long period, as in the 1970s.[17]

Inheritances. The current generation of elderly has amassed tremendous wealth. Although a substantial portion is in the form of annuities—Social Security and pensions—that cannot be bequeathed, a large amount of resources will be passed on to the baby-boom generation. This will be a boon for selected families. It will not in and of itself "solve" the saving problem for the boomer generation, but it certainly will not hurt. In terms of dollar value, most inheritances involve extremely wealthy decedents giving to very wealthy recipients. Relative to retirement income needs, the typical boomer household will likely gain little if anything from inheritances, perhaps on the order of $10,000–$30,000.

THE ROLE OF PRIVATE PENSIONS

The retirement status of future generations of Americans will depend to a large extent on the evolution of the private pension system. Pension wealth is a sizable component of total household resources. In 1993, 47 percent of civilian nonagricultural workers participated in pension plans.[18] The present value of future income flows from private pensions accounted for 20 percent of the wealth of households aged sixty-five to sixty-nine.[19]

The private pension system grew rapidly in the twenty-five years after World War II. In 1940, 15 percent of private sector workers were covered by pensions. By 1970, the figure had risen to 45 percent.[20] Since then, however, pension coverage has either remained constant, fallen a bit, or increased slightly depending on the definition of coverage, the data source, the sample, and the end years chosen.[21]

Stagnating pension coverage, however, masks a major shift in the composition of private pensions toward defined contribution plans and away from defined benefit plans. In defined benefit plans, annuity benefits are stipulated as a percentage of years worked, average or maximum salaries, and other considerations. In defined contribution plans, contributions are stipulated. The account balances build up over time, and whatever is in the account at the time of retirement is available for retirement consumption. From 1975 to 1992, the share of defined contribution plans rose from 29 percent to 60 percent of all active pension participants, and from 35 percent to 72 percent of all contributions.

Since the early 1980s, almost all of the rise in defined contribution plans has taken the form of 401(k) plans. For example, total contributions to defined contribution plans rose by $49 billion from 1984 to 1992, of which $48 billion represented increased contributions to 401(k)s. A recent, related trend is the evident growth in hybrid retirement plans, which combine features of defined benefit and defined contribution plans. While less is known about these plans, they may be seen as an attempt generally to balance the costs and benefits of defined contribution and defined benefit plans.

Two main hypotheses have been examined concerning the secular rise of defined contribution plans: increased regulation of defined benefit plans following the passage of the Employee Retirement Income Security Act (ERISA) in 1974; and the changing composition of the workforce. These hypotheses, of course, need not be mutually exclusive.[22] The appeal of plans with 401(k) characteristics undoubtedly springs in part from the fact that employees may make tax-deductible contributions. Further,

Richard Ippolito also shows that the matching features of 401(k) plans are likely to be relatively more attractive to more productive workers, so that 401(k)s can help firms attract and retain the right type of people.[23]

The implications for retirement saving of the shift to defined contribution plans can be divided into two parts: first, the effects of pensions on saving behavior generally; second, differences in the effects of defined benefit and defined contribution plans on saving. The interaction between pensions and other saving can be complex. In the simplest life cycle models, workers save only for retirement. Changing the form of workers' compensation from current wages to future pension benefits has no effect on consumption, and no effect on overall (pension plus nonpension) wealth or saving. Increases in pension wealth are offset completely by reductions in other wealth. A number of issues in the real world, however, complicate this analysis. First, unlike conventional, taxable assets, pensions are typically illiquid, tax-deferred annuities. Second, people save for reasons other than retirement. Third, alternative models of saving have been proposed, in which households make saving decisions based on psychological or behavioral models[24] or people lack the basics of economic literacy.[25] Given all of the theoretical variants, the range of possible outcomes is wide: pensions can have any effect, from reducing nonpension wealth by more than pension wealth adds to raising nonpension wealth.

Taken at face value, the literature to date suggests with only a few exceptions that pensions raise household wealth overall and cause almost no reduction in households' nonpension wealth. However, my previous research notes that several features of earlier empirical work impose a series of systematic statistical biases, implying that such previous studies overstate the effect of pensions on other wealth.[26] Correcting for none of the biases, my estimates were that a dollar increase in pension wealth reduces other wealth by 10 percent or less. Correcting for five (of the eight) biases yielded the finding that a dollar increase in pension wealth reduces other wealth by forty to eighty cents, depending on the specification of the regression equation. Some analyses also suggest considerable heterogeneity in how households respond to pension wealth.[27] Thus, there remains substantial uncertainty concerning the impact of traditional pensions on households' wealth accumulation.

Like the literature on traditional pensions, studies examining the impact of 401(k)s have produced disparate results.[28] Estimates from this literature also suffer from a series of econometric biases, most of which tend to overstate the impact of 401(k) plans on saving but at least one of which may lead to an understatement of the effects.

There are several significant differences in the operation of defined benefit and defined contribution plans that could influence the adequacy of retirement saving.[29] In defined contribution plans, employees typically have much more control over not only whether to participate but also how much to contribute, where to invest, and how and when to withdraw funds. All of these options raise concerns about the adequacy of retirement saving. Participation rates among workers eligible for 401(k) plans hover around 70 percent. This is much higher than, say, IRA participation rates but of course lower than the almost 100 percent participation rates that prevail for defined benefit plans. There is also concern that workers in defined contribution plans are not contributing enough and are investing too conservatively (and hence earning too low a return).

In addition, defined contribution plans are more liquid than defined benefit plans. Workers can make use of the money in 401(k)s under circumstances of personal hardship and other considerations and can access all of the funds, subject to a penalty, should they leave the firm. Evidence suggests that most people with the option of taking an early, lump-sum distribution choose to take the funds in cash. But these are mainly younger workers who have built up only small amounts in their accounts. Most of the funds that are eligible for lump-sum distribution are in fact rolled over into other retirement accounts.[30] Although defined benefit plans can be cashed in upon exiting the firm in certain circumstances (mainly when the present value of future benefits is low), the benefits offered are in general much less liquid than benefits in defined contribution plans.

The increased liquidity of defined contribution plans may make them more attractive relative to defined benefit plans. This would attract contributions to defined contribution plans, but the contributions would be more likely to be removed before retirement. The net effect on saving seems to be uncertain.

Defined benefit and defined contribution plans create different kinds of risks. In the former, benefits are linked to the highest few years of earnings, whereas in the latter, benefits are essentially a weighted average of earnings over many years. Rules regarding (nominal) benefits in a defined benefit plan are set by the employer, typically many years in advance. Benefits in a defined contribution plan depend on the rate of return earned on pension assets, based on choices made by the participant. Both types of benefits are subject to inflation risk. Andrew Samwick and Jonathan Skinner conclude that defined contribution plans present less overall risk than defined benefit plans do.[31] If so, then defined contribution plans may well engender less precautionary saving and so have a larger negative impact on other saving.

Accruing balances and account statements are probably simpler to understand in defined contribution plans than in defined benefit plans. Whether increased visibility of earnings raises or reduces households' other saving depends in part on whether the household accrues more or less than its members would otherwise have expected in its plan. An added effect is that by providing periodic updates on balances, defined contribution plans may do a better job of constantly reminding households of the need to save for retirement. Of course, there is no reason why such updates could not also be provided in a defined benefit plan.

Although it is in general quite difficult to pin down the implications of these differences for how pensions affect wealth, several points are worth emphasizing. First, the mechanisms through which pensions affect wealth can be exceedingly complex. Second, there is no reason to expect defined benefit and defined contribution plans to have identical impacts on the level or structure of household wealth, even if the benefit levels are held constant. The shift toward defined contribution plans creates opportunities as well as risks. Secular shifts in preferences in the pension system may be altering the way pensions affect retirement wealth accumulation.

A final consideration concerns substitution between 401(k) plans and other pension plans at the firm level. Many 401(k)s appear to have been converted directly from previously existing pension or thrift plans. Because 401(k)s were not popular until the IRS issued clarifying regulations in 1981, most plans created before 1982 are thought to have been conversions. In 1985, these plans accounted for 39 percent of the 401(k) plans, 85 percent of balances, 65 percent of participants with nonzero balances, and two-thirds of contributions.[32] Even as recently as 1991, the majority of assets, 42 percent of participants, and 47 percent of contributions were in plans created before 1982. This suggests the possibility that much of 401(k) wealth in 1991 would have existed in other pensions even in the absence of 401(k) plans.

For 401(k)s created after 1985, other mechanisms may be at work. Leslie Papke uses panel data from 1985 to 1992 and estimates that for every ten plan sponsors that started out in 1985 with no 401(k) or other defined contribution plan and then added a 401(k) over time, the number of defined benefit plans offered by those sponsors fell by at least three more than it otherwise would have over this period.[33] Plan-level estimates imply that if a 401(k) plan is added by a sponsor, the probability that a defined benefit plan is terminated approximately doubles or increases from about 18 percent to about 36 percent. These results imply that a sizable minority of 401(k) plans are replacing defined benefit plans.[34]

Another channel of substitution can occur on the margin—firms may cut back on existing plans in other ways such as restricting or reducing benefit increases. Casual observation suggests that this form of substitution could be quite important, but there is as yet no hard evidence.[35] It is also possible (but difficult to verify) that some 401(k) plans are being established at firms that would have created another plan had 401(k)s not existed. Taken together, these trends and possibilities suggest that a substantial portion of 401(k)s may be replacing other pensions.

To the extent that 401(k)s displace other plans completely or at the margin, an additional issue comes into play. All workers covered by traditional plans participate, but workers may well opt out of a 401(k). Thus, the saving impact of the 401(k) may be less than that of the traditional plan it displaces.[36] If so, a 401(k) plan that substituted for a terminated defined benefit plan could actually reduce private saving on average.

CONCLUSION

Retirement prospects for the baby boomers are marked by heterogeneity and uncertainty. The heterogeneity stems from the fact that some households save much more than others. While some part of this difference is likely the result of government policies, much of it must ultimately be attributed to households' observable characteristics—number of children, age, income, and others—and, just as important, households' unobserved characteristics—their patience, risk aversion, valuation of the future. There are several sources of uncertainty, including what policymakers and boomers themselves will accept as a reasonable goal for retirement living standards and the functioning of the economy as a whole. This diagnosis of the problem indicates that the adequacy and distribution of retirement saving will continue to be an important topic in policy debates in the future.

8

FAMILY FINANCES AND AGING

Linda K. George

Economic resources and financial security are typically viewed as objective phenomena that are the purview of economists and financial analysts. There is truth, of course, in this perception. But the realities of personal wealth, societal wealth, and economic policies are but part of the picture. Economic decisions—whether individual, societal, or global—are made by people. And people's lives encompass much more than objective considerations. Indeed, most people describe their "richest" experiences as lying outside the realm of economics. Social and behavioral scientists typically study people in a more holistic sense than economists, striving to understand individuals' attitudes and behaviors—and finding that such understanding requires more than an inventory of the objective realities of human existence. Subjective perceptions and social context have emerged as two particularly important determinants of personal attitudes, behaviors, and well-being.

The purpose of this chapter is to supplement traditional economic views of aging with information about the social and psychological aspects of financial security in later life. The chapter is organized into three sections. The first examines the social psychology of financial well-being. The second section examines the vital role of families as the vehicles for substantial transfers of money, goods, and services for the elderly population. The final section briefly addresses some of the broader implications of social and psychological processes for understanding financial security in later life.

THE SOCIAL PSYCHOLOGY OF FINANCIAL SECURITY

There are both objective and subjective dimensions of financial well-being. The objective dimension, of course, refers to financial resources, such as amount of income or net worth. The subjective dimension has several components; the one examined here will be financial satisfaction—the extent to which people are satisfied with the financial resources available to them. A key reason to examine both objective and subjective dimensions of financial security is that they differ in several important ways. These differences are best contrasted when observations are made across age groups or across time. The nature of these differences will be delineated first, followed by an examination of how subjective perceptions of financial security affect economic decisionmaking in ways that would not be predicted by knowing about *only* financial resources.

During the past thirty to thirty-five years, the economic status of the older population has increased significantly—both in absolute levels and relative to young and middle-aged adults.[1] Despite the more favorable economic condition of the older population as a whole, however, at the individual level, old age is characterized by income loss. Retirement results in a substantial drop in earnings, and financial resources tend to decline throughout old age[2]—usually gradually but occasionally precipitously as a result of catastrophic events.

Turning to the subjective dimension of financial security, research evidence indicates that approximately 85 percent of older Americans are "satisfied" or "very satisfied" with their incomes and their financial status more broadly.[3] In fact, substantially higher proportions of older adults than young and middle-aged adults feel this way. The proportion of older adults who report that they are content with their financial resources has been stable for the past thirty to thirty-five years. Thus, the real increase in economic resources among persons who recently entered old age has not resulted in greater satisfaction. The same pattern is observed in longitudinal studies of older adults. Those studies find no evidence that perceptions of well-being decline with age or time since retirement, despite tangible decreases in economic resources.[4] Certainly personal disasters can create economic problems, but overall, regardless of whether one examines generations of older people who entered life with different degrees of prosperity or whether one observes the same individuals over time, levels of financial satisfaction remain remarkably constant. It should be noted, however, that virtually all evidence regarding satisfaction with finances is based on data collected after Medicare and Medicaid were instituted.

It is already obvious that very different patterns emerge, depending upon whether the focus of concern is objective levels of economic resources or subjective perceptions of financial well-being during later life. This can be better understood by examining the relationship between objective and subjective dimensions of financial security. The natural hypothesis is that financial satisfaction will be strongly related to actual economic status. And there is support for that hypothesis: there is a moderately strong relationship between levels of economic resources and perceptions of the adequacy of those resources.[5] But the lack of overlap between objective and subjective dimensions of financial well-being also is substantial. In quantitative terms, economic resources explain only about half of financial satisfaction for the adult population of the United States. Also important, economic resources are a less important predictor of financial satisfaction for older adults than for middle-aged and younger adults. Income and assets explain only about 25 percent of the perceptions of financial well-being for older adults, compared to 50 percent for the total population.

Thus far, the economic picture for older adults has been rather rosy—improving economic status in objective terms and high, stable levels of financial satisfaction. But older adults also experience a form of discomfort with regard to their financial security. Although it has received less attention in previous research, there is strong evidence that a majority of older adults are afraid that their economic resources will not be sufficient to meet their future needs.[6] And, as was true in the case of financial satisfaction, one observes a surprising relationship between objective levels of financial resources and fear that those resources will not be sufficient for future needs. In studies of representative samples of older adults, my colleagues and I have found essentially no relationship between income and worries about economic security.[7] That is, older people with high incomes are as likely as older people with low incomes to be worried about their futures.

Thus, with regard to the present, the vast majority of older adults are satisfied with their financial resources, regardless of level of objective wealth. In contrast, with regard to the future, most older adults are worried about the adequacy of their economic resources—again, regardless of degree of affluence. Moreover, in the studies just cited, this pattern is as strong among the oldest members of the samples as among those who are somewhat younger. Intuitively, it seems that there would come a point in the life course where people believed that their economic assets were sufficient to meet the needs of a future that, realistically, would be relatively short. But such is not the case. Persons age eighty and older are as worried about future financial demands as persons aged sixty-five to seventy-nine are—again, high levels of income and assets do not significantly dampen this fear.

One cannot understand the financial decisions and behaviors of older adults without taking into account their subjective perceptions of their economic needs and means. As documented repeatedly in the social and behavioral sciences, individual behavior is based on perceptions of reality rather than reality itself. Knowledge of the typical patterns of perceptions of economic security among the elderly, coupled with information about objective financial resources, suggests a number of ways that individual economic decisions during later life may be affected and public policy concerns may in turn take a different shape.

First, the high levels of financial satisfaction reported by older adults undoubtedly contribute to public perceptions that the elderly are pampered, resource-rich, and benefiting excessively from public economic transfers. What is not recognized is that these high levels of declared financial satisfaction are only modestly related to actual economic well-being and are highly insensitive to change, even as people's resources decline over time. For example, a series of studies conducted by the Social Security Administration examined older adults' perceptions of income adequacy, with the goal of determining whether those perceptions might be used for policy purposes.[8] The conclusion was that subjective perceptions should *not* be used for income policies because of the degree to which the attributions of adequacy made by older adults were unrealistic; in particular, large proportions of older adults living below the official poverty line described their economic resources as sufficient. Undoubtedly the broader public is unaware of the fact that older adults' perceptions are so weakly related to their true living standards.

Second, these findings have important implications for the development of public policies that are sensitive to the needs and concerns of older adults, keeping in mind that the major economic worries among the elderly concern the future. Most obvious, of course, is the need for policies that provide adequate coverage for catastrophic events of all kinds—illness, of course, but also natural disasters, forced relocation, and so forth. In addition, fear of the future undoubtedly accounts for behavior by some older adults that appears to be greedy or self-centered. For example, when older adults with high incomes resist policies that would require them to pay for a portion of their benefits, they may well be motivated by fear that their savings will be depleted rather than from a desire for more afternoons on the golf course. As things stand, it is clear that the majority of older adults do not believe that public policies provide enough of a safety net to meet their needs if their personal resources are exhausted.

Third, and perhaps most important, understanding typical patterns of subjective views on financial security helps to explain some personal economic decisions that otherwise appear ill-advised at best and illogical at worst. There is a large research base documenting the fact that many fewer older adults use health and social services than would profit from them.[9] Indeed, an active area of practical research is the development of effective strategies for overcoming barriers to appropriate use of services. It is commonly noted in this research that cognitive and attitudinal barriers are among the most common. This pattern was vividly brought to attention during the development and evaluation of an in-home respite care program for the caregivers of demented older adults, conducted at the Duke University Center for the Study of Aging and Human Development.

Similar to other researchers and clinicians, the author's study team developed a respite care program designed to give family caregivers a break from the demands of caregiving. Using this program, families could obtain the services of a trained respite care worker, who would come to the home and care for the demented older adult for periods ranging from four to sixteen hours a week. Because the program was supported by a grant from a private foundation, we were able to subsidize the services. A sliding scale, ranging from $1 to $8 per hour, was developed, with the amount of subsidy contingent on the caregiver's income. Our study, in common with others like it, experienced three significant difficulties. First, few caregivers chose to use the program, despite the fact that they had expressed interest in it. Second, the primary reason given for not using the program was that it cost too much, which surprised us greatly. Indeed, as months went by and our subsidies became more generous, we encountered caregivers with annual incomes of $50,000 or more who were unwilling to pay $1 per hour for respite services. Third, despite targeting the respite care program at middle-stage dementia patients, most of those who used the program were caring for family members in the final stages of dementia. Intensive fieldwork demonstrated that fear that economic resources would be insufficient for future needs underlay all three of these difficulties. Even caregivers who were objectively financially well-off were frightened to pay for respite services—even when these were subsidized—if they were unsure whether their economic resources would see them through a disease that could last for years and require institutional care. This same fear explained why most of the respite care was reserved for persons with advanced dementia. It was only when the "end was in sight" that family members felt sufficiently confident to spend their financial resources on relief from caregiving duties. This experience and other research indicates that there is a tremendous lack of awareness about the many ways in which older adults' behavior is affected by such fears. As this brief review documents, a true sense of financial security rests on the perception that economic resources are sufficient for future as well as current needs.

INTERGENERATIONAL TRANSFERS:
WHO GIVES AND WHO GETS

It is only relatively recently that economists have come to take nonmonetary transfers of goods and services seriously when attempting to assess the economic status of the elderly and other subgroups of interest. This kind of resource flow is referred to as in-kind transfers. Initial efforts to assess the importance of in-kind transfers focused on resources provided through formal means (for example, tax breaks or transportation services for the elderly). Even more recent is recognition by economists that vast volumes of money, goods, and services are routinely transferred between adult children and elderly parents in multigenerational families. Obviously, it was generally known that family members help each other; the dramatic shift has been in acknowledging that the economic value of these patterns of family assistance is extraordinarily large—probably rivaling that of public transfers to the elderly.

This examination of intergenerational transfers among American families—with specific focus on the transfer of money, goods, and services between adult children and their parents—will, because of space limitations, be restricted in two ways. First, intergenerational transfers conferred after the death of older parents will not be looked at, although a great deal of personal wealth is transferred via inheritance. Second, the review will be restricted to interhousehold intergenerational transfers. The direction of transfers across generations in shared households is very difficult to disentangle. It should be noted, however, that these restrictions of scope result in underestimates of the incidence of intergenerational transfers throughout society.

Transfers between adult children and aging parents occur in two primary "currencies": money and time. Time transfers will be disaggregated into two categories: household assistance and personal care. Household assistance includes all types of household help: repairs, maintenance, cleaning, yard work, and so forth. Personal care refers to help with fundamental skills such as bathing, eating, dressing, moving about, and so forth. Both household assistance and personal care clearly have economic value, but previous research has documented the importance of distinguishing between time and money transfers since these have different predictors.

The topic of intergenerational transfers is one that highlights the differences in the core assumptions that economists and sociologists rely upon for understanding human behavior. The key assumption of economic theory is that individuals are rational and make rational choices—that is, that the major motive of human behavior is to maximize rewards. Rewards may be monetary or nonmonetary, but it is held that even nonmonetary rewards can be quantified in terms of their value. Sociologists do not dispute the assumption that the quest for rewards is a driving force in human behavior. But they also emphasize that behavior occurs in a social context—and that social context provides sets of opportunities and constraints that operate independently of individual desires to maximize rewards. Perhaps the most dramatic evidence of the power of social context is its potential to elicit behaviors from individuals that are at odds with objective personal rewards. Social norms in context create behavior patterns that often are at odds with such rewards. In order to maximize *subjective* rewards and social approval, individuals often subjugate objective rewards to compliance with social norms. Sociological theories view this conflict between objective and subjective rewards as a core tension of social life. Individuals face a myriad of decisions daily that involve the choice between maximizing purely personal and social gratification. Empirical investigation of the choices that individuals make and whether these choices can be predicted is a primary focus of sociological inquiry.

Economists and sociologists, operating on the core assumptions of their disciplines, would make different predictions about intergenerational transfers. From the economic, rational choice perspective, older adults would wish to maximize the rewards (money and time) that they receive from their children, whereas adult children would wish to minimize the flow of resources to their older parents. Thus, one would expect resource transfers to be relatively rare, to occur only when the need for them is strong, and to be made by those children for whom the transfer is least costly (those with the greatest resources). From the sociological perspective, both the incidence of transfers and the forecast of who gives and receives such transfers would vary by social context and norms. Consequently, sociologists would expect patterns that deviate from rational choice if there are norms that support such a departure.

MONEY TRANSFERS

Despite the normative ideal that all adults are economically self-sufficient, financial transfers between adult children and their parents are far from rare. Even excluding transfers by inheritance, the dominant direction of intergenerational transfers of money is from older parents to their adult children.[10] In the population as a whole, the incidence of money transfers is greater from parents to adult children than from adult children to parents; in addition, the *value* of intergenerational transfers is greater for parent to adult child transfers, on average, than for the reverse. Transfers from the elder generation take two primary forms. One is equal disbursement of financial resources to all children, regardless of personal need. This pattern is the less frequent one and is used primarily by wealthy elders who wish to disburse their estates partially prior to death.[11] More commonly, money transfers appear to be occasional and targeted toward helping children who are in need of additional economic resources.[12] In these transfers, there is no attempt to treat all one's children equally. Thus, older Americans, though viewed by economists as part of the dependency ratio, are in fact more likely to be donors than recipients in intergenerational financial transfers.

Despite the dominant pattern of financial transfers, the reverse also occurs. Estimates from representative national samples suggest that between 3 and 10 percent of middle-aged adults with living parents transfer $500 or more to them during a one-year interval.[13] These estimates are the best available and are useful. Nonetheless, they are incomplete. First, there is a lack of information on the frequency of transfers over long periods of time. That is, the degree to which financial transfers tend to be onetime, occasional, or regular events cannot be determined on the basis of available data. Second, the *lifetime* risk of making financial transfers to aging parents is unknown—but the proportion of those assisting the elder generation over the course of a lifetime is certainly substantially larger than the slim percentage who make transfers in a given year. Third, although there are now data from representative national samples about the incidence of transfers, there are no data about the actual value of those transfers. Available evidence indicates that the primary characteristics of elderly parents associated with the likelihood of receipt of a financial transfer from an adult child are indicators of need. Transfers to parents are obviously most likely when the parent is poor or when the adult child perceives the parent to be financially needy.[14] Other characteristics associated with receipt of a financial transfer from children are being unmarried and having significant health problems.[15] These also reflect need. Health problems clearly can require large expenditures. Being unmarried also may generate more need for money especially among widowed women. Finally, the more children one has, the higher the odds that a parent will receive financial assistance from at least one of them.[16]

The primary characteristics of adult children who make financial transfers to aging parents appear to reflect both resources and obligations. That is, children are especially likely to transfer money to their aging parents when they are relatively well-off and have fewer competing demands on their assets. For adult children, higher levels of education and income are associated with greater probability of making a transfer.[17] Unmarried adult children also are more likely than their married peers to transfer money to their parents.[18] Contrary to the competing demands hypothesis, however, the number of children (of the adult child) is not associated with the likelihood of making a transfer.[19]

Other considerations seem to reflect subcultural family traditions. Middle-aged daughters are more likely to transfer money to their parents than middle-aged sons,[20] suggesting either that women sustain closer ties with their parents than men or that cultural norms place disproportionate responsibility for parent care on women's shoulders. Birth order also affects the likelihood that one will make a financial transfer to one's parents, with older children most likely to be supportive.[21] This pattern also may reflect cultural norms about filial responsibility. Having siblings, however, appears modestly to affect transfers to aging parents—the odds of helping out economically are slightly higher if one has a sibling who has done the same.[22]

In research to date, race differences have not been shown to have an effect on the likelihood that money transfers will be made to aging parents. Some investigators find that racial/ethnic minorities are more likely than whites to make transfers;[23] others report that they are less likely to do so.[24] At this point, it seems likely that results are dependent on specific sample characteristics and reflect two countervailing trends: On the one hand, older minority individuals are more in need of financial transfers. On the other hand, middle-aged members of minority groups have fewer resources of their own—a pattern that is being reinforced over time because of growing income inequalities in this society.[25]

PERSONAL CARE TRANSFERS

Transfers in terms of time devoted to personal care of aging parents are only slightly more common than money transfers. Available research suggests that 7 to 15 percent of middle-aged Americans provide personal care assistance to their parents over a one-year interval.[26] As is true for financial transfers, data remain unavailable for purposes of gauging the frequency and duration of personal care transfers and estimating the likelihood over a lifetime that one will provide personal care assistance to aging parents.

Characteristics of older parents are strongly related to the likelihood of their receiving personal care assistance from one or more of their children. As might be expected, a parent's health or ability to function is the strongest predictor of personal care assistance.[27] Available evidence indicates that parents who receive assistance with personal care from their children typically report high levels of chronic illness and have multiple functional impairments. Three demographic characteristics also are strongly related to the receipt of personal care assistance from children: gender, age, and marital status. Mothers receive more intergenerational transfers of personal assistance than fathers,[28] the oldest old get more attention than the others,[29] and the unmarried (typically widows) receive more than the married.[30] This all makes sense in recalling that older women live longer than men but suffer higher levels of impairment; advanced age often reflects a general frailty not captured by conventional measures of physical health and functioning; and the unmarried do not have a husband or wife to assist with personal care.

Evidence concerning the linkage between the parent's financial status and personal care transfers from children has been inconsistent. Some investigators observe no relationship between the two.[31] Others, however, report a moderately strong relationship such that greater parental affluence is associated with reduced likelihood of personal care assistance from children.[32] The most obvious inference to draw from this is that well-off parents purchase personal care assistance rather than rely on their children for it.

Only two characteristics of adult children are consistently related to providing personal care assistance to a parent: gender and marital status. As has been widely documented, daughters are responsible for the vast majority of personal care for parents.[33] Indeed, if there are no daughters available, daughters-in-law rather than sons give personal care assistance to their parents-in-law.[34] The strong role of gender in determining who provides personal care to aging parents appears to be purely normative and speaks to the deeply ingrained sex roles that continue as a cultural force in allocating privileges and responsibilities to American adults. Unmarried children are more likely to give personal care to aging parents than married children.[35] This pattern may reflect the practical issue that unmarried adults have fewer competing demands on their time than their married peers. Alternatively, unmarried children may simply sustain clos-er relationships with their parents.

Data permitting examination of sibling structure and its effects on time transfers is slowly becoming available, although research on this issue remains relatively scarce. Results to date suggest that siblings are more likely to share responsibilities for personal care assistance than to allocate them to a single brother or sister.[36] Thus, the odds of an adult child pro-viding some level of personal care assistance to a parent are greater if at least one sibling is doing the same.

Evidence based on representative samples of the population indicates no racial/ethnic differences in supplying intergenerational personal care.[37] This pattern is somewhat unexpected in that other research strongly sug-gests that the social support networks of racial and ethnic minorities are characterized by higher levels of shared resources.[38] It is possible that a higher proportion of personal care assistance among racial and ethnic minorities occurs in the context of shared residences than is true for whites.

HOUSEHOLD ASSISTANCE TRANSFERS

Among the forms that intergenerational transfers take, household assistance transfers are most common. Research suggests that 23 to 32 percent of older parents receive some form of household assistance from their children in a given month.[39] Again, data are lacking about the fre-quency and duration of household assistance. Nonetheless, it is clear that a significant minority of older parents receive at least occasional household assistance from one or more of their children.

Parents who are in poor health or have significant functional limita-tions are more likely to receive household assistance from children than their healthier peers.[40] Unmarried parents also benefit from more house-hold assistance than married parents—and widowed mothers are espe-cially likely to get help.[41] The more children an older parent has, the more likely that he or she will obtain household assistance from one or more of them. In addition, higher levels of contact between older parents and their adult children increase the likelihood of household aid.[42] This rela-tionship is not surprising—the more interesting issue is that this is the only transfer "currency" in which it is observed.

The relationship between gender and the likelihood of an adult child furnishing household assistance is unclear. Hoyert[43] reports that daughters are more likely than sons to provide household help to aging parents.

Eggebeen and Hogan,[44] however, report higher levels of assistance by sons. The economic status of the adult child affects the likelihood of household assistance transfers in ways that are more readily apparent. Children with higher levels of education and income are more likely to contribute time around the house to their parents than their less socioeconomically advantaged peers.[45]

Evidence about the division of responsibility for household assistance transfers among siblings is scant in volume but intriguing. As was true for personal care assistance, there is evidence that siblings attempt to "share the load."[46] The odds that an adult child will provide household assistance to a parent are increased if there is at least one sibling who also is providing such assistance.

Research to date indicates that intergenerational transfers of household assistance are more common among whites than among racial and ethnic minorities, even after controlling for adult children's socioeconomic status.[47] As with personal care assistance, this pattern is surprising in light of other findings that highlight the strong patterns of shared resources and mutual aid characteristic of minority families.

One other issue merits brief consideration. For both personal care assistance transfers and household assistance, geographic proximity of parent and child is strongly associated with the likelihood that a transfer will occur.[48] At one level, this relationship is so obvious that it scarcely merits note. At another level, it is an important reminder that structural elements play a large role in intergenerational family relationships. Regardless of ties of affection and commitment to filial responsibility, intergenerational time transfers require propinquity and are unlikely to occur otherwise.

In summary, intergenerational transfers of money and time are quite common. Moreover, since current estimates are for very limited time periods (past year or month), they consequently underestimate such transfers over the life course. It is clear that parents' needs are the major trigger for intergenerational assistance. Older adults in poor health or with low levels of economic resources are the primary recipients. Relationships between adult child characteristics and transfer behavior are less clear-cut. Certainly the resources available to adult children affect their generosity toward parents, especially in terms of money and time for household assistance. However, norms also appear to have a clear role in transfer behavior. Gender distinctions in who provides what kind of help to aging parents are strong and tend to fall in line with traditional sex roles. Norms of equity also appear to influence transfer behavior, as best illustrated by the fact that siblings tend to share responsibility for time devoted to aging parents.

There is much yet to be learned about intergenerational transfer behavior throughout the life course. Little is known, for example, about the degree to which aid from parents to children earlier in life affects later treatment by adult children of aging parents. In the first study to examine this issue using a high-quality national sample, Henretta and colleagues[49] found that past financial transfers from parents to children increased the likelihood that the child would subsequently provide personal care assistance to the parent. Clearly, more research is needed on this critically important topic. The extent to which transfers of one kind are used to substitute for another is not known either. For example, do adult children offer time to their parents in an effort to avoid direct economic support? Are children who are geographically distant from their aging parents more likely to provide financial assistance to substitute for being unavailable to spend time with their parents?

TIME TRANSFERS FROM OLDER TO YOUNGER GENERATIONS

There also is a limited research base on time transfers from older adults to their adult children and grandchildren. The distinction between personal care and household assistance has not been made in this research. Large numbers of older persons spend time caring for their younger family members, especially unmarried children and grandchildren.[50] However, unlike in the case of financial transfers, the intergenerational flow of time transfers is larger from adult children to parents than the reverse. Also, those older adults who spend time with their children and grandchildren are unlikely to be receiving financial or other assistance from their children.

INTERGENERATIONAL TRANSFERS: RATIONAL CHOICES OR NOT?

In light of the empirical evidence concerning the incidence of intergenerational transfers and the characteristics of recipients and donors, it is now possible to assess such behavior from the rational choice and social context perspectives. Rational choice can readily explain money transfers from adult children to aging parents. Such transfers are quite rare (at least over a one-year interval), are made almost exclusively to older adults who are demonstrably in need, and are most likely to be made by adult children with relatively high levels of economic resources.

However, the rational choice perspective fails to account for many of the patterns of intergenerational transfers. First, sacrifices of time are far from rare and are of significant economic value, suggesting that adult children are not attempting to shirk filial responsibilities. Second, although the relationship between parental need and assistance from adult children supports rational choice theory with regard to the behavior of donors, that is not the case for the behavior of recipients. There is no evidence that older parents are attempting to maximize the rewards they receive from their children; they apparently accept such transfers only when they are in need.

Third, and most impressive in demonstrating the limits of rational choice as an explanation for intergenerational transfers, many of the strongly established predictors of transfer behaviors are irrelevant or even contrary to purely economic models of exchange. Especially important in this regard are the effects of gender and the sibling network. Women are, without question, the primary donors to aging parents, in both time and money terms. This pattern does not reflect higher levels of resources among women than men, as the rational choice perspective would predict. Sex role norms and the special quality and intimacy of daughters' relationships with parents are more intuitively sensible explanations. With regard to sibling structure, the rational choice perspective would suggest that adult children with siblings who are already making transfers to their elderly parents would be less likely to follow suit. But the opposite is observed empirically—the presence of one or more siblings giving aid to older parents increases the likelihood that the adult child will do the same. These patterns are much more compatible with explanations based on normative expectations, family solidarity, and ties of affection.[51]

CONCLUSIONS AND IMPLICATIONS

This has been a brief review of the impact of two noneconomic determinants of the economic behavior and financial well-being of older adults: subjective perceptions of economic well-being and the social contexts within which intergenerational transfers occur. The degree of satisfaction with one's financial status and fears that economic resources will not be sufficient to meet future needs are important foundations of economic behavior during later life. In addition, they have clear policy implications, highlighting the need for public policies that protect older adults from economic ruin as a result of catastrophic events. Thus, any comprehensive assessment of the economic status of the elderly must include attention to perceptions of the current and anticipated adequacy of financial resources. As is true for their younger peers, it is subjective assessments of reality, rather than objective reality itself, that form the bedrock of attitudes and behavior for the elderly. Financial resources may be largely a matter of income and assets, but financial security is not.

Intergenerational transfers are common between older adults and their children. For financial flows the dominant pattern is from parents to their adult children; for time devoted to household assistance and personal care, adult children are usually the donors and their parents are the recipients. Available research indicates that economic models explain some, but not all, of the predictors of transfer behavior. Other predictors are the opposite of what one would expect on the basis of rational choice theory, suggesting the importance of social norms. Indeed, even those that are compatible with economic models may reflect societal norms as well (for example, that transfers should be made by those who can best afford them, that transfers should be restricted to situations where there is clear need). Thus, it is doubtful there are any purely "economic" predictors.

Just as academic disciplines rest upon core assumptions, so does public opinion. Two of the most widespread assumptions in American society are that individuals are responsible for their own decisions and behaviors and that reality is primarily objective and therefore a solid basis for understanding behavior and its consequences. Precisely because these assumptions are subscribed to widely, they are incorporated into the guidelines set for the conduct of public and private life. Underlying the veneer of individualism and objective reality, however, are other truths. Individual behavior is more strongly affected by subjective perceptions than by external reality. And despite the premium on individualism in our society, research evidence documents that individuals function within complex social contexts—contexts that account for much of one's behavior and quality of life. Thus, an appropriate scientific view of the human condition will take into consideration objective life circumstances, subjective perceptions of reality, the social networks in which individuals are involved, and convergences and divergences across these strata of human existence. Financial status in later life is clearly affected by all these layers of reality.

9

THE OLDER WORKER IN A GRAYING AMERICA:
INNOVATION, CHOICE, AND CHANGE

Sara E. Rix*

OLDER WORKERS IN THE POSTWAR YEARS

EARLY LABOR FORCE WITHDRAWAL

For many Americans, the term "older worker" is all but an oxymoron, given the work and retirement trends of the second half of the twentieth century. Indeed, paid employment has characterized an ever smaller percentage of the older population for much of the post-World War II era. Declining labor force participation has been most pronounced among men aged sixty-five and older, whose participation rate has fallen by more than thirty percentage points since 1945 (see Table 9.1, page 188). At the end of World War II, nearly half the men in this age group were working or looking for work, but by 1998 that was the case for only one in six. Though not shown in Table 1, an especially dramatic decline occurred among men between the ages of sixty-five and sixty-nine, slightly more than one-fourth (28 percent) of whom were in the labor force in 1998, down from nearly two-thirds (63.9 percent) in 1950.[1]

---

* The views expressed in this paper are those of the author and not necessarily those of AARP.

TABLE 9.1
CIVILIAN LABOR FORCE PARTICIPATION RATES OF MIDDLE-AGED
AND OLDER MEN AND WOMEN, SELECTED YEARS 1945–1998

Year	Men		Women	
	55–64	65+	55–64	65+
1945	—	48.7	—	9.0
1950	86.9	45.8	27.0	9.7
1955	87.9	39.6	32.5	10.6
1960	86.8	33.1	37.2	10.8
1965	84.6	27.9	41.1	10.0
1970	83.0	26.8	43.0	9.7
1975	75.6	21.6	40.9	8.2
1980	72.1	19.0	41.3	8.1
1985	67.9	15.8	42.0	7.3
1990	67.7	16.4	45.3	8.7
1995	66.0	16.8	49.2	8.8
1996	67.0	16.9	49.6	8.6
1997	67.6	17.1	50.9	8.6
1998	68.1	16.5	51.2	8.6

Sources: U.S. Department of Commerce, Bureau of the Census, *Historical Statistics of the United States: Colonial Times to 1970, Part 1* (Washington, D.C.: U.S. Government Printing Office, 1975); U.S. Department of Labor, Bureau of Labor Statistics, *Handbook of Labor Statistics* (Washington, D.C.: U.S. Government Printing Office, 1985); U.S. Department of Labor, Bureau of Labor Statistics, *Employment and Earnings* 33, no. 1 (January 1986); 38, no. 1 (January 1991); 43, no. 1 (January 1996); 44, no. 1 (January 1997); 45, no. 1 (January 1998); 46, no. 1 (January 1999).

Older men actually began withdrawing from the labor force well before World War II, a decline that was temporarily halted when wartime labor shortages prompted employers to recruit workers, including those sixty-five and older, whom they might have passed over under other circumstances. Answering the call, older men increased their participation rate from just under 42 percent in 1940 to a peak exceeding 49 percent in 1944. Not to be outdone, older women also demonstrated increasing labor force activity during the war, with a participation rate that rose from 6.1 percent in 1940 to a high of 9.6 percent in 1943.[2]

Assessing the performance of older wartime workers is somewhat difficult in view of the paucity of relevant data; age comparisons of worker absenteeism, injuries, accidents, and the like are sadly lacking. Hence, one might simply conclude that the proof of older worker performance lies in the pudding—victory. Nonetheless, if employers were sorry to see their older employees depart at war's end, they were silent on the matter. Once the war machine began to wind down, participation rates for the oldest workers resumed a decline that showed few signs of abatement until the mid-1980s.

MIDDLE-AGED MEN FOLLOW SUIT; WOMEN BREAK THE MOLD

The oldest men have not been alone in demonstrating a weakening attachment to the labor force. Middle-aged men, especially those between the ages of fifty-five and sixty-four, are also far less likely to be in the labor force today than they were in the early postwar years—68 percent in 1998 versus nearly 87 percent in 1950.

Women, on the other hand, have been marching in a different direction. The past fifty years have seen growing numbers of women at almost all ages entering or remaining in the labor force. As of 1998, more than half of women between the ages of fifty-five and sixty-four were working or looking for work, up from 27 percent in 1950.

With a labor force participation rate that has fluctuated only very modestly over the past half-century, women aged sixty-five and older resemble neither their younger female counterparts nor men of the same age. In 1998, fewer than one in ten women who were sixty-five-plus could be found in the labor force.

Though middle-aged women's participation rate has risen sharply, the increase has not been sufficient to offset the decrease among men. Consequently, the labor force participation rate for the group commonly viewed as the "older" workforce—fifty-five-plus—has fallen and remains below its level of five decades ago (see Figure 9.1, page 190).

As of 1950, only 23 percent of the older labor force was female; by 1998, that figure had risen to 44 percent. And although many of these women came of age at a time when women were not expected to have long-term jobs or careers, their work histories and earnings were by no means insignificant. According to one report, women at age fifty-five, having worked longer than half of their adult lives, had "market earnings [that] exceeded $119 billion in 1992."[3] There is no reason to expect a diminution of women's contribution to the workforce. In fact, one forecasting firm projects that, by about 2011, the number of middle-aged women in the labor force will exceed that of men of comparable age.[4]

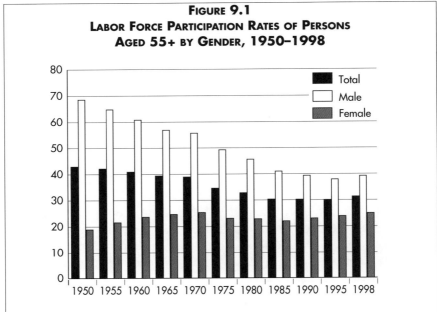

FIGURE 9.1
LABOR FORCE PARTICIPATION RATES OF PERSONS
AGED 55+ BY GENDER, 1950–1998

Sources: U.S. Department of Labor, Bureau of Labor Statistics, *Handbook of Labor Statistics* (Washington, D.C.: U.S. Government Printing Office, 1985); U.S. Department of Labor, Bureau of Labor Statistics, *Employment and Earnings* 33, no. 1 (January 1986); 38, no. 1 (January 1991);43, no. 1 (January 1996); 44, no. 1 (January 1997); 46, no. 1 (January 1999).

A GLANCE AT THE FUTURE

For much of the postwar era, workers were retiring at what appeared to be ever-younger ages. Faced with an adequate supply of labor as baby boomers and women entered the labor force in large numbers, employers saw little need to discourage this behavior. A number of considerations influence the retirement decision, not the least of which is the availability of Social Security and pension benefits at relatively early ages. Though job loss, disability, ill health, and employer preferences for younger workers also play their part, workers tend to retire when they think they can afford to retire. For many workers, that has been at age sixty-two or even younger. The baby boomers, however, might well rewrite retirement history.

As of 1995, the federal Bureau of Labor Statistics (BLS) was projecting relatively little change in the labor force participation rates for men between the ages of fifty-five and sixty-four or for those sixty-five and older over the near future. Rates for middle-aged women were expected to continue to rise, while a slight increase was projected for the oldest women.[5] Only two years later, however, BLS released projections to 2006 that suggest greater labor force attachment on the part of older men, particularly those ages fifty-five to sixty-four, than had been earlier projected.

BLS might still be underestimating the baby boomers' need or desire to work longer and/or employers' interest in fostering greater labor force attachment, at least among those still considered middle-aged. Baby boomers may end up working longer than their parents for a variety of reasons, one of which is that many of them may be ill-prepared financially to leave the labor force at the relatively young ages characteristic of recent retirees.

Predictions about worker behavior are risky, but it seems increasingly likely that baby boomers and those who follow them will push up the average age of retirement. Not only does current law provide for a gradual increase in the age of eligibility for full Social Security benefits beginning in the year 2000, but also many of the proposals to restore long-term solvency to the Social Security system include further or speedier increases. Unpopular as such increases might be to many workers, improvements in life expectancy, coupled with the associated costs of retirement, call into question the ability of future cohorts of workers to support the baby boomers adequately in their old age.

Retiree health benefits are being scaled back, which might prompt future retirees to reevaluate the costs of early retirement. In addition, although recent efforts to raise the age of eligibility for Medicare were thwarted, such proposals are likely to resurface and might well pass in the future. That, too, would likely affect retirement decisions.

Private pension coverage has shown little overall increase since the 1970s. Recent years have also been marked by a decline in the proportion of defined benefit plans, which promise workers a specified benefit in retirement, and the spread of defined contribution plans, for which the retirement benefit depends on the size and success of investments. As baby boomers in particular reach retirement age with insufficient savings and still heavily dependent on Social Security, greater emphasis may be placed on the fourth leg of the retirement income stool—earnings.

Finally, employer demand, which could increase should low unemployment rates persist, must be taken into account. If job growth continues to be robust, employers will have to find workers somewhere. Older workers could meet some of the need, and more employers might begin to adopt policies and programs to keep them working longer.

A LOOK TO THE PAST:
PRESSURES AND INDUCEMENTS TO RETIRE

Though legal and common in many large companies after the war, manda-tory retirement rules appear to have had little influence on the timing of the labor force departure by older men. Observing that even workers who reached the required retirement age were not necessarily involuntary retirees—they may have been ready to go by then—James H. Schulz has calculated that less than 10 percent of retired men in a sample of Social Security beneficiaries were prevented from working by mandatory retire-ment policies that were legal at the time they left.[6] Other researchers have come to a similar conclusion.[7]

Had mandatory retirement rules been a significant determinant of labor force withdrawal, some rise in participation would have been expected among age groups affected by legislated changes in the legal mandatory retirement age. The 1978 amendments to the Age Discrimination in Employment Act (ADEA), for example, raised the allowable mandatory retirement age from sixty-five to seventy, but the change occasioned no increase in participation rates among persons between the ages of sixty-five and sixty-nine, 21.1 per-cent of whom were in the labor force in 1977 compared to less than 20 per-cent ten years later. Nor do workers seem to have taken advantage of the opportunity now that mandatory retirement has been eliminated for all but a handful of occupations. Not only can most workers legally remain on the job after age seventy, but workers aged seventy and older are not subject to the Social Security earnings test. Even so, few stay.

The availability of Social Security benefits to a growing number of older workers by the late 1940s, coupled with an expanding private pen-sion system, made it possible for workers to withdraw from the labor force at relatively young ages. Eligible workers can begin collecting retired work-er benefits from Social Security at age sixty-two. Even though the benefits of workers who receive Social Security before age sixty-five (the normal or full retirement age) are actuarially reduced, most workers opt for the lower benefits rather than waiting until full retirement.

Reduced benefits for early retirement were not always available. Women earned the right to collect benefits at age sixty-two in 1956, men in 1961, and as soon as they could collect early benefits, they began doing so in growing numbers (see Table 9.2). In 1960, the year before they became eligible for early benefits, men were an average of 66.8 years old when they were awarded Social Security benefits; by 1996, they were only 63.6. Among women, the average award age fell from 67.8 in 1955 to 63.4 in 1996.

TABLE 9.2
Percentage of Men and Women Awarded Early (Prior to Age 65)
Social Security Retired Worker Benefits, 1960–1996

Year	Men	Women
1960	—	48.5
1965	30.2	48.4
1970	39.4	56.0
1975	48.9	62.3
1980	51.7	63.9
1985	65.7	75.2
1990	66.1	72.9
1995	67.1	72.1
1996	66.7	72.7

Source: Social Security Administration, *Annual Statistical Supplement to the Social Security Bulletin, 1997* (Washington, D.C.: U.S. Government Printing Office, 1997), Table 6.B5.

The enthusiasm manifested for early retirement benefits is especially evident in how the percentages of retired workers choosing to receive benefits at various ages changed over time. By 1965, just a few years after early retirement provisions took effect, only 70 percent of men were waiting until age sixty-five (or later) for their Social Security benefits, and, as of 1996, just one-third were awarded benefits at or after the full retirement age. The pattern for women has been similar, except that women are typically younger than men when they are awarded retired worker benefits.

Private pension benefits, which may be available to workers as early as age fifty-five or even fifty, have contributed to the early retirement trend as well. Private pension plans may be structured in such a way that premature retirement is almost guaranteed. Laurence Kotlikoff and David Wise, among others, have shown how defined pension plans can "penalize" participants who remain on the job after some—often early—age.[8] Workers may find that any increase in pension benefits realized as a result of delaying retirement is not enough to make up for the benefits they forgo by continuing to work. In other words, delayed retirement may result in less in lifetime pension benefits rather than more, hardly an outcome apt to encourage continued employment. In addition, employers have commonly offered *special* retirement incentives to encourage even earlier departure of workers who might have preferred to remain in the labor force longer.

The availability of retiree health insurance has also been found to affect the timing of labor force withdrawal, especially among early retirees.[9] Workers whose employers provide health insurance to retirees are, not surprisingly, more likely to retire early than those who would cease to be covered by an employer health plan. At age sixty-five, of course, workers become eligible for Medicare, so the loss of employer-provided health insurance upon retirement carries less risk than it does for younger retirees. At the same time, an employer's health insurance remains the primary payer for workers who remain on the job after becoming eligible for Medicare. As discussed subsequently, the higher costs of insuring older workers might well dampen employer interest in hiring or retaining older workers.

Job loss and ill health may propel workers out of the labor force before they are ready to go. For example, unemployed older workers confront more barriers in their job search than younger workers and are more likely to find themselves among the long-term unemployed; they are also far more likely to drop out of the labor force. More favorable employment prospects conceivably would keep them in it.

Murray Gendell and Jacob Siegel, among others, have found that it is not uncommon for workers to leave the labor force *before* becoming eligible for early Social Security benefits. In one study, perhaps as many as one-fourth of men and one-half of women had stopped working more than one year before age sixty-two.[10] Numerous studies over the years have documented the role that declining health plays in the decision to retire, especially at relatively young ages. Poor health appears to be a particular problem for workers retiring earlier than planned. Minorities may be especially disadvantaged when it comes to health status, as well as to reemployment prospects after job loss.

The retirement decision is also influenced by education and occupation, with better-educated workers tending to retire later than those with less education. Not only are the jobs of the better educated less physically demanding and conducive to longer work lives, but the "opportunity costs" of retirement are greater, since pensions and Social Security tend to replace a lower proportion of preretirement earnings among such workers.[11] Professionals are likely to retire later than those in many other occupations;[12] workers whose occupations are more "substantively complex"— and presumably more challenging but less arduous—are more apt to delay departure.[13] Blue-collar workers have shorter work life expectancies.[14] With the growing dominance of service sector employment, continued technological developments that reduce the physical demands of many jobs, and the expansion of alternative work options such as homework, the significance of some of the current motivations driving the retirement decision should dwindle.

WORK IN RETIREMENT

Neither labor force withdrawal nor receipt of Social Security benefits is synonymous with "retirement." Many pensioners continue to work, and some, including the "triple-dippers" (for example, retirees who get a military pension, Social Security, and a private pension), eventually retire from a second or subsequent career. Diane Herz reports that, although the proportion of fifty-five- to sixty-one-year-old men receiving a pension changed little between 1984 and 1993, the percentage of pensioners who worked rose from 37 to 49 percent.[15] Among pensioners aged sixty-five and older, though, no appreciable increase in working activity occurred. Unfortunately, it is not known just how many of the early retirees could, had they chosen, have begun collecting pension benefits and remained with their employer until eligible for Social Security benefits, but the number is likely to have been low, as private pension plans typically require workers to leave their job in order to qualify for benefits.

Quite possibly, many of the young pension recipients Herz studied accepted a pension offer with the expectation that they would continue working elsewhere until they could collect Social Security. That many young pensioners were *not* working might, of course, simply mean that they did not need the money or want to work, but it could just as easily reflect the difficulties that job seekers of this age face when looking for employment.

Social Security beneficiaries also continue to work, although they may be penalized for doing so. Earnings account for about 16 percent of the aggregate income of beneficiaries sixty-five and older.[16] Yet employed beneficiaries face benefit losses if their earnings exceed a certain amount, which in 1999 was $9,600 for sixty-two- to sixty-four-year-old beneficiaries and $15,500 for beneficiaries between the ages of sixty-five and sixty-nine. The younger workers lose $1 in benefits for every $2 of earnings above the limit, and the older ones lose $1 for every $3 of excess earnings; both continue to make payroll contributions and face taxes on their earnings.

The prospect of benefit loss is held by many to serve as a work disincentive, and it may well do so. Nonetheless, relatively few Social Security beneficiaries experience any loss because for the most part they are not in the labor force in the first place. Still, some of those who have jobs may curtail work hours in response to the limit, and some nonworking beneficiaries may be under the misunderstanding that any amount of earnings puts benefits at risk.

The fact that many pensioners, especially young ones, continue to work while collecting pension benefits, and that some Social Security recipients remain in or return to the labor force, makes it difficult to define exactly when retirement occurs. Hence, queries about "average" retirement age are usually met with qualifications about the limitations of the data. One effort to come up with an average—actually median—retirement age was undertaken by Gendell and Siegel, who computed an approximate measure of permanent labor force withdrawal.[17] They concluded that the median retirement age was about one year lower than the average age of award of Social Security retirement benefits—62.7 years for men and 62.6 years for women in the period 1990–95. This comports with the contention by Richard Burkhauser and Joseph Quinn that if "normal" retirement age is the age at which half remain in the labor force, then sixty-two is the normal retirement age for men today.[18]

PATHS TO RETIREMENT

For perhaps the majority of workers, retirement is a well-defined event that represents a complete and permanent cessation of paid work activity. But for a sizable minority, retirement is neither abrupt nor final. Jan Mutchler and colleagues refer to "blurred" retirement, a process that may involve repeated moves in and out of the labor force, especially on the part of workers without pension income.[19] These workers most likely remain attached to the labor force out of financial necessity. The "crisp" labor force exits of Mutchler et al. seem to be far more common among workers receiving or eligible for pension income.

BRIDGE WORK

A growing literature documents older workers' experiences with what is known as "bridge" employment that carries workers from long-term or "career" employment to short-term, transitional employment, often but not always part-time. While the estimates of the proportion of workers that ease into retirement via bridge or transitional arrangements differ depending on what is considered bridge work, such employment is believed to be substantial—experienced by perhaps as many as one-third to one-half of eventual retirees.[20] Moreover, the duration of employment in a postcareer or bridge job may be quite lengthy. For workers who end up in bridge employment, retirement is a process, not an event, and it is one that often begins at a rather young age.

The nature of bridge work varies. For many workers, the shift out of career or long-term employment signals downward occupational mobility. Wage cuts in bridge employment may be quite substantial, as may be the decreases in responsibility and job status. Bridge employment, however, does not necessarily involve declining rank or prestige.[21]

Christopher Ruhm's research points to less desirable forms of bridge employment among workers who moved from their longest job into unrelated bridge employment, as opposed to those whose bridge work occurred within their longest occupation.[22] The downward mobility characteristic of the former type in the United States, as well as the fact that it is more common among workers without pensions, would seem to indicate that some, if not much, of this kind of work results from an involuntary move, such as job loss or premature retirement. The experiences of older displaced workers would seem to confirm this observation.[23]

Though the literature documents a fairly high degree of transitional employment between full-time work and full-time retirement, very little of it is the result of formal, phased retirement programs. According to the benefits consulting firm Watson Wyatt, only 8 percent of the five hundred companies responding to a recent survey have implemented phased retirement arrangements,[24] a figure likely to be high as this was not a random sample.

Lacking access to formal gradual retirement programs, millions of older Americans find or create their own transitions to retirement. They may, for example, obtain employment in the nearly 50 percent of firms with twenty or more employees that say they hire retirees.[25] Still, a major concern identified by Ruhm is the "limited ability of many workers to either retain longest jobs or to obtain acceptable bridge employment."[26] This group is perhaps least likely to have resources to live comfortably in retirement. Workers with what Mutchler and associates call "multiple, short-term forays into and out of labor force" may get a taste of what is in store for the baby boomers whose financial resources do not allow for a comfortable retirement at an early age.[27]

CONTINGENT WORK

Contingent work, which is employment that lacks any promise of permanence—for example, contract and temporary work as well as leased employment—may also serve as a bridge to retirement. Additionally, it may provide retired workers with the flexibility to work when and at whatever they please. The flexibility works both ways. Because employers find it easier to terminate unsatisfactory workers when they are contingent, such employment eliminates one of the disincentives to hiring costly older workers. Add to that the fact that contingent employees are frequently not provided expensive fringe benefits and another impediment to hiring older workers is eliminated. Older workers may even be viewed as something of a bargain by employers if they are contingent.[28]

While occasional news stories might have readers concluding that the number of contingent workers has been soaring, good baseline data on this type of employment are unavailable for years before 1995. Estimates from the Bureau of Labor Statistics indicate that under the most expansive definition of "contingent," only about 6 million workers qualified in 1995 and 1997.[29] Such workers are also more likely to be young.

Though at best contingent workers represent less than 5 percent of the workforce, it seems reasonable to predict an increase as employers continue to seek ways to reduce labor costs and maintain maximum flexibility in an environment of growing competition and rapidly changing markets. Large numbers of employers report relying on temporary and contract workers,[30] at least on occasion, and no longer just for clerical work.

Contingent work may fill a need for retired workers, especially those who can afford to be choosy about when and where to work. Less financially secure retirees might find the lack of permanence and benefits to constitute real hardships. The same may be the case for middle-aged workers, especially women with spotty work histories, who need the assurance of stable wages and present and future (retirement) benefits. Particularly troublesome is what contingent work means for workforce training and retraining, most of which occurs within firms. Contingent workers will generally lack access to firm-provided training, but their skills will require repeated sharpening to keep them marketable. The cost, uncertainty about the most useful types, and lack of time to participate in training programs may limit the ability of many contingent workers to compete successfully for the more lucrative jobs.

Self-Employment

Bridge employment may also be in the form of self-employment, which Joseph Quinn and Michael Kozy, observing the greater self-employment in later life, suggest can be a means of phasing gradually into retirement.[31] David Evans and Linda Leighton also report a slight increase in self-employment among people in their early to mid-sixties.[32]

Older workers are clearly disproportionately represented among the self-employed; they were only 12 percent of the nonagricultural workforce in 1998 but 23 percent of the self-employed.[33] Not all of these workers, to be sure, started working for themselves late in life, but anecdotal evidence suggests that downsizing of the late 1980s drove some older workers into self-employment (such as consulting).

Regardless of whether workers became self-employed when old or grew old as self-employed, self-employment appears conducive to a longer worklife. Self-employed workers may need to delay retirement (for reasons of insufficient pension coverage or lack of retiree health benefits) but clearly may also find it far easier than wage and salary workers to tailor work schedules to changing physical status, interests, and income needs.

Though the data fail to document recent increase in self-employment (see Table 9.3), self-employment's potential for the elderly, especially the better-educated and skilled workers, could be considerable. Still, it is undoubtedly not a panacea for the older worker employment "problem." Most older workers probably lack the financial resources and/or the marketable products or services necessary to succeed in business. For some older individuals, however, self-employment is the path to a longer worklife.

Table 9.3
Percentage of Nonagricultural Workers Who Are Self-Employed, 1986 and 1998

Age	1986	1998
Total, 16+	7.4	7.0
55–64	10.9	11.2
65+	20.1	18.5

Source: U.S. Department of Labor, Bureau of Labor Statistics, *Employment and Earnings* 34, no. 1 (January 1987), Table 23; 46, no. 1 (January 1998), Table 15.

WILL TWENTIETH-CENTURY TRENDS PREVAIL?

SIGNS OF A HALT

Forecasters inclined to predict ever earlier labor force departure by older Americans might have begun to have second thoughts by the mid- to late 1980s, when the steady decline in the labor force participation rates of middle-aged and older men appeared to cease. Moreover, although the participation rate for the fifty-five-plus population has fluctuated around 30 percent since 1990, there have been some noticeable increases within that broad age group. In particular, between 1995 and 1998, the participation rate of men between the ages of sixty and sixty-four rose by more than two percentage points. Other age groups showed less marked increases, but that could well change if the unemployment rate, which had fallen to 4.5 percent by 1998, remains low. The increased labor force participation rate among middle-aged workers could be a sign that a rising tide is beginning to lift all boats.

DESIRE FOR EMPLOYMENT

Public opinion polls and surveys have long highlighted an interest in postretirement employment on the part of workers. As a case in point, 51 percent of the preretirees in a 1979 Louis Harris survey asserted that they would like some type of work after retirement; part-time work was the most popular option.[34] More recently, the longitudinal Health and Retirement Study (HRS) funded by the National Institute on Aging found that three-fourths of employed respondents, who were largely between the ages of fifty-one and sixty-one, wanted to keep on working in some capacity after retirement, yet few believed that their employers would facilitate their doing so.[35] The "leading edge" of the baby boomers—the first to turn fifty—expect to continue working in some capacity, typically part-time, in retirement.[36] The large majority (88 percent) of the nonretired respondents in the 1996 Retirement Confidence Survey also say they will retire at age sixty-five or earlier—21 percent before age sixty—but many plan on working in retirement; one in four contends that employment will be the most important or a major source of income in retirement.[37]

A logical question is why, if so many preretirees want postretirement employment, so few older persons remain in the labor force. One explanation involves the types of jobs that are available to retired job seekers, many of whom express a distinct interest in suitable part-time work. Part-time jobs often lack appeal for a variety of reasons; not only are many of them low-skill, demanding, and yet not very challenging, but wages are also often lower than for comparable full-time work. While the reasons for the lower compensation may be understandable—part-time work generates greater administrative costs, and recruitment and training costs that apply to two workers instead of one will naturally be higher—the reduced wages, coupled with the nature of the work, may temper the enthusiasm for part-time jobs, especially in the case of retirees who do not need the income.

Discouraged Workers

Older workers also face employment barriers that may discourage them from even looking for work, regardless of the kinds of jobs that are available. Employment analysts express concern about the extent to which discouragement in job seeking causes older workers to leave the labor force prematurely. Why look for work, people might ask, if employers are only going to find them too old or obsolete?

As it turns out, official discouraged-worker figures from the Bureau of Labor Statistics suggest that few older persons suffer from job-seeking discouragement. As of 1998, less than two-tenths of 1 percent of nonworking men and women aged fifty-five or older could be classified as discouraged using BLS criteria. This figure, which seems exceptionally low, is undoubtedly a function of recent changes in the way BLS classifies workers. To qualify as discouraged, potential workers must want a job, must have searched for one in the previous year, and must be available for work at the time of the interview. Once all that is established, they must give a "discouraged" reason for not looking; for example, they believe that they lack the necessary training or that employers would think them too old.

Having looked for work may certainly be a sign of commitment; nonetheless, the bureau's definition may be too restrictive in view of all that is known about the problems older workers face in finding positions. Surely, many older workers shy away from even starting to search, given the reception they expect to encounter from many employers.

A more liberal definition of job-seeking discouragement would encompass anyone who is out of the labor force but who would like a job, regardless of whether a search was undertaken. Even the figure generated in this context is hardly startling: only 2.2 percent of the fifty-five-and-older population not in the labor force admitted to wanting a job in

1998.[38] However, this translates into more than 800,000 older men and women who might return to the labor force if they thought they had a decent chance of finding suitable employment.

That the number of potential workers is higher than official discouraged-worker figures indicate is suggested in the results of a 1989 survey of fifty- to sixty-four-year-olds conducted for the Commonwealth Fund. Louis Harris and Associates reported that 1.9 million nonworking men and women in this age group were ready and able to return to work; 1.1 million of these had passed several commitment tests and were "most ready and able to work." The latter group of respondents insisted that they were willing to work in available occupations, needed a job for financial reasons, could accomplish critical job-related tasks, had looked for or were discouraged about finding employment, and were willing to accept difficult work conditions. Under the right conditions, more than 5 million older persons might be enticed to go back to work.[39]

It is true that the "would-be workers" in the Commonwealth Fund study were younger than those surveyed by the Bureau of Labor Statistics, who could be in their late seventies or older. Herbert Parnes and David Sommers found that few men in their seventies and above who were not working already expressed any interest in employment, but, again, these men were relatively old.[40] A greater work interest on the part of the younger elderly is to be expected. The point is not that official discouraged-worker figures are so low but that a sizable number of nonworkers say they would like to be working.

Once workers are out of the labor force for any length of time, enthusiasm for employment seems to weaken. The pull of working life may lessen; inertia may set in; volunteer work may meet the need for meaningful activity. Hence, it is not known how many workers would reenter the labor force if attractive opportunities presented themselves. Many retirement-age workers do move in and out of the labor force, but if Michael Hurd is correct, workers over the age of sixty who have left the labor force have a very low probability of returning after a year or more's absence; regarding them as permanently retired would be wrong in few cases.[41] Indeed, moves to rejoin the labor force among older men, who have been the subject of most research on this subject, tend to occur early, before sixty-five and generally before sixty-two, according to Mark Hayward, Eileen Crimmins, and Linda Wray.[42] Though it might be easier to get workers to delay retirement than to give it up, the right conditions could induce more workers to return to the workforce.

WILL BABY BOOMERS REVERSE THE TREND?

The expectation that baby boomers may have to work longer is reflected in revised BLS projections in 1997 as well as in higher labor force participation projections from at least one forecaster. The Bureau of Labor Statistics predicts that some 70 percent of men between the ages of fifty-five and sixty-four will be in the labor force in 2006, very close to the 72 percent estimate by NPA Data Services, Inc.[43] Moreover, this figure will rise to 83 percent in 2025 if NPA Data's projections prove accurate. NPA Data's projections for middle-aged women are dramatic; they foresee participation rising to 62.3 percent in 2006 (compared with a BLS projection of 55.8 percent), and reaching 78.2 percent twenty years later.

EMPLOYERS EYE THE OLDER WORKER

NEGATIVE PERCEPTIONS OUTWEIGH THE POSITIVE

Today's older men and women who want to work may find themselves stymied by the ambivalent attitudes employers have toward older workers. On the one hand, these workers are spoken of in glowing terms; on the other, they are regarded as deficient in the attributes that employers say they need today. In survey after survey, employers give high marks to older workers. Such workers are viewed as more conscientious and loyal than younger workers and as possessing a good attitude, a commitment to quality, and a solid, reliable performance record. However, two "overpowering obstacles" to their hiring and retraining appear to be a greater problem today than in the mid-1980s.[44] These involve perceptions about older worker adaptability and comfort with new technology, qualities that have become more important over time as businesses attempt to cope with technological change, global competition, and rapidly changing consumer demands that require maximum flexibility and technological proficiency. So, although employers and human resource managers find much to praise in older workers, they also often complain that those same workers are too costly and lacking in the skills that they seek in an increasingly global economy. Employer concerns about older worker flexibility and adaptability conspire against those workers; thus, it often is the case that, by age fifty, workers' best years—at least in terms of employment opportunities—are behind them.

Several hundred human resource executives studied by Michael Barth, William McNaught, and Philip Rizzi ranked older workers worse than "average workers" when it came to flexibility in accepting new assignments.[45] Apparently, "the traits that managers most admire in older workers—and which older workers themselves report as their most positive attributes—are not highly valued in human resource decisions related to hiring, promotion, job assignment, and retention," according to another recent study.[46] Doing things the old way is out, and older workers often fail to pass muster in the eyes of their supervisors when it comes to the new ways.

"In the technology industry, [forty is] clearly over the hill," asserts Internet wonder Marc Andreessen.[47] Quite likely, Mr. Andreessen will be singing a different tune as he approaches the top of the hill, but he is not alone in his disparaging opinion of the technical capabilities of older workers. The good news is that perceptions about older workers' ability and their ease with new technology have improved somewhat. The bad news is that those attributes have become more important since 1985 or 1989, resulting in a wider gap between what employers rank as very important and what their assessments of older workers reveal (see Table 9.4).

TABLE 9.4
HUMAN RESOURCE MANAGERS' RATINGS OF WORKER CHARACTERISTICS AND OLDER WORKERS' PERFORMANCE RATINGS, 1985, 1989, AND 1994
(in percentages)

ISSUE	RATED ESSENTIAL/ VERY IMPORTANT			OLDER WORKERS RATED EXCELLENT/VERY GOOD			IMPORTANCE/ PERFORMANCE GAP		
	1994	1989	1985	1994	1989	1985	1994	1989	1985
Flexibility	81	72	61	45	46	28	+36	+26	+33
Comfort with new technology	55	48	32	23	22	10	+32	+26	+22

Source: *American Business and Older Workers: A Road Map to the 21st Century* (Washington, D.C.: AARP, 1995), p. 10.

TRAINING SHORTSIGHTEDNESS

Despite the growing gap between what employers view as important and what older workers have, employers were *less* likely in 1994 than they had been in 1989 (the time of earlier interviews) to have implemented skills training for older workers.[48] In like vein, Barth, McNaught, and Rizzi noted that human resource executives were spending less on older worker training than on younger worker training, and that that held true even if they had an aging workforce.[49] These managers were cognizant of the workforce demographics, but, like those interviewed for AARP for a study titled *American Business and Older Workers*, were doing little to prepare for it. BLS data confirm that older workers are less likely to participate in employer-provided training activities than younger workers, although there was an increase in the percentage undergoing skills improvement training between 1983 and 1991.[50] A more recent BLS survey finds that the youngest workers (less than twenty-five) and the oldest (fifty-five-plus) were less likely than other age groups to have received training over the previous twelve months.[51] In addition, the oldest trainees received about half as many hours of training as all age groups combined.

Older workers thus find themselves caught up in a vicious cycle: Employers perceive them as less technologically adept than younger workers but are less likely to take steps to correct their shortcomings. Older workers find it difficult to keep up with new technology or other needed skills and consequently do become less relevant to their employers, who can then, with justification, accuse them of lacking the requisite preparation.

AGE-RELATED PRODUCTIVITY IN TRAINING

There tends to be rather general agreement that time needed for learning increases with age: Not only do older individuals take more time than younger ones to master new subject matter, they apparently need more time than they themselves did when they were younger. However, the extent to which differences are due to age per se as opposed to health status, educational attainment, motivation, familiarity with learning materials, or anxiety is by no means certain.

Moreover, some of what appears to be time required for learning may actually involve reviving learning skills that have atrophied after years of disuse. In addition, instructors' and supervisors' negative stereotypes about older worker trainability may undermine older trainees' attempts to master new skills.

In a now dated but classic review of the literature on older workers, Mildred Doering, Susan Rhodes, and Michael Schuster concluded that older workers can "continue to learn and learn well."[52] However, the available sources were limited; the researchers based their findings on a relatively small number of studies and participants. Though subsequent studies seem to confirm their conclusion, Harvey L. Sterns and Michael McDaniel nonetheless complain about the paucity of "research that evaluates the effectiveness of training interventions with workers of various ages."[53] Workplace demands (current and anticipated) are considerably different from what they were when Doering and her colleagues were writing in the early 1980s. Training research that showed few differences among the age groups in its effect on performance in the 1970s and 1980s may not be relevant to the workplace of today. More recent research on computer and noncomputer training found that older workers did learn less than younger workers; age differences were greater for training involving computer skills.[54]

These findings may or may not have practical relevance. For example, age differences may be meaningless if they are small or if workers need infrequent training. If, however, frequent updating is required, age differences could have significant cost implications. However, the fact that older workers remain longer on the job after training than younger workers do[55] suggests an offset to any higher costs of retraining older workers. A key point is that older workers, with enough time, can master new, highly technical skills and activities.

Another important issue involves the relevance of the research to the real workplace. Much of the research examines relatively small numbers of individuals in experimental settings that may or may not magnify age-related differences. Furthermore, it is not clear that any differences measured in experimental settings transfer, in the same way, to on-the-job performance, where success or failure has demonstrable consequences.

A further problem involves the scarcity of training studies with many trainees older than, say, sixty-five or seventy, or with sufficient numbers of participants in real-world training situations that permit reasonable recommendations for employers and potential trainers. To the extent that serious attention is given to raising the retirement age above that currently legislated, how these questions are resolved will have critical implications for employer productivity, labor costs, and opportunities for older workers in the future.

COSTS AND PERFORMANCE OF OLDER WORKERS

COSTS

On a dollar-for-dollar basis, older workers tend to cost more than younger workers, which may make their departure attractive to bottom-liners. As noted by Barth, McNaught, and Rizzi, wages and salaries typically rise with age because of the implicit contract that promises workers employment security and relatively steady wage progress in return for "loyalty and exemplary work behavior."[56] Other costs go up as well. Health expenditures show a sharp increase with age, more notably among men than women. Contributions to defined benefit pension plans may also rise rapidly with age. Defined contribution pension plans generally set aside the same percentage for all participants regardless of age, but if the wage base is higher, the pension contribution will be higher as well. The same will be true for any benefits that are wage-based. Generally, older workers will thus have the higher benefits.

What is not known, however, is the extent to which older workers' salaries are increased less sharply than those of younger workers to compensate for the higher costs.[57] In addition, it is important to keep in mind that the "equal cost or equal benefit" rule under the ADEA enables employers to reduce some benefits for older workers (for example, life insurance) to keep costs the same for old and younger workers. Finally, there is the issue of turnover costs, which can be considerable, especially when it comes to the recruitment and training of replacement workers. If sufficiently high, these costs might discourage employers from getting rid of their more experienced workers.

AGE AND PERFORMANCE

Data on age and work quality lead to the conclusion that age is a poor predictor of performance. If anything, as age rises, performance does as well, but the relationship is very weak.[58] Thus, it probably is not true that older workers are less productive on average than younger workers. None of the executives in a twelve-company study conducted for AARP were willing to admit that "age is a useful predictor of performance when making human resource decisions,"[59] and the research would seem to underscore the soundness of their position.

Nonetheless, research on on-the-job performance also suffers from a number of deficiencies, including a dearth of studies with adequate numbers of workers of various ages in real work situations. The problem is especially noticeable when it comes to workers in their upper sixties or beyond, not many of whom can be found in the labor force to participate in any type of study. The few older workers who do remain at work may be generally healthier and more productive than those who have left. Hence, what applies to the "older" worker in much of the available research may not apply to the typical sixty-five-year-old, another unresolved issue that may assume greater import if proposals to raise the retirement age further prove successful. Older-worker advocates must be prepared to address the issues of age, performance, and productivity in the workforce of today.

PRIVATE AND PUBLIC SECTOR RESPONSES TO AN AGING POPULATION

THE PRIVATE SECTOR

At the beginning of the 1980s, chief executives of 550 of the nation's largest industrial and service companies were contending that, by the end of the decade, employers would "have to develop benefit plans to attract and maintain older workers," and early retirement plans would have to be replaced.[60] Only 10 percent of the CEOs at that time saw encouraging early retirement as a company goal over the next ten years; 80 percent felt they would be moving in the direction of allowing workers to decide when they want to retire.

As quickly became clear, efforts to attract and retain older workers failed to take shape over the decade, and progress has been slow well into the 1990s. To date, private sector programs to put older people to work or keep them there have added up to very little. About 140 examples of programs that facilitate the employment of older workers can be found in AARP's National Older Workers Information System (NOWIS), which periodically queries firms on their employment initiatives that are either age-neutral or specifically targeted to older workers. NOWIS describes a variety of public and private sector "experienced worker" programs that include part-time opportunities, rehiring retirees, training programs, and job sharing. On the whole, however, special programs and policies to hire or keep older workers are rare.

Yet, programs need not "target" older workers to facilitate their employment. Part-time, contingent, and alternative work options may be exactly what some older workers are seeking, and some of these employment arrangements are proliferating. Part-time employment in the United States rose by about three percentage points over the past quarter-century; this might not seem like very much, but it translates into about 10 million more part-time workers, nearly one in five of whom was aged fifty-five or older in 1993. Watson Wyatt reports that a sizable proportion of firms in one of its recent surveys have implemented flexible work schedules,[61] which are ideal for many older (and younger) workers.

In fact, it is of considerable interest that the firms that actually hire retirees do so for the most part without specific policies or formal programs to hire retirees; rather they find them in the normal applicant pool.[62] This suggests a perhaps overlooked, obvious idea: If older workers make themselves available, that is, if they go out and look for work, they increase their chances of finding a job, even if they heighten their exposure to discrimination at the same time.

PUBLIC SECTOR RESPONSE

If examination of public policy and the older worker over the past fifty years points to anything, it is that, with the possible exception of age discrimination legislation, advances on behalf of the nation's aged during this period have not extended to older workers to any significant extent. Government efforts aimed at elder employment are perhaps best reflected in the 1983 amendments to the Social Security Act, which were designed to foster later retirement through an increase in the delayed retirement credit and gradual increments in the age of eligibility for full Social Security benefits starting in the year 2000. By requiring workers to remain in the labor force longer or else suffer a greater reduction in Social Security benefits, the higher retirement age may serve as a disincentive to departure from the working world. The delayed retirement credit, on the other hand, may encourage prolonged work by introducing actuarial fairness to the "credit" that workers receive by delaying receipt of Social Security benefits until age seventy. Whatever these provisions are intended to do, analysts are not convinced that either of them alone, when fully in effect, will be decisive in lengthening the span of a working life.

More recently, Congress approved a liberalization of the earnings limit for retired Social Security beneficiaries. It is too soon to assess the impact, but it seems unlikely to result in an increase in the number or proportion of older persons in the workforce. It could, however, encourage some persons who are already in to work more hours.

THE BABY BOOMERS MARCH ON

John Besl and Balkrishna Kale argue that the high levels of education of the baby boomers, higher than those of the working generations that preceded them, may foster labor force attachment, as better-educated persons tend to work longer than those with less education.[63] Rising educational attainment is frequently advanced as a reason why employers will find future older workers more attractive than those of today. As noted earlier, there are many reasons to assume that baby boomers will work longer. Education will surely play its part, but there is a danger that older worker advocates and workers themselves may be too complacent about the relevance of their higher educational achievement to employers. Formal educational achievement may be a measure of certain skills and ability to learn, but it might not be enough. Younger workers will always be more recently trained and more up-to-date than older workers, an advantage that years of schooling alone will not eliminate.

The Census Bureau concludes that "for the next 15 years, the choices made by Americans aged 55 and older will largely determine the size of the U.S. labor force."[64] This large group of prospective older workers—76 million strong—is aware of the power of its numbers; they have had a major impact on virtually everything they have encountered in the past and will continue to do so as they age. Should they want to continue working, they may make demands that employers could find hard to resist. Better training and work-related educational opportunities, telecommuting and other alternative work options, phased retirement programs, and benefits for part-time and contingent work may become part of their game plan. Employers would also do well to keep in mind that the Age Discrimination in Employment Act, which protects workers and job seekers aged forty and older, represents tremendous leverage for workers willing and able to take advantage of it. Baby boomers—never given reason to question their self-importance—might be just the cohort that realizes the potential of this legislation.

EMPLOYMENT POLICIES FOR AN AGING AMERICA

Economist James Schulz has written that most people adjust quickly and well to retirement, and the data seem to bear him out.[65] The institutionalization of retirement has become one of the great success stories of the twentieth century. Nonetheless, there is rising concern about the continued affordability to society of a retirement that typically begins in a person's early sixties. In addition, there are questions about the wisdom of encouraging retirement on the part of increasingly better-educated older individuals who could have years of productive contributions ahead of them. Tomorrow's elderly—the baby boomers—themselves may have a thing or two to say about that as they contemplate twenty or more years of nonworking life and a retirement income system with fewer guarantees than today's. Faced with labor and skills shortages, employers might turn a less jaundiced eye toward previously disposable older workers.

Whether there is a role for the federal government in promoting older worker employment beyond what has already been done and just what any government intervention might entail are a matter of some debate. At a recent forum on employment and the baby boomers' retirement sponsored by the Senate Special Committee on Aging, Michael Barth concluded that there is no "silver bullet" the federal government can deliver that would solve the problems faced by older workers. Rather, he contended that, "no matter how unfair, older persons must accept the burden of proof and overcompensate, if necessary."[66] This would include going after the training they need and demonstrating their flexibility to employers.

Other employment experts see a far greater role for government. Recommendations call for raising the age of eligibility for early Social Security benefits, further increases in the age of eligibility for full retirement benefits under Social Security, eliminating the Social Security earnings test, eliminating payroll taxes (and subsequent benefit increases) for older workers, or providing tax incentives to employers for hiring and training older workers.[67] Marcus Rebick has suggested that if employers were allowed to pay less to older workers whose productivity has presumably declined, as is done in Japan, employment rates among U.S. elderly might be higher.[68]

The fact is that it is not certain just what policies and programs would have a sizable impact on older worker employment. Certainly a sharp rise in the early retirement age would force more workers to remain in the workforce longer. However, a higher retirement age would also pose serious problems for the many workers who must leave the labor force before they turn sixty-two or who manage to hang onto a job only until that age.

As noted, health and job problems push many workers out of the labor force before age sixty-two. Some of these workers are eligible for pension or disability benefits, but others lack alternative sources of income and take Social Security at the earliest possible instance because they have no choice.

A higher retirement age assumes that there will be jobs for all who need or want them, but jobs might not be available for workers with few or obsolete skills or whose health problems limit what they can do. Despite documented declines stemming from disability in old age, not much is known about health status, stamina, and work ability for the sixty-five-plus group. Furthermore, chronic health conditions often emerge well before age sixty-five. There is little research at hand on the effects of accumulated health problems for prolonged, productive work. In some cases, health difficulties may mean nothing or require little beyond modest workplace or scheduling adjustments. In other cases, they may have significant cost and productivity implications.

A higher retirement age also requires assurances that an adequate safety net exists for those who cannot work longer. The safety net is especially critical if employers respond to changing retirement rules by culling their less productive workers at even younger ages.

The report *Workforce 2020* worries that a sizable increase in the number of baby boomers remaining at work could block opportunities for younger workers and suggests that "new 'off-line' or part-time positions for senior employees" might be needed "to provide younger workers with opportunities for advancement."[69] Numerous special elder employment programs can be found in Japan, where employment rates for older workers exceed those of the United States. However, unless the shift to one of these options were truly voluntary, these programs, like lower wages based solely on age, would violate the ADEA.

Recommendations to eliminate the Social Security earnings test are common, but there is little evidence that this would keep more people in the workforce longer. Rather, it might encourage some higher earners to work more, as they are the ones likely to bump up against the limit. This in itself might be a good thing, though.

Because health costs are a major expense to employers, and because it costs more to insure older workers, some older-worker advocates recommend repealing legislation that makes employers' health insurance the primary payer for Medicare-covered workers. Repeal would obviously have no impact on aging workers who have not yet turned sixty-five—many of whom have trouble finding employment or staying employed. Nor would it affect the high proportion of part-time older workers whose employers do not provide health benefits to part-timers. Nonetheless, it might help some older workers get or keep jobs. However, unless outweighed by increasing revenues generated by the older workers, the added costs of making Medicare the primary payer, given the critical fiscal status of the Medicare Trust Fund, could prove hard to justify.

Some observers have gone so far as to suggest eliminating the Social Security payroll tax (and subsequent benefit increases) for older workers, which would certainly make work more appealing to older workers themselves. Nevertheless, unless there were an urgent need to keep older workers in the labor force, this recommendation also seems hard to justify on several grounds. First, it would run counter to the spirit of the Age Discrimination in Employment Act, which calls for equal treatment of workers, regardless of age. Second, the payroll tax is especially onerous for young, lower-income families, who might question why older persons with income from sources other than work are entitled to this tax break. Third, if payroll tax increases become part of a Social Security reform package, Congress might find it politically difficult to exempt one group from assuming some of that burden of restoring solvency.

Incentives to employers to hire and train older workers are also debatable. In the first place, such incentives have not proved very effective in getting employers to hire or train workers they otherwise would have overlooked. In the second place, such measures seem to emphasize that there is something "wrong" with the workers in question, and it is these very negative perceptions that so bedevil older workers already. Third, incentives would be another example of favoritism that seems questionable in light of efforts to eliminate all forms of discrimination. And fourth, when it comes to training, if employers offer it, they cannot legally prevent older workers from taking part in it. Older workers must become more aggressive in obtaining their fare share of employer-provided training.

The answers to prolonging working life to any appreciable extent most likely lie with the private sector. Ample empirical support is available to support the notion that employers who need workers will do what they must to get them, using nontraditional methods and looking in nontraditional places if required. So, for instance, a study of medium-sized and large businesses found that firms facing labor shortages were more likely than other firms to accommodate older workers.[70] Confronted with a shrinking pool of young applicants, who had formed the core of employment in the fast-food industry, enterprises like McDonald's turned to older people and implemented policies to entice them to return to work.

Days Inns, a large hotel chain, was another business in need of workers in the 1980s that began systematically to hire and train older persons for employment in reservations centers and hotels. By all accounts, this program was a great success; according to research by the Commonwealth Fund, older Days Inns workers were productive, trainable, and less of a problem than their younger counterparts when it came to absenteeism and turnover.

If employers do not want older workers, of course, they will find ways of getting rid of them, despite public policies to the contrary. Special early retirement incentive offers have been a useful tool for companies in recent years. In the future, employers may be less inclined to want or need retirement incentive programs, seeing instead a demand for policies and programs that entice older workers to remain in or return to the labor force. These inducements will likely include more flexible work schedules, alternative work opportunities, the development and expansion of phased retirement options, and greater availability of challenging part-time work. Employers who want to retain older workers might also have to rethink pension policies that prevent workers from remaining on the job once they begin collecting benefits and/or essentially penalize them by not increasing pension benefits enough to compensate for the benefits lost by not retiring earlier.

Since the process of retirement often begins early and is blurred, the provision of benefits to "nontraditional" workers might tempt older workers to remain in or return to the labor force. This is perhaps one area where legislation could have a significant impact on the economic well-being of workers of all ages who cannot count on permanent employment. Congress might be encouraged to enact legislation requiring prorated benefits for less than full-time work.

For workers of all ages, the working world of the coming decades will be far less certain than that of the past. In some respects, older workers should find themselves on more equal footing with younger workers, all of whom will be required to "produce" in order to remain employed. However, it is imperative to keep in mind that "older" workers are, and will remain, an extremely diverse segment of the population. Under the Age Discrimination in Employment Act, an older worker is aged forty or above. The challenge facing workers, employers, and older-worker advocates, will be keeping this multifarious and growing group fit, productive, and gainfully employed until its members are ready and able to retire. Work incentives and retirement disincentives will be part of the mix. There shall indeed be no single silver bullet, whether public or private, but a range of programs and policies to meet a variety of employer and employee needs and interests.

Over the somewhat longer run, older workers themselves may prove collectively to be such a mighty force that employers are compelled to deal with them. As baby boomers have shaped virtually every institution with which they have come into contact in the second half of the twentieth century, they seem poised to reshape the world of work in the twenty-first. The savvy employer would do well to recognize that probability and take advantage of its potential.

10

THE MATURING OF MARKETING

John Zweig

We humans are at the tip of time's arrow. . . . We live at the first moments of a newly becoming creation, not at its dwindling end.
—Brian Josephson

So much information has been gathered, analyzed, and published on the subject of our nation's aging population that we need to question the point of any additional perspective. It is abundantly clear and widely accepted that people sixty-five and older will transform every aspect of our culture, including commerce. Accordingly, industry is responding to the challenge with a flood of new products and services, along with targeted advertising and marketing campaigns extolling their virtues, all designed to cater to the needs of this "special" marketplace. An increasingly older population, accounting for a growing share of our nation's resources, potential, and problems, has become one of the standard assumptions in the internal strategic planning and external communications of many of the Fortune 500 corporations.

Yet, despite this new emphasis, there are still plenty of examples of companies missing out entirely on the commercial implications of the mature market; alternatively, when this market is being pursued, many of the messages targeted to older consumers are off the mark, or they offend or alienate. It is not difficult to make the case that mass media, reflecting our prevailing cultural values particularly as expressed through entertainment, are as youth worshiping and "gerontophobic" as advocates for the aging have maintained for more than a decade.

How can this be the case? The neglect of older consumers partly has to do with the average age of the people creating the ads and images that fill the media channels—writers and art directors are usually between twenty-five and thirty-five years old, anyone older having either made it to the executive floor, beyond the day-to-day marketing activities, or been pushed out altogether as a result of corporate reengineering and "downsizing." Beyond this, however, there are subtle forces that affect even those who are older. Such forces still play a role in perpetuating ageism through fear, denial, or loathing for the later stage of life. As Robert Butler has pointed out, "Behind ageism ultimately is corrosive narcissism, the inability to accept our own . . . fate."

This chapter will review some specific trends in changing consumer markets, allocation of corporate resources, and communications focus. In addition to describing these commercial trends, it will reflect on questions that get less attention but are clearly more important: Are older consumers coming to terms with the meanings of their extended lives? How is industry responding? These questions have more significant implications for advertising, marketing, and business in general, given the widely held assumption that consumer appetites for greater comfort and status will never be satisfied. If such motivations were to diminish with age, commerce would suffer despite the greater spending power of an aging marketplace. As arguably the nation's most powerful social institution, business is well equipped to meet evolving needs and aspirations, but confronted with the demographic realities corporate America must change its approach to an older society in fundamental ways. To rise to this challenge, marketing—which is how business communicates its values—cannot be synonymous in people's minds with "hucksterism," in which the point of the exercise is to lure, trick, or manipulate foolish older consumers into parting with their money. Rather, those in the field need to employ their creative capacities to generate insight and mobilize communication tools in ways that serve and deeply inform people.

An aging population is a "lead market," from which a great deal can be learned about what will work and what will fail in the new global society that is emerging, giving business a critical opportunity to make the coming era a rich and rewarding one. In this sense the new business frontier is first and foremost a new *human* frontier.

Facts and Implications

People in business generally keep themselves busy responding to changes in market forces: consumer demand, competitive threats, and other economic conditions. Accordingly, there has been plenty to do over the past several years reacting to obvious opportunities inherent in the demographic shift toward aging consumers. At the simplest, factual level, start with the consideration that the "mature market" comprises only about 25 percent of the U.S. population yet controls three-fourths of financial assets. The U.S. Census Bureau report *65 Plus in the United States* found the number of older Americans (sixty-five and over) had grown elevenfold since the turn of the century, while the under-sixty-five population only tripled. Not only are the ranks of the elderly growing explosively, but they spend more per capita on average than those aged twenty-five to thirty-four across many product categories. Figure 10.1 indicates some of the specific areas where older

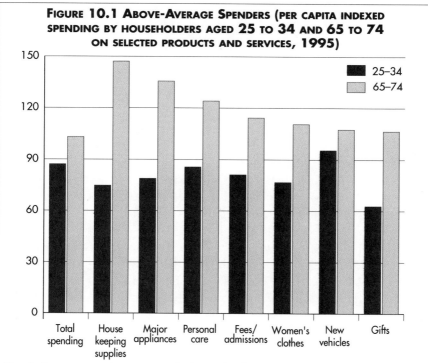

FIGURE 10.1 ABOVE-AVERAGE SPENDERS (PER CAPITA INDEXED SPENDING BY HOUSEHOLDERS AGED 25 TO 34 AND 65 TO 74 ON SELECTED PRODUCTS AND SERVICES, 1995)

Note: Index represents the extent to which spending by a specific age group is higher or lower than average; the U.S. average = 100 percent.

Source: U.S. Department of Labor, Bureau of Labor Statistics, *Consumer Expenditure Survey*, cited in "The Ungraying of America," *American Demographics* (July 1997): 12.

consumers outspend their younger counterparts. The message has been received by commercial America, as highlighted by a few market facts and product and service illustrations below:

- A study by Age Wave Communications of more than one thousand new empty nesters with $50,000-plus in annual incomes found better than one-third reporting $10,000 or more and two-thirds indicating $5,000 or more in "empty-nest bonuses." These extra financial resources have been primarily used by people for "new experiences" such as vacations.

- People over fifty-five travel more frequently and stay longer than younger people—three-quarters have taken a trip of five nights or more within the past year, according to the American Association of Retired Persons and the Travel Industry Association of America. This has stimulated the construction of rooms specifically designed for older people, with larger buttons on remote controls, grab rails in showers, etc.

- Studies conducted by the Center for Mature Consumer Studies in Atlanta found that seniors are more likely than baby boomers to read newspapers on a daily basis (85 percent versus 47 percent); and community newspapers have been shown to be a remarkably effective advertising and information medium.

- Diet is playing an increasingly important role in maintaining health and vigor according to the Food Marketing Institute, which found 65 percent of older consumers "very" concerned about nutritional content. They are demanding more variety and assortment of foods, with an increase in products developed to get around problems associated with aging, such as the ability to digest lactose.

- Far from being "technophobic," 30 percent of seniors between fifty-five and seventy-five own their own computer (according to Senior-Com, a website specializing in marketing to seniors). The same source indicates that seniors are more likely to make a purchase via the World Wide Web than any other age group.

- Also contrary to stereotypes of older consumers, 78 percent of Americans aged fifty-six to ninety are likely or very likely to try new products, according to a national research survey conducted by ProMatura Group. Brand name is cited by two-thirds of the respondents as important in their selection of products.

- Three out of five Americans over fifty-five work to maintain their health through regular exercise and fitness activities, according to the Sporting Goods Manufacturing Association. The most popular sports among Americans over fifty-five are fitness walking, to which the people who practice it devote a significant amount of time (one hundred plus days/year), golf (twenty-five plus days/year), recreational vehicle camping, stationary bike riding, use of a treadmill, and even free weights (also one hundred-plus days/year).

- Roper Starch Worldwide reported in 1996 that grandparents have become a critical link to the children's market and spend an average of $400 per year on their grandchildren. Highest on the list of purchases are clothing, toys, games, books, and videos.

- Among the hottest sellers in videotapes are nostalgia movies and reruns of "The Honeymooners" and "I Love Lucy"; Nat King Cole was brought back from the dead in a remix of his music performed by his daughter Natalie.

- Mature Americans are as fashion conscious as their younger counterparts—categories such as apparel, footwear, and cosmetics are being repositioned, and new products are being launched in terms of their appeal to older consumers.

- The models in Ralph Lauren's and Calvin Klein's newest advertising campaigns are over forty and in some cases over fifty—indicating that it is becoming "hip" to be older. Sean Connery was recently named *People Magazine*'s sexiest man.

- The cosmetics industry is experiencing its biggest boom in history, with every imaginable wrinkle cream, skin softener, age-spot remover, tooth whitener, herbal and vitamin-containing products.

- Examples of advertising attacking aging head on include slogans like "I don't intend to grow old gracefully" and a skin product with a well-recognized actress asserting, "Don't hide your age, defy it."

- The new senior leisure class is being courted with targeted programs from YMCAs, country clubs, elder hostels, and the like. Adult theme parks are now geared to older audiences. Former president Bush was recently seen jumping out of an airplane in a parachute. The Senior Olympics now has a seventy-and-over ski club.

THE EVOLUTION OF MARKETING TECHNIQUES

Interest in the commercial potential of the older consumer market started about twenty years ago and is now at an all-time high. As the demographics have splintered and fragmented—that is, as more and more differences among groups have been noted—so have marketing techniques evolved in their sophistication and precision. Ken Dychtwald was among the first to recognize both the potential of this market and the problems created by a "gerontophobic" culture, and his 1989 book *Age Wave* is still one of the most comprehensive and insightful explorations of both the problems and the opportunities available to date. Calling this a "demographic revolution that has no precedent in history," Dychtwald demonstrated how the increase in numbers and the swelling resources of older Americans could make obsolete many of the current assumptions about the life cycle and about serving the needs of the people who are in the later phases of theirs.

The fascination with aging is mirrored in the number of people studying the field, the publications targeted to mature readers, and the number and variety of advocacy groups. *Age Wave* was also among the first to implore decisionmakers in business and social institutions to acknowledge that this is a powerful buying and voting population that is not reticent about communicating its views and desires. As a result, by now most marketing departments and advertising agencies have been forced to confront the myth that anyone over fifty is tight with what little money he or she has, or that the only desirable television audiences are in the eighteen to forty-nine range. Syndicated research services like Nielsen and Simmons MRB, which previously had classified many and varied segments of audiences in younger groups but tended to lump all elders together, have changed their categories as well. Simmons now recognizes four distinct types of older consumers, each with its own unique attitudes and behavior.

Through the deepening of research into older consumers, it has become evident that these are people who rarely think of themselves as "old" and would rather see themselves portrayed in attractive and positive ways; however, from their perspective, security, safety, and comfort are more important psychological and product needs to be fulfilled. Convenience in both purchasing and the use of a product has become as important as the product itself.

Arguing for a shift in cultural perception that provides a better framework for what it means to become older, Dychtwald noted that "the question of whether an aged America turns out to be good or bad news will depend on whether we can grow beyond the values and expectations of youth to discover a positive and expanded vision of who we might become." It is, however, difficult to find examples that point to the fulfillment of this vision in the years since it was first described.

Another perspective is presented in a recent book entitled *Rocking the Ages: The Yankelovich Report on Generational Marketing*. Authors J. Walker Smith and Ann Clurman utilize data gathered through the twenty-five-year Yankelovich tracking of America's living habits and values to illustrate how the marketplace evolves in response to the different needs of different generations. In their view, the proper frame of reference is one that puts the emphasis on the unifying experiences of various cohorts labeled "Matures," "Boomers," and "Xers." The assumption here is that a central tendency within each generation is expressed in common values, motivations, and the lifestyles that grow out of these. As a result, marketing and communication should be tailored along the lines laid out in Figure 10.2.

FIGURE 10.2 GENERATIONS AT A GLANCE			
	Matures	**Boomers**	**Xers**
Defining Idea . . .	DUTY	INDIVIDUALITY	DIVERSITY
Celebrating . . .	Victory	Youth	Savvy
Success because . . .	Fought hard and won	Were born, therefore should be a winner	Have two jobs
Style . . .	Team player	Self-absorbed	Entrepreneur
Rewards because . . .	You've earned	You deserve it	You need it
Work is . . .	An inevitable obligation	An exciting adventure	A difficult challenge
Surprises in life . . .	Some good, some bad	All good	Avoid it—all bad
Leisure is . . .	Reward for hard work	The point of life	Relief
Education is . . .	A dream	A birthright	A way to get ahead
Future . . .	Rainy day to work for	"Now" is more important	Uncertain but manageable
Managing money . . .	Save	Spend	Hedge
"Program" means . . .	Social program	Cult deprogrammers	Software programs
Go watch . . .	*The Best Years of Our Lives*	*The Big Chill*	*Reality Bites*

In other words, *when* we were born is more important than how old we are. This may certainly be true taken as a snapshot in time, but presumably even Boomers will shed some of their self-indulgent traits as mortality looms.

Another recently published book, *Gerontographics: Life Stage Segmentation for Marketing Strategy Development* by George P. Moschis, makes a studied and well-documented case for the *dissimilarity* of people comprising "the" mature market. He demonstrates through attitudinal as well as behavioral research that these differences have more to do with outlook on life than chronological or biological age, and therefore are not explained by a simple "cohort effect." In fact, the older we get, the more pronounced our differentiation in terms of needs, lifestyles, and purchasing habits. Gerontographics is an approach that recognizes individuals' movement through different phases based upon changing life conditions—not just physical well-being, as commonly conceived, but also psychological and social states as well. The gerontographics life-stage model classifies older adults into the four groups shown in Figure 10.3, each with its own product and service implications.

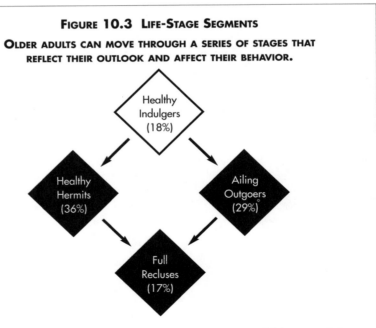

FIGURE 10.3 LIFE-STAGE SEGMENTS

OLDER ADULTS CAN MOVE THROUGH A SERIES OF STAGES THAT REFLECT THEIR OUTLOOK AND AFFECT THEIR BEHAVIOR.

Healthy
Indulgers
(18%)

Healthy
Hermits
(36%)

Ailing
Outgoers
(29%)

Full
Recluses
(17%)

Note: Arrows indicate that people may move to the next stage in life because of physiological, psychological, and social aging. Arrows pointing to the left denote psychosocial aging; arrows pointing to the right denote physical aging.

"Healthy Indulgers" have experienced fewer pivotal life events such as the loss of a spouse, chronic illness, or retirement than those in the other classifications. As a consequence, this is a group most likely to have similarities in attitudes and values to younger consumers. However, because they are economically in better shape than their juniors, they tend to look toward enjoyment of activities rather than to strive continuously for status and power.

People within the segment described as "Healthy Hermits" have had their self-image shaken by challenging life events and as a result tend to withdraw. According to Moschis, many of these people "resent the isolation and the fact that they are expected to behave like old people." Unlike Healthy Hermits, "Ailing Outgoers" are accepting of their status and limitations—but still want to get something out of life.

Finally, "Frail Recluses" may also accept their old age and have adjusted their lifestyles accordingly; however, they need the greatest level of support in terms of health-related products and services. They move toward spiritual fulfillment as compensation for their physical deterioration.

As a model for product developers and creators of advertising, gerontographics is obviously different from traditional demographic structures, and because these new classifications suggest values are a state of mind, there is a basis for more thoughtful and responsive marketing tools, as it fosters hypotheses that stimulate thinking.

CONFUSION AND CONTRADICTION

All the information and literature on the subject notwithstanding, the field of consumer marketing is still relatively primitive. If this were not so, success rates would consistently be much higher. Even according to studies Moschis cites, no single factor explains consumer responses to marketing offerings on average more than 5 percent of the time. The behavior of older consumers is perhaps most fraught with uncertainties, and a *Wall Street Journal* piece as long ago as October 1987, after attempting to sort out fact and fiction about the older consumer, incorporated in its headline the message "the mature market is full of contradictions."

For example, some statistics support the premise that older consumers are more likely to spend their money, while other information indicates that they are holding onto it as their needs for products and services lessen and their concern about unanticipated, major expenses like health care and long-term care mounts. The *Journal of Consumer Marketing* in 1991 stated that older people are "inherently thrifty and more careful with the money they spend."

It is universally acknowledged among marketers that the best way to influence older people is through messages and branding they can identify with. Yet, there are many examples of products that have tried to do so and have failed, such as the shampoo "For 50 Plus" (the only people who bought it were generally over sixty, representing a much smaller market). Many people obviously do not want to identify themselves as older. And while well-off older people are indeed more active than ever before— shopping, playing golf and cards—this does not necessarily mean they are getting as much out of these activities as they did from the social and economic functions they might have pursued in the past. Indeed, according to Harvey L. Sterns and Anthony A. Sterns in the collection of articles entitled *Older and Active: How Americans over 55 Are Contributing to Society*, "evidence is mounting that intrinsic rewards—satisfaction, relationships with co-workers, and a sense of participating in meaningful activity— become more important as an individual ages."

These intrinsic benefits are hard to come by whether in work or in life more generally, for all people. Even in health, where there have clearly been miraculous advances in our ability to treat illness, extend life, and promote health objectively, our subjective quality of life may not necessarily be improving. John Knowles, previously director of the Rockefeller Foundation, described this phenomenon as "doing better, but feeling worse." Our scientific and industrial revolution has done much to better our material world, but it has also had side effects. In fact, stress-related and psychosomatic illness, alcohol and drug abuse, are all on the increase. For many, part of maturing is the deepening of our values and growth of our motivation beyond objects, activities, and other external sources or stimuli. It is imperative that those leading marketing and communication firms and advising manufacturer clients develop new pathways that address meaning as well as consumption and acquisition.

Mass marketing continues to decline according to many measures of its effectiveness, including brand loyalty and new product success rates, and advertising has steadily lost credibility. One explanation is that our national culture coming out of World War II was relatively homogeneous—making a living, raising a family, owning a home, and building the future were shared experiences. Today, there are not the same shared values and patterns of behavior. The unifying symbols, myths, and rituals in every culture play a critical role in creating and readjusting our worldview, without which there is a feeling of being adrift. For many people in our society there may be infinite possibilities for material advancement; however, what good is the ability and freedom to satisfy our whims if life has relatively little meaning? At a certain point, we will not be able to deal with all that we have accumulated. Meanwhile, ongoing "improvements" through technology evolve further and faster than our ability to apply them and derive human value from them.

Let us assume that it will become clear as we age that continuous consumption is not as satisfying as it once was, and that the thing we are granted in greatest abundance is more time to think about our mortality. People would understandably experience feelings of isolation and anxiety; if marketing in turn continued to try to fill the void with *more* goods, services, and entertainment, the feelings of emptiness would be intensified. This negative cycle threatens the effectiveness of business to a greater degree than simply failing to put older actors in commercials. Samuel Johnson's observation that "being hanged in a fortnight can concentrate the mind wonderfully" is the dynamic that can be put to productive use by marketers on behalf of the hidden needs of the elderly. By making good use of this opportunity to learn and grow and benefit from all the latent potential of an aging population, marketers can break the cycle by latching onto values that have more relevance in an older society.

Albert Einstein once said, "Knowledge cannot come from experience alone, but only from the inventions of the intellect as compared to observable fact." Since most business does tend to be reactive, its strategies are based on historical analysis rather than on hypotheses or intuition, which rarely plays well up the chain of management command. The effect is that those working in advertising are missing what may be lurking beneath the easily accessible data. While market segmentation clearly does improve targeting efficiency, the pieces are becoming so small that they slip through one's fingers. We need models that allow us to put things back into coherent wholes, metaphors or maps to stimulate and access our imagination, which has always been the most powerful creative resource.

A Broader Definition of Health

One of the most helpful models for exploring what it means to grow as we age is based in the conception of health. Health is in a sense really another word for wholeness; in fact, the word "health" has the same root as the words "hale" and "whole." It is based on the recognition that, in the broadest sense, our bodies, minds, and social and physical environments are all critical dimensions of well-being, each interacting with and impinging upon the others. (See Figure 10.4.)

The best marketing recognizes that products and services are most readily embraced by consumers when something is evoked from the inside rather than imposed from the outside, so the potential of a commercial approach based on the innate desire for better health can help to identify underlying areas of dissatisfaction and launch new dimensions of consumer value.

The emotional problems often cited in the literature on aging include loss of power, loss of a feeling of connection with others, a sense of dependence, and awareness of the inevitable shortening of life. Their positive mirror images, however, can become the basis for fertile opportunities in providing products or services of value. (See Figure 10.5.)

Imagine the largest and most economically powerful segment of our population—comprising many subsegments of lifestyle, taste, socioeconomic and demographic distinctions but united by a continuous striving for growth or health in the broadest sense. It has never been established

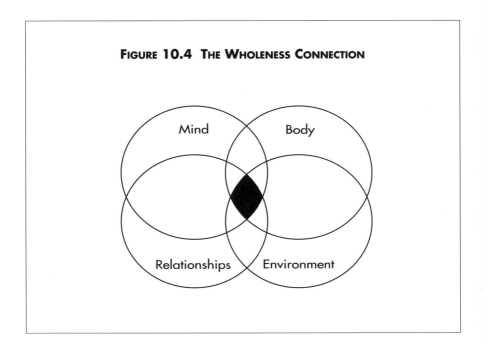

FIGURE 10.4 THE WHOLENESS CONNECTION

FIGURE 10.5

FROM UNHEALTHY AGING . . .	TO HEALTHY AGING
Dependence	Autonomy
Powerlessness	Power
Transience	Durability
Isolation	Unity

---

whether marketing actually influences consumer values or merely reflects the prevailing values of the culture. What is clear, though, is that we have an opportunity unlike that of any other time in history, where the success of a commercial enterprise can at the same time deal with the growth of human beings to their fullest.

In a maturing marketplace, the two might actually need each other.

11

THE MEDIA'S ROLE:
LIFE IN AN OLDER AMERICA

Lawrence K. Grossman

One of the biggest and most important stories of our time—indeed, one of the miracles of the twentieth century—has been mostly ignored so far by the nation's mainstream media. It is a little-known fact that the equivalent of an *entire generation* has been added to the average person's life span. In 1900, the average American lived to age forty-seven and 75 percent of all Americans died before age sixty-five. Today, the average American lives until seventy-six, and 70 percent of all Americans live beyond sixty-five. What may be even more newsworthy, most of those who live longer are also living healthier, more vigorous lives. Older people are living better and leading more active lives than most younger people enjoyed when the century began. The aging generation is no longer the rocking chair generation.

That news is just starting to get around. According to a recent special edition of *New York Times Magazine*, devoted entirely to "The Age Boom," America is discovering "a new stage of life—*after middle age*." The press has been slow to discern other major social trends as well—the civil rights movement, the feminist movement, the gay rights movement, the evangelical movement. But once it did, it propelled them into the headlines and gave them mainstream status and attention. Now the press is finally beginning to catch on to the fast expanding "after middle age" movement. This new stage of life manifests itself more clearly every day, redefining

economic and political power, generating social change, stimulating scientific breakthroughs and shaping artistic, cultural, fashion, travel, and
entertainment trends.

One would not know it, however, from looking at American television, the nation's dominant communications medium. Any time of the
day or night, virtually all there is to be seen are programs aimed at young
people, ages eighteen to forty-nine, or even eighteen to thirty-five, the
group that is most sought after because it is most prized by advertisers.
Advertisers pay a premium for young adults because, with their expanding
families and recent entry into the grown-up marketplace, they are supposed to spend the most on packaged goods and services that advertise on
television. Despite all the channels that have been added during the past
twenty years, the rule has been the same for all—reach out for the young
audiences, the ones for whom advertisers will pay the most money. Adults
aged eighteen to thirty-four command an average of $23.54 per thousand
from advertisers, compared to a mere $9.57 per thousand for adults over age
thirty-four, in a survey by ratings research firm A. C. Nielsen.

That is largely what accounts for the relentless sameness of commercial television, no matter how many channels there are. The mass media's
comparative disinterest in an older America bespeaks neither a dark con-
spiracy nor a limit of imagination. It stems from commercial television's
zealous pursuit of the easiest path to profits in a consumer society that, so
far at least, has been preoccupied by youth. A 1995 study of how the elderly were portrayed in one hundred prime-time television shows found that
people over age sixty-five make up only 2.8 percent of all adult characters
with speaking parts. And only 8.8 percent of those were cast in major
roles, which actually represented a decline since the 1970s, according to
the summer 1995 issue of the newsletter *Communication Reports*. An analysis of twenty-eight studies of characters on television and in children's
books and magazines revealed that elderly people, especially women, not
only were underrepresented and rarely cast in prime roles but also were
depicted in a negative light as reported in the January/February 1993 issue
of *Educational Gerontology*.

In May 1997, former CBS chairman and chief executive officer
Michael Jordan revealed that his company had commissioned Nielsen
Media Research to help it identify the 20 percent of consumers who make
80 percent of the household purchases. "It makes good sense," Jordan said,
"to pay a premium for those programs that reach the viewers who spend the
most money on advertiser products." In fact, most of the big-spending viewers, who prefer news magazine shows to sitcoms, are adults over age thirty-

five. In today's graying marketplace, the median age of adults is forty-three, and it will rise to fifty in less than a decade. But despite the CBS chairman's rhetoric, the network's actual program strategy for the new season was targeted squarely on fresher-faced audiences. CBS president Leslie Moonves unveiled seven new prime-time series aimed, he said, at broadening CBS's audience base to include younger, more urban viewers.

A print journalist, after appearing as a guest on a widely syndicated radio call-in show, expressed surprise at how young the show's callers seemed to be, judging by their voices and the nature of their comments. "The reason is simple," the producer explained, pointing into the control room. "Our telephone operators filter out older people just in case any advertisers happen to be listening. We don't want them coming away with the impression that our show appeals to older folks. It's bad for sales."

Some researchers have attempted to show "that the youthfulness of ad agency creative teams and media planners and buyers is at the core of the issue," according to the July/August 1997 issue of *Aging Today*. "Others fault ad agency clients who insist on youthful values in both commercials and the shows. . . . Still others say the anxiety many decision makers have about their own aging unconsciously biases them against giving aging any positive face, even when money is to be made by doing so." Meanwhile TV network audiences are eroding at an increasing rate—by 22 percent over the past three seasons and climbing. Their cherished eighteen to forty-nine age group is shrinking by nearly 7 million in this decade, while the only real growth in viewership is among the thirty-five- to sixty-four-year-old cohort.

As for newspapers, publishers are terrified as the age of their newspaper readers inexorably rises. Worse, young people are no longer in the habit of reading; newspaper readers who die are not being replaced. There are, of course, publications geared specifically for older audiences. But service to older people is largely confined to niche publications such as the American Association of Retired Persons' *Modern Maturity*, which has a massive circulation but does not enjoy the clout of the mainstream media. Still, this is more than the electronic media can offer. Such a niche cannot be found at all in television, not even in cable TV, which originally held out the promise of offering networks that would cater to audiences with all manner of specific interests.

The mainstream media mostly continue to operate amid the legacy of an American society dominated by the culture of youth, in its clothes, language, music, movies, and overall lifestyle. But now a new century looms. The baby boomers have turned fifty, rounding the corner into upper middle age and beyond. The mainstream media have been slow to awaken to that major demographic shift and its implications for marketing. Paul Kleyman, editor of *Aging Today*, asked the relatively few reporters for the mainstream media who cover the aging field how they got their assignments. Almost all of them revealed that they had the idea themselves and had to sell it to their editors. The commitment to the aging beat did not come from the top down but from the bottom up.

Still, after decades of chasing the eighteen- to forty-nine-year-old and ignoring the mature market, even television will have to begin to show signs of change. The core of its audience—the 76 million baby boomers who were weaned on television, who remain hale and hearty, and who have the disposable income that advertisers would love to tap—are putting the medium through its own midlife crisis. Media ad buyers, who have consistently devalued the over-fifty crowd, will have to awaken to the fact of an implacable core audience shift that they no longer can afford to overlook. In the decade ahead, nearly one-half of the projected growth in the American population will come from an increase in the number of people between the ages of thirty-five and fifty-nine, a study by economist-demographers William Serow and David Sly of the Population Center at Florida State University asserts. In terms of income, the ages between nineteen and sixty-five (in other words, the full span of a working life, not just the younger years) are now "the period of the life course where labor force participation, income and productivity are the greatest." A torrent of survey data shows that people older than forty-five buy most of the new cars and trucks; those over fifty-five buy almost a third of all new vehicles; and according to the *New York Times*, "people over fifty take 163 million trips a year and a third of all overseas packaged tours."

Even more significant, especially to companies looking for opportunities to expand their markets, not only in the United States but throughout the world, "population growth will be minimal among children and *negative among young adults*," a trend that may actually come as good news for newspapers. It is to the seasoned adults rather than to the young people that the mainstream media must look for their future. For the next twenty-five years, as Serow and Sly point out, "[U.S.] population growth will be concentrated in those age groups which are either in the peak years of earnings and productivity or in those age groups where discretionary retirement income and spending are comparatively high." And the older age groups, with their higher median income, now consist of people who do not suffer nearly the amount of debilitating and chronic illness that their predecessors did. Leading active and vital lives, they should be prime targets for advertisers. Maturity will come back into marketing fashion.

Journalistically, the most interesting aspect of the "grown-ups' movement" is that it represents not a special interest beat, or what in current media jargon is called a "niche" beat, but one of the most important *general interest* beats of the coming century. "Follow the money," the classic advice from the Watergate scandal, is also appropriate advice for the mainstream media in their competitive pursuit of audiences and advertisers. And the money will be found in serving an older crowd. As the baby-boomer generation matures, its sheer numbers, significant financial resources, personal and professional interests, and shared worries will dominate the news. That was true as well, of course, during the years that this generation was growing up. But now the focus will come from the mature perspective of an older population.

By the year 2005, one-half of the U.S. labor force will be over forty years of age. Television viewers, radio listeners, newspaper and magazine readers, and Internet participants will include more older people and fewer young ones than ever before. The new maturity beat is going mainstream. For journalists, that automatically helps define what their most interesting, most important, and, above all, most newsworthy issues will be.

In the words of advertising executive Jerry Della Femina,

> The boomer market represents a pot of gold for any advertiser with the intelligence and guts to go after it. . . . You're talking about an incredible concentration of wealth and power. Boomers have the best jobs. They have the most money. . . . There are more of them, and every seven seconds another one turns fifty.

When advertisers go after the boomer market, the media are bound to follow.

While the over-fifty group represents a core readership or viewership for magazines, book publishers, and broadcasters, it probably will constitute the single most important market for the nation's daily newspapers. For newspapers to survive in the face of their continuous and precipitous circulation decline, they will have to concentrate on serving the maturing boomer market. The major newspapers will need to sharpen their focus to reach out to their most likely audience. And because this maturing population cohort is the most politically active and influential, it also suggests that America will be adapting its institutions—including the media—public policies, and priorities to reflect the growing clout of its elder and near-elder citizens.

By contrast with issues that resonate with the younger generation, like abortion, premarital sex, teen crime, smoking, and drugs, which have dominated the news for so long, issues that primarily reflect the concerns of the older population are starting to gain more media attention because they are becoming important to more people. Today's lead stories ask whether it is proper to become a mother at age sixty-three, or a father at age seventy-seven; whether elderly patients have the right to choose to die; whether doctors should help the terminally ill commit suicide; what determines when life comes to an end; whether illegal drugs should be prescribed to reduce pain and suffering among the seriously ill; what responsibilities the family and the government have for long-term care; whether health care for the elderly should be rationed; and whether strict limits should be placed on expensive, advanced medical care. Financial stories primarily affecting seniors are finding their way into the day's headlines because of their enormous impact on the economy and on federal and state budgets. Examples include proposals to lower inheritance and capital gains taxes and debates over the solvency of Social Security and the future of Medicare. When it comes to the major entitlement programs for the elderly, the sheer numbers involved are on a scale huge enough to upset the entire economy. A recent proposal to convert Social Security into individual pension investment programs could generate an estimated $10 to $40 billion in new annual fees alone for Wall Street. That is big news.

The focus on "fixing" Medicare reflects not only the maturing population's growing influence on how health care is delivered but also the rising importance of the health care industry to the nation's economy. Approximately 15 percent of the U.S. gross domestic product is being spent on medical care today, twice what the percentage was in 1970. This is now the third-largest industry in the United States, and older Americans, more than any other segment of the population, make up its primary market. As economist Paul Krugman points out, "Almost one worker in ten is employed in the health care service industry; if this trend continues, in a few years there will be more people working in doctors' offices and hospitals than factories. . . . Medical expenditures used to be small, not because doctors were cheap or hospitals well managed but because there was only so much medicine had to offer, no matter how much you were willing to spend." Now, new medical advances—new diagnostic techniques, new surgical procedures, new therapies—are either curing or alleviating conditions that previously had to be endured or allowed to take their inevitable downward and debilitating course.

Prodded by the population shift toward older boomers, the United States will be embarking on new approaches to education, work, and productivity. To the traditional emphasis on instruction for children will be added vital new priorities: the need to upgrade adult skills, expand job retraining, and provide lifelong educational resources and opportunities for the maturing population.

While many in journalism persist in expressing Cassandra-like alarm at the rise of an older America, the news is actually good. Remarkable progress in the quality of the nation's life and health has produced a senior generation capable of determining its own destiny and enjoying the fruits of years of labor. Prevailing images of a frail, weak, and dependent elderly population are being replaced by images of a nation of vital, active, sensible, independent adults.

As every chapter in this volume demonstrates, the nation is seeing striking changes in its living conditions, consumption, and employment. The retirement age is being postponed as the working population grows older. The demand for products and services is being redefined by older people in every area, affecting the nature of travel and leisure, education and jobs, entertainment, information, and industry. It is the nature of news reporting, however, to feature conflict and controversy rather than cooperation and unity. Stories are beginning to appear about the growing conflict between the generations and the government's tendency to transfer wealth to the old at the expense of the young. The "greedy geezer" image has become a nationwide editorial staple.

It can only be hoped that with more journalism training, education, and experience, coverage of generational issues will become more practiced and therefore more intelligent and sophisticated. As older people lead younger lifestyles, society will have little choice but to adopt patterns of relationships that reflect not generational battles but integrated living among the generations. Generational separation and segregation should give way to community models in which vigorous older people serve as valuable resources for the young—grandparents helping working parents bring up their children and filling the shameful gaps in our society's opportunities for education and day care. Older citizens can engage in neighborhood and political activities for which members of the younger generation, struggling to gain their foothold, have neither the time nor energy nor resources.

The political clout of the growing cohort of mature citizens is reflected not only in the sheer magnitude of numbers but also in the fact that, by contrast with young adults, a higher proportion of them vote, contribute to political causes and election campaigns, and participate in civic affairs. The process will accelerate as interactive media spread and older people become more accustomed to using e-mail, computers, the Internet, and other media resources to call up the information and data they need. If the traditional press will not supply what they want, in the telecommunications age they will be able to summon it for themselves. While older people tend to resist new technologies, the first generation of computer users is turning sixty. Eventually, the Internet and its variations will become a central focus of attention for the old as well as the young.

Much of journalism is personal, as those who practice it know. The decisions that editors, news directors, producers, and reporters make are greatly influenced by what experiences affect them in their own daily lives. It was mentioned earlier that age beat reporters typically originate the coverage themselves, sometimes only after years of requesting the assignment. One notable exception to this occurred recently at the *Philadelphia Inquirer*, where a receptive editor's interest in aging was triggered by his own searing personal experience. Reporter Mike Vitez, winner of the 1997 Pulitzer Prize for his extraordinary five-part series on death and dying, revealed that he had been assigned the story after his newspaper's executive editor watched the death struggle of a much-loved, terminally ill aunt. With 33 million Americans now over age sixty-five and more approaching, aging and longevity issues will increasingly frame our experience and our conversations, and consequently the content of our media for the next twenty years or more.

By gaining dominance in America through its numbers alone, the "grown-ups' movement" is likely to become the twenty-first century's successor to the civil rights movement, the women's movement, and the gay and lesbian movement. We are on the verge of a great population transformation. And the mainstream media, reflecting their role as society's central nervous system in the information age, will report on and interpret that transformation if for no other reason than that it now engages most journalists and media professionals, as well as the majority of the nation's citizens, personally and directly.

NOTES

INTRODUCTION

1. Robert N. Butler, "Ageism: Another Form of Bigotry," *Gerontologist* 9 (1969): 243–46.

2. Robert N. Butler and Herbert P. Gleason, *Productive Aging: Enhancing Vitality in Later Life* (New York: Springer Publishing Company, 1985).

3. Philippe Aries, *Centuries of Childhood: A Social History of Family Life*, trans. R. Baldick (New York: Alfred A. Knopf, 1962).

CHAPTER 2

1. Board of Trustees of the Federal Hospital Insurance Trust Fund, *1999 Annual Report* (Washington, D.C.: Government Printing Office, 1999).

2. Haiden A. Huskamp and Joseph Newhouse, "Is Health Spending Slowing Down?" *Health Affairs* 13, no. 5 (1994): 32–38.

3. Health Care Financing Administration, *Health Care Financing Review—Medicare and Medicaid Statistical Supplement* (Baltimore: U.S. Department of Health and Human Services, 1996).

4. "Budgetary Implication of the Balanced Budget Act."

5. Marilyn Moon and Stephen Zuckerman, "Are Private Insurers Really Controlling Spending Better than Medicare?" Henry J. Kaiser Family Foundation, Washington, D.C., July 1995; Katherine Levit et al., "National Health Expenditures, 1994," *Health Care Financing Review* 18, no. 3 (Spring 1996): 205–42.

6. *Health Benefits in 1996* (Newark: KPMG Peat Marwick, 1997).

7. Prospective Payment Assessment Commission, *Report and Recommendations to the Congress* (Washington, D.C.: U.S. Government Printing Office, 1997).

8. Stephen Zuckerman and Diana Verrilli, "The Medicare Relative Value Scale and Private Payers: The Potential Impact on Physician Payments," prepared for U.S. Department of Health and Human Services, Health Care Financing Administration, 1995.

9. "Status of the Social Security and Medicare Programs: A Summary of the 1997 Annual Reports," Social Security and Medicare Boards of Trustees, 1997, mimeograph.

10. U.S. Congress, Senate Committee on Education and Labor, "Health Insurance and the Uninsured: Background Data and Analysis," 101st Cong., 1st sess., 1989, pp. 122–23.

11. Testimony of George F. Grob, U.S. Congress, Senate Special Committee on Aging, "Medicare: Home Health Benefit," 105th Cong., 1st sess., July 28, 1997.

12. Huskamp and Newhouse, "Is Health Spending Slowing Down?"

13. Charles M. Winslow et al., "The Appropriateness of Performing Coronary Artery Bypass Surgery," *Journal of the American Medical Association* 260 (1988): 505–9; Mark R. Chassin et al., "Does Inappropriate Use Explain Geographic Variations in the Use of Health Care Services?" *Journal of the American Medical Association* 258 (1987): 2533–37.

14. William B. Schwartz, "In the Pipeline: A Wave of Valuable Medical Technology," *Health Affairs* 13, no. 3 (Summer 1994): 70–79.

15. Kenneth G. Manton et al., "Chronic Disability Trends in Elderly United States Populations: 1982–1994," *Proceeding of the National Academy of Sciences* 94 (March 1997): 2593–98.

16. John Ratner, "Medicare: Rapid Spending Growth Calls for More Prudent Purchasing," U.S. General Accounting Office, 1995.

17. Gerald Riley et al., "Health Status of Medicare Enrollees in HMOs and Fee-for-Service in 1994," *Health Care Financing Review* 17, no. 4 (Summer 1996): 65–76; Kathryn M. Langwell and Laura A. Esslinger, *Medicaid Managed Care: Evidence on Use, Costs, and Quality of Care* (New York: The Commonwealth Fund, 1997).

18. Greater cost sharing in areas such as home health could reduce the use of services and perhaps could be viewed as enhancing efficiency. But since most elderly persons have some supplemental insurance that would likely shield them from behavioral incentives, even such changes are more likely to represent a shifting of costs rather than a force for putting the use of services on a more rational basis.

19. Marilyn Moon, *Medicare Now and in the Future*, 2d ed. (Washington, D.C.: Urban Institute Press, 1996).

20. Marilyn Moon, *Restructuring Medicare's Cost-Sharing* (New York: The Commonwealth Fund, 1996).

21. U.S. Department of Commerce, Bureau of the Census, *Current Population Survey, 1997*.

22. Marilyn Moon, Barbara Gage, and Alison Evans, *An Examination of Key Medicare Provisions in the Balanced Budget Act of 1997* (New York: The Commonwealth Fund, 1997).

23. Medical savings account options are actually a combination of a high deductible, a catastrophic insurance plan, and the creation of a savings account from any of the dollars left over after purchasing the less expensive insurance. Many analysts have written about the attractiveness of such options to those who can afford to risk the higher deductible and who expect to spend less on medical care than others. Jack Rogers and James W. Mays, *Medical Savings Accounts for Medicare Beneficiaries* (Washington, D.C.: Henry J. Kaiser Family Foundation, 1995).

24. This option results in a substantial change in policy, one that would add considerably to the complexity of the program while raising relatively small amounts for Medicare. Critics of this approach also argue that it is unfair to tax some in-kind benefits and not others. Consistency implies that health benefits provided by employers to their workers should be taxed as well—a very controversial policy. Notwithstanding the outcry from affected parties, this would be perhaps the most equitable way to require higher-income beneficiaries to pay more toward the cost of their care.

25. See *Congressional Record*, July 29, 1997, p. H6.

26. Federal Hospital Insurance Trust Fund, Annual Report, 1997.

27. Ibid.

28. Timothy Waidmann, "Potential Effects of an Increase in Medicare's Age of Eligibility" *Health Affairs* 17, no. 2 (Spring 1998): 156–64.

29. U.S. Department of Commerce, *Current Population Survey*, selected tables on income by age.

30. Ibid.

31. Joshua M. Wiener, "How to Pay for Long-Term Care," *Washington Post*, April 21, 1997.

CHAPTER 3

1. *Informal Caregiving: Compassion in Action*, The Assistant Secretary for Planning and Evaluation and The Administration on Aging, Washington, D.C., 1998.

2. U.S. Department of Commerce, Bureau of the Census, "Population Projections of the United States by Age, Sex, Race, and Hispanic Origin: 1995 to 2050," *Current Population Reports*, P25–1130, 1996, p. 9.

3. Kenneth G. Manton, Larry Corder, and Eric Stallard, "Chronic Disability Trends in Elderly United States Populations: 1982–1994," *Proceedings of the National Academy of Science* 94 (1997): 2593–98.

4. Lisa Maria B. Alecxih, "What It Is, Who Needs It, and Who Provides It," in B. L. Boyd, ed., *Long-term Care: Knowing the Risk, Paying the Price* (Washington, D.C.: Health Insurance Association of America, 1997), pp. 1–17.

5. *Facts on Long-term Care*, National Academy on Aging, Washington, D.C., 1997, available online at http://geron.org/NAA/ltc.html.

6. Alecxih, "What It Is"; ibid.

7. *Facts on Long-term Care*.

8. Harriet L. Komisar, Jeanne M. Lambrew, and Judith Feder, *Long-term Care for the Elderly* (New York: Commonwealth Fund, 1996), p. 7.

9. Alecxih, "What It Is."

10. Brenda Spillman, Nancy Krauss, and Barbara Altman, "A Comparison of Nursing Home Resident Characteristics: 1987–1996," unpublished paper, Agency for Health Care Policy and Research, Rockville, Md., 1997.

11. Alecxih, "What It Is."

12. Elizabeth B. Jackson and Pamela Doty, "Unmet and Undermet Need for Functional Assistance among the U.S. Disabled Elderly" (paper presented at the annual meeting of the Gerontological Society of America, Cincinnati, November 14–18, 1997).

13. *Informal Caregiving: Compassion in Action*, The Assistant Secretary for Planning and Evaluating and The Administration on Aging, Washington, D.C., 1998.

14. *Facts on Long-term Care*.

15. Alecxih, "What It Is"; Christopher M. Murtaugh, Peter G. Kemper, and Brenda C. Spillman, "The Risk of Nursing Home Use in Later Life," *Medical Care* 28, no. 10 (October 1990): 952–62.

16. Alecxih, "What It Is."

17. Lisa Maria Alecxih, "Who Pays, How Much?" in Boyd, *Long-term Care*, pp. 19–27.

18. Robyn I. Stone and Pamela F. Short, "The Competing Demands of Employment and Informal Caregiving to Disabled Elders," *Medical Care* 28, no. 6 (June 1990): 513–26.

19. Natalie Graves Tucker and Robert W. Bectel, *Across the States 1996: Profiles of Long-term Care Systems* (Washington, D.C.: American Association of Retired Persons, 1996), p. 228.

20. Genevieve Kenney, Shruti Rajan, and Stephanie Soscia, "State Spending for Medicare and Medicaid Home Care Programs," *Health Affairs* 17, no. 1 (January/February 1998): 201–12.

21. Barbara Coleman, *New Directions for State Long-term Care Systems, Vol. IV: Limiting State Medicaid Spending on Nursing Home Care* (Washington, D.C.: American Association of Retired Persons, 1997), p. 14.

22. "Hamilton County's Elderly Services Program" (unpublished document, Council on Aging of the Cincinnati Area, Inc., Cincinnati, Ohio, 1997).

23. Harriet L. Komisar and Judith Feder, *The Balanced Budget Act of 1997: Effects on Medicare's Home Health Benefit and Beneficiaries Who Need*

Long-term Care (New York: Commonwealth Fund, 1998), available online at http://www.cmwf.org/fraileld/kobba258.html.

24. Kenney, Rajan, and Soscia, "State Spending for Medicare and Medicaid Home Care Programs."

25. Komisar and Feder, *Balanced Budget Act of 1997*.

26. Ibid.

27. Kenney, Rajan, and Soscia, "State Spending for Medicare and Medicaid Home Care Programs."

28. Ibid.

29. Jennie Harvell, "Subacute Care: Its Role and the Assurance of Quality," in Robert J. Newcomer, Anne M. Wilkinson, and M. Powell Lawton, eds., *Annual Review of Gerontology and Geriatrics* 16 (New York: Springer Publishing Company, 1997), pp. 37–59.

30. Gary W. Singleton, "Subacute Care: An Emerging Industry," *Brown University Long-term Care Quality Letter* 5, no. 1 (1993). Cited in Harvell, "Subacute Care: Its Role and the Assurance of Quality."

31. Laura Hyatt, "ASCA Unites Subacute Care Professionals," *American Subacute Care Association Quarterly* 3, no. 1 (1993). Cited in Harvell, "Subacute Care: Its Role and the Assurance of Quality."

32. Carlos Gonzales, "Subacute Care: Preparing for a New Market," *Provider* 20 (1994): 55–56. Cited in Harvell, "Subacute Care: Its Role and the Assurance of Quality."

33. Alecxih, "What It Is."

34. Barbara Gage et al., *Medicare Savings: Options and Opportunities* (Washington, D.C.: Urban Institute, 1997), p. 33.

35. Barbara Manard et al., "Subacute Care: Policy Synthesis and Market Area Analysis," Lewin-VHI for the Office of the Assistant Secretary for Planning and Evaluation, U.S. Department of Health and Human Services 1995. Cited in Harvell, "Subacute Care: Its Role and the Assurance of Quality."

36. *Facts on Long-term Care*.

37. Gail P. Schaeffer, "An Evolving Product," in Boyd, *Long-term Care*, pp. 49–73.

38. Ibid.

39. Robert B. Friedland, *Facing the Costs of Long-term Care* (Washington, D.C.: Employee Benefit Research Institute, 1990).

40. Susan E. Polniaszek, "Consumer Issues," in Boyd, *Long-term Care*, pp. 129–46.

41. "How Will You Pay for Your Old Age? A Special Report on Long-term Care Insurance," *Consumer Reports*, October 1997, pp. 36–50.

42. Marc A. Cohen, "Future Directions," in Boyd, *Long-term Care*, pp. 147–65; Nelda McCall, "Insurance Regulation and the Partnership for Long-term Care," *Journal of Insurance Regulation* 16, no. 1 (Fall 1997): 73–101.

43. Mark Meiners and Hunter McKay, "Developing Public-Private Long-term Care Insurance Partnerships," *Pride Institute Journal of Long Term Home Health Care* 8, no. 4 (Fall 1989): 35–40.

44. Nelda McCall et al., "The Partnership for Long-term Care: Who Are the Partnership Policy Purchasers?" *Medical Care Research and Review* 54, no. 4 (December 1997): 472–89.

45. Robyn I. Stone and Marlene R. Niefeld, "Medicare Managed Care: Sinking or Swimming with the Tide," *Journal of Long-Term Home Health Care* 17, no. 1 (Winter 1998): 7–16.

46. Jo Ann Lamphere et al., "The Surge in Medicare Managed Care: An Update," *Health Affairs* 16, no. 3 (May/June 1997): 127–33.

47. Randell S. Brown et al., "Do Health Maintenance Organizations Work for Medicare?" *Health Care Financing Review* 15, no. 1 (Fall 1993): 7–23.

48. Maureen Booth et al., "Integration of Acute and Long-term Care for Dually Eligible Beneficiaries through Managed Care," technical assistance paper prepared by the Muskie School of Public Service, University of Southern Maine, and the National Academy for State Health Policy, Portland, Maine, 1997, under a grant from the Robert Wood Johnson Foundation Medicare/Medicaid Integration Program.

49. Cohen, "Future Directions"; Laurence G. Branch, Robert F. Coulam, and Yvonne A. Zimmerman, "The PACE Evaluation: Initial Findings," *Gerontologist* 35, no. 3 (June 1995): 349–59.

50. Robert Newcomer et al., "Case Mix Controlled Service Use and Expenditures in the Social/Health Maintenance Organization Demonstration," *Journal of Gerontology: Medical Sciences* 50A, no. 1 (January 1995): M35–44; Joshua M. Wiener and Jason Skaggs, *Current Approaches to Integrating Acute and Long-term Care Financing and Services* (Washington, D.C.: American Association of Retired Persons, 1995).

51. Leonard Gruenberg et al., "An Analysis of Expected Medicare Costs for Participants in the PACE Demonstration," paper presented at the PACE annual demonstration meeting Baltimore, Maryland, 1993, cited in Robyn I. Stone, "Integration of Home- and Community-based Services: Issues for the 1990s," in Daniel M. Fox and Carol Raphael, eds., *Home-based Care for a New Century* (Malden, Mass.: Blackwell Publishers, 1997), pp. 71–98.

52. John K. Shen, "Program of All-Inclusive Care for the Elderly (PACE)," from session 9 of "Long-term Care: A Workshop for Senior State and Local Health Officials," Miami, 1993, cited in Stone, "Integration of Home- and Community-based Services."

53. Branch, Coulam, and Zimmerman, "The PACE Evaluation."

54. Robert L. Kane et al., "S/HMOs, the Second Generation: Building on the Experience of the First Social Health Maintenance Organization Demonstrations," *Journal of the American Geriatrics Society* 45, no. 1, January 1997): 101–7.

55. Booth et al., "Integration of Acute and Long-term Care."

56. Catherine Hawes, Judith B. Wildfire, and Linda J. Lux, *Regulation of Board and Care Homes: Results of a Survey in the 50 States and the District of Columbia* (Washington, D.C.: American Association of Retired Persons, 1993).

57. Robert Newcomer, Keren Brown Wilson, and Paul Lee, "Residential Care for the Frail Elderly: State Innovations in Placement, Financing, and Governance," In Robert J. Newcomer, Anne M. Wilkinson, and M. Powell Lawton, eds., *Annual Review of Gerontology and Geriatrics* 16, pp. 162–82.

58. William D. Spector, James D. Reschovsky, and Joel W. Cohen, "Appropriate Placement of Nursing-Home Residents in Lower Levels of Care," *Milbank Quarterly* 74, no. 1 (Spring 1996) 139–60.

59. Rosalie A. Kane, "Boundaries of Home Care: Can a Home-Care Approach Transform LTC Institutions?" in Fox and Raphael, *Home-based Care for a New Century*, pp. 23–46.

60. Alan Friedlob, "The Use of Physical Restraints in Nursing Homes and the Allocation of Nursing Resources," Ph.D. diss., University of Minnesota, 1993, cited in Kane, "Boundaries of Home Care."

61. Sylvia Sherwood and John N. Morris, "The Pennsylvania Domiciliary Care Experiment: Impact on Quality Life," *American Journal of Public Health* 73, no. 6 (June 1983): 646–53; Rosalie A. Kane et al., "Adult Foster Care for the Elderly in Oregon: A Mainstream Alternative to Nursing Homes?" *American Journal of Public Health* 81, no. 9 (September 1991): 1113–20; Robert Newcomer, Steven Preston, and Sue Roderick, "Assisted Living and Nursing Unit Use among Continuing Care Retirement Community Residents," *Research on Aging* 17, no. 9 (June 1995): 149–67.

62. Kane, "Boundaries of Home Care."

63. Robert L. Mollica and Kimberly I. Snow, *State Assisted Living Policy: 1996*, report prepared under contract DHHS–100–94–0044 for the U.S. Department of Health and Human Services, 1996.

64. Kane, "Boundaries of Home Care."

65. Nathan L. Linsk et al., *Wages for Caring: Compensating Family Care of the Elderly* (New York: Praeger, 1992).

66. Sharon Keigher and Robyn I. Stone, "Payment for Care in the US: A Very Mixed Policy Bag," paper presented at the International Meeting on Payment for Dependent Care, Vienna, July 4–7, 1992, cited in Stone, "Integration of Home- and Community-based Services."

67. Ulrike Shneider, "Germany's New Long-term Care Policy: Profile and Assessment of the Social Dependency Insurance," policy paper no. 5, American Institute for Contemporary German Studies, Johns Hopkins University, 1997.

68. Penny H. Feldman, "Labor Market Issues in Home Care," in Fox and Raphael, *Home-based Care for a New Century*, pp. 155–83.

69. Friedland, *Facing the Costs of Long-term Care*; Joshua M. Wiener, Laurel Hixon Illston, and Raymond J. Hanley, *Sharing the Burden: Strategies for Public and Private Long-term Care Insurance* (Washington, D.C.: Brookings Institution, 1994); Pepper Commission, *A Call for Action: Final Report*, S.Prt. 101–114, prepared by the staff of the U.S. Bipartisan Commission on Comprehensive Health Care (Washington, D.C.: U.S. Government Printing Office, 1990).

CHAPTER 4

1. U.S. Congress, Senate, Special Committee on Aging, *Developments in Aging: 1993*, vol. I, S. Rept. 103–403, 103d Cong., 2d sess., October 7, 1994.

2. Katherine R. Levit et al., "National Health Expenditures in 1997: More Slow Growth," *Health Affairs* 17, no. 6 (November/December 1998): 99–110.

3. Congressional Budget Office, *The Economic and Budget Outlook: Fiscal Years 2000–2009* (Washington, D.C.: U.S. Government Printing Office, 1999).

4. U.S. Department of Health and Human Services, Health Care Financing Administration, "Medicare and Medicaid Statistical Supplement, 1998," *Health Care Financing Review*, statistical supplement, 1998.

5. Congressional Budget Office, *Projections of Expenditures for Long-Term Care Services for the Elderly* (Washington, D.C.: U.S. Government Printing Office, 1999).

6. Public Law 105–33, The Balanced Budget Act of 1997.

7. Frank B. Hobbs, "65+ in the United States," U.S. Department of Commerce, Bureau of the Census, *Current Population Reports*, Special Studies, P23–190 (Washington, D.C.: U.S. Government Printing Office, 1996).

8. Edward L. Schneider and Jack M. Guralnik, "The Aging of America: Impact on Health Care Costs," *Journal of the American Medical Association* 263, no. 17 (May 2, 1990): 2335–40.

9. Congressional Budget Office, *Projections of Expenditures for Long-Term Care Services for the Elderly*.

10. See, for example, the findings of the Bipartisan Commission on Entitlement and Tax Reform, issued in 1994.

11. Daniel Callahan, *Setting Limits: Medical Goals in an Aging Society* (New York: Simon and Schuster, 1987), p. 20.

12. Hobbs, "65+ in the United States."

13. *Old Age in the 21st Century* (Washington, D.C.: National Academy on Aging, Syracuse University, 1994).

14. A. P. Polednak, "Projected Numbers of Cancers Diagnosed in the U.S. Elderly Population, 1990 through 2030," *American Journal of Public Health* 84, no. 8 (August 1994): 1313–16.

15. Christine K. Cassel, Mark A. Rudberg, and S. Jay Olshansky, "The Price of Success: Health Care in an Aging Society," *Health Affairs* 11, no. 2 (Summer 1992): 87–99.

16. Congressional Budget Office, *Projections of Expenditures for Long-Term Care Services for the Elderly*.

17. See, e.g., Kenneth G. Manton, Larry S. Corder, and Eric Stallard, "Chronic Disability in Elderly United States Populations: 1982–1994," *Proceedings of the National Academy of Sciences, USA* 94 (1997): 2593–98; Kenneth G. Manton, Larry S. Corder, and Eric Stallard, "Estimates of Change in Chronic Disability

and Institutional Incidence and Prevalence Rates in the U.S. Elderly Population from the 1982, 1984, and 1989 National Long Term Care Survey," *Journal of Gerontology: Social Sciences* 48, no. 4 (July 1993): S153–66.

18. See, e.g., U. S. General Accounting Office, *Health Care Spending Control: The Experience of France, Germany, and Japan* (Washington, D.C.: U.S. Government Printing Office, 1991).

19. D. N. Mendelson, and William B. Schwartz, "The Effects of Aging and Population Growth on Health Care Costs," *Health Affairs* 12, no. 1 (Spring 1993): 119–25.

20. See Ross H. Arnett III et al., "Projections of Health Care Spending to 1990," *Health Care Financing Review* 7, no. 3 (Spring 1986): 1–36; Thomas E. Getzen, "Population Aging and the Growth of Health Expenditures," *Journal of Gerontology* 47, no. 3 (May 1992): S98–104; Martin Pfaff, "Differences in Health Care Spending across Countries: Statistical Evidence," *Journal of Health Politics, Policy, and Law* 15, no. 1 (Spring 1990): 1–67; and Sally T. Sonnefeld et al., "Projections of National Health Expenditures through the Year 2000," *Health Care Financing Review* 13, no. 1 (Fall 1991): 1–27.

21. Senate Special Committee on Aging, *Developments in Aging*.

22. George J. Schieber, Jean-Pierre Poullier, and Leslie M. Greenwald, "U.S. Health Expenditure Performance: An International Comparison and Update," *Health Care Financing Review* 13, no. 4 (Summer 1992): 1–87.

23. Henry J. Aaron and William B. Schwartz, *The Painful Prescription: Rationing Hospital Care* (Washington, D.C.: Brookings Institution, 1984).

24. Deborah J. Chollet, *Health Care Spending by the Elderly Population: A Comparison of Selected Countries and the United States*, research report no. 91–4, Center for Risk Management and Insurance Research, Georgia State University, Atlanta, 1991.

25. Deborah J. Chollet, "The Impact of Aging on National Health Care Spending: Cross-National Estimates for Selected Countries," paper delivered at the annual meeting of the American Risk and Insurance Association, Washington, D.C., August 18, 1992.

26. Reiner Leidel, "Effects of Population Aging on Health Care Expenditure and Financing: Some Illustrations," in Daniel Callahan, Ruud H. J. Ter Meulen, and Eva Topinková, eds., *A World Growing Old: The Coming Health Care Challenges* (Washington, D.C.: Georgetown University Press, 1995), p. 60.

27. The term "voodoo demographics" was coined in James H. Schulz, Allan Borowski, and William H. Crown, *Economics of Population Aging: The "Graying" of Australia, Japan, and the United States* (New York: Auburn House, 1991).

28. The term "apocalyptic demography" was coined in Ann Robertson, "The Politics of Alzheimer's Disease: A Case Study in Apocalyptic Demography," in Meredith Minkler and Carroll L. Estes, eds., *Critical Perspectives on Aging: The Political and Moral Economy of Growing Old* (Amityville, N.Y.: Baywood Publishing Company, Inc., 1991), pp. 135–50.

29. J. Schulte, "Terminal Patients Deplete Medicare, Greenspan Says," *Dallas Morning News*, April 26, 1983, p. 1.

30. W. Slater, "Latest Lamm Remark Angers the Elderly," *Arizona Daily Star*, March 29, 1984, p. 1.

31. Richard D. Lamm, "A Debate: Medicare in 2020," in *Medicare Reform and the Baby Boom Generation*, edited proceedings of the second annual conference of Americans for Generational Equity, Washington, D.C., April 30–May 1, 1987, pp. 77–88; Richard D. Lamm, "Columbus and Copernicus: New Wine in Old Wineskins," *Mount Sinai Journal of Medicine* 56, no. 1 (1989): 1–10; Richard D. Lamm, "The Crime of the Century," *Christian Science Monitor*, July 8, 1996, p. 18.

32. See, e.g., Norman Daniels, *Am I My Parents' Keeper? An Essay on Justice between the Young and the Old* (New York: Oxford University Press, 1988); Paul T. Menzel, *Strong Medicine: The Ethical Rationing of Health Care* (New York: Oxford University Press, 1990).

33. For example, Timothy M. Smeeding et al., eds., *Should Medical Care Be Rationed by Age?* (Totowa, N.J.: Rowman & Littlefield, 1987).

34. Callahan, *Setting Limits*, p. 171.

35. See, e.g., Robert H. Binstock and Stephen G. Post, eds., *Too Old for Health Care? Controversies in Medicine, Law, Economics, and Ethics* (Baltimore: Johns Hopkins University Press, 1991); Robert L. Barry and Gerard V. Bradley, eds., *Set No Limits: A Rebuttal to Daniel Callahan's Proposal to Limit Health Care for the Elderly* (Urbana, Ill.: University of Illinois Press, 1991); Paul Homer and Martha Holstein, eds., *A Good Old Age? The Paradox of Setting Limits* (New York: Simon and Schuster, 1990).

36. Daniel Callahan, "Setting Limits: A Response," *Gerontologist* 34, no. 3 (June 1994): 393–98; Callahan, Ter Meulen, and Topinková, *A World Growing Old*.

37. James D. Lubitz and Gerald F. Riley, "Trends in Medicare Payments in the Last Year of Life," *New England Journal of Medicine* 328, no. 15 (April 15, 1993): 1092–96.

38. National Center for Health Statistics, *Births, Marriages, Divorces, and Deaths for August 1993*, Monthly Vital Statistics Report 42, no. 8 (Hyattsville, Md.: U.S. Public Health Service, 1994).

39. James D. Lubitz and Ronald Prihoda, "The Use and Costs of Medicare Services in the Last Two Years of Life," *Health Care Financing Review* 5, no. 3 (Spring 1984): 117–31; Anne A. Scitovsky, "'The High Cost of Dying': What Do the Data Show?" *Milbank Memorial Fund Quarterly/Health and Society* 62, no. 4 (1984): 591–608; Anne A. Scitovsky, "Medical Care in the Last Twelve Months of Life: The Relation between Age, Functional Status, and Medical Care Expenditures," *Milbank Memorial Fund Quarterly/Health and Society* 66, no. 4 (1988): 640–60.

40. U.S. Department of Health and Human Services, "Medicare and Medicaid Statistical Supplement, 1998."

41. Ibid.

42. Ezekiel J. Emanuel and Linda L. Emanuel, "The Economics of Dying: The Illusion of Cost Savings at the End of Life," *New England Journal of Medicine* 330, no. 8 (February 24, 1994): 540–44.

43. See *Seven Deadly Myths: Uncovering the Facts about the High Cost of the Last Year of Life* (Washington, D.C.: Alliance for Aging Research, 1997).

44. Richard H. Fortinsky, Robert H. Binstock, and Alfred Rimm, "Some Age-based Rationing Scenarios: How Much Money Would Be Saved?" paper delivered at the 122d annual meeting of the American Public Health Association, Washington, D.C., November 2, 1994.

45. Robert Pear, "House Panel Votes Changes to Try to Keep Medicare Solvent," *New York Times*, June 10, 1997, p. A19.

46. Robert L. Kane and Rosalie A. Kane, "Effects of the Clinton Health Reform on Older Persons and Their Families: A Health Care Systems Perspective," *Gerontologist* 34, no. 5 (October 1994): 598–605.

47. Lyle Nelson et al., "Access to Care in Medicare HMOs, 1996," *Health Affairs* 16, no. 2 (March/April 1997): 148–56; Peter W. Shaughnessy, "Home Health Care Outcomes under Capitated and Fee-for-Service Payment," *Health Care Financing Review* 16, no. 1 (Fall 1994): 187–222; John E. Ware et al., "Differences in 4-Year Health Outcomes for Elderly and Poor, Chronically-Ill Patients Treated in HMO and Fee-for-Service Systems: Results from the Medical Outcomes Study," *Journal of the American Medical Association* 276, no. 13 (October 2, 1996): 1039–47.

48. Joshua M. Wiener and Jason Skaggs, *Current Approaches to Integrating Acute and Long-Term Care Financing and Services* (Washington, D.C.: Public Policy Institute, American Association of Retired Persons, 1995).

49. U.S. Department of Commerce, Bureau of the Census, "Poverty in the United States: 1995," *Current Population Reports*, Consumer Income, P60–194 (Washington, D.C.: U.S. Government Printing Office, 1996).

50. Stephanie A. Robert and James S. House, "Socioeconomic Status and Health over the Life Course," in Ronald A. Abeles, Helen C. Gift, and Marcia G. Ory, eds., *Aging and Quality of Life* (New York: Springer Publishing Company, 1994), pp. 253–74.

51. R. R. Shield, "Managing the Care of Nursing Home Residents: The Challenge of Integration," in R. J. Newcomer and A. M. Wilkinson, eds., *Focus on Managed Care and Quality Assurance: Integrating Acute and Chronic Care*, Annual Review of Gerontology and Geriatrics 16 (New York: Springer Publishing Company, 1996), pp. 60–77.

52. David Mechanic, "Managed Care: Rhetoric and Realities," *Inquiry* 31, no. 2 (1994): 124–28.

53. See Robert H. Binstock and William D. Spector, "Five Priority Areas for Research on Long-Term Care," *Health Services Research* 32, no. 5 (December 1997): 715–30.

54. See Newcomer and Wilkinson, *Focus on Managed Care and Quality Assurance*; T. Franklin Williams and Helena Temkin-Greener, "Older People, Dependency, and Trends in Supportive Care," in Robert H. Binstock, Leighton E. Cluff, and Otto von Mering, eds., *The Future of Long-Term Care: Social and Policy Issues* (Baltimore: Johns Hopkins University Press, 1996), pp. 51–74.

55. See D. Balaban, N. McCall, and L. Paringer, *Quality of Care in the Arizona Long-term Care System (ALTCS): A Study of Quality Indicators among Nursing Home Residents* (San Francisco: Laguna Research Associates, 1994); Laurence G. Branch, Robert F. Coulam, and Yvonne A. Zimmerman, "The PACE Evaluation: Initial Findings," *Gerontologist* 35, no. 3 (June 1995): 349–59; Charlene Harrington and Robert J. Newcomer, "A Comparison of S/HMO Disenrollees and Continuing Members," *Inquiry* 30, no. 4 (1993): 429–40; Robert L. Kane, Laurel Hixon Illston, and Nancy A. Miller, "Qualitative Analysis of the Program of All-Inclusive Care for the Elderly (PACE)," *Gerontologist* 32, no. 6 (December 1992): 771–80; Kenneth G. Manton et al., "Social/Health Maintenance Organization and Fee-for-Service Health Outcomes over Time," *Health Care Financing Review* 15, no. 2 (Winter 1993): 173–202; Joshua M. Wiener, "Managed Care and Long-Term Care: The Integration of Financing and Services," *Generations* 20, no. 2 (Summer 1996): 47–52.

56. Lester C. Thurow, "The Birth of a Revolutionary Class," *New York Times Magazine*, May 19, 1996, pp. 46–47.

57. Gerdt Sundstrom, "Ageing Is Riskier Than It Looks," *Age and Ageing* 24, no. 5 (1995): 373–74.

58. Robert H. Binstock and Christine L. Day, "Aging and Politics," in Robert H. Binstock and Linda K. George, eds., *Handbook of Aging and the Social Sciences*, 4th ed. (San Diego: Academic Press, 1995), pp. 362–87.

59. Ibid.

60. Robert H. Binstock, "The 1996 Election: Older Voters and Implications for Policies on Aging," *Gerontologist* 37, no. 1 (February 1997): 15–19; Robert H. Binstock, "Older Voters and the 1992 Presidential Election," *Gerontologist* 32, no. 5 (October 1992): 601–6; Binstock and Day, "Aging and Politics."

61. See "Portrait of the Electorate," *New York Times*, November 10, 1996, p. A16.

62. See transcript of the first televised debate between Clinton and Dole, printed in *New York Times*, October 8, 1996, pp. A14–17; excerpts from the second televised debate between Clinton and Dole, printed in *New York Times*, October 18, 1996, pp. C22–23.

63. "Portrait of the Electorate."

64. Herbert A. Simon, "Human Nature in Politics: The Dialogue of Psychology with Political Science," *American Political Science Review* 79, no. 2 (June 1985): 293–304.

65. Binstock and Day, "Aging and Politics."

66. Robert H. Binstock, "Changing Criteria in Old-Age Programs: The Introduction of Economic Status and Need for Services," *Gerontologist* 34, no. 6 (December 1994): 726–30.

67. Robert H. Binstock, "The Old-Age Lobby in a New Political Era," in Robert B. Hudson, ed., *The Future of Age-Based Public Policy* (Baltimore: Johns Hopkins University Press, 1997).

68. See, e.g., Neal E. Cutler, "Demographic, Social-Psychological, and Political Factors in the Politics of Aging: A Foundation for Research in 'Political Gerontology,'" *American Political Science Review* 71, no. 4 (December 1977): 1011–25.

CHAPTER 5

1. U.S. Department of Commerce, Bureau of the Census, *Statistical Abstract of the United States 1995* (Washington, D.C.: U.S. Government Printing Office, 1995), Table 24.

2. Frank B. Hobbs and Bonnie L. Damon, *65+ in the United States*, U.S. Department of Commerce, Bureau of the Census, *Current Population Reports*, Special Studies, P23-190 (Washington, D.C.: U.S. Government Printing Office, 1996), Table 4–4.

3. Susan Grad, "Income of the Population 55 or Older," publication no. 13–11871, Social Security Administration, January 1996, Table 1.7.

4. EBRI Notes, No. 1, *Women and Saving: Results of the 1998 Women's Retirement Confidence Survey*, Employee Benefit Research Institute, February, 1999.

5. Marjorie Honig, "Retirement Expectations: Differences by Race, Ethnicity, and Gender," *Gerontologist* 36, no. 3 (1996): 373–82.

6. Francine Blau and Lawrence M. Kahn, "Swimming Upstream: Trends in the Gender Wage Differential in the 1980's," *Journal of Labor Economics* 15, no. 1, part 1 (1997): 1–42.

7. U.S. Department of Commerce, Bureau of the Census, *Statistical Abstract of the United States 1995*, Table 638.

8. U.S. Department of Commerce, *Statistical Abstract of the United States 1996*, Table 637.

9. U.S. Department of Health and Human Services, Health Care Financing Administration, Medicare Managed Care Operational Policy Letter no. 49, February 12, 1997; *Aging News Alert* no. 97–6, Silver Spring, Md., March 31, 1997.

10. "Older Women Are Less Likely to Receive Chemotherapy and Radiation Treatment after Breast Surgery," *Research Activities* no. 201, U.S. Department of

Health and Human Services, Agency for Health Care Policy and Research, February 1997.

11. Council on Ethical and Judicial Affairs, American Medical Association, "Gender Disparities in Clinical Decision Making," *Journal of the American Medical Association* 266, no. 4 (July 24/31, 1991): 559–62.

12. Robert N. Butler et al., *Aging and Mental Health: Positive Psychosocial and Biomedical Approaches*, 5th ed. (Englewood Cliffs, N.J.: Prentice Hall, 1998), Chapter 7.

13. U.S. Department of Commerce, *Statistical Abstract 1995*, Table 748.

14. Ibid.

15. U.S. Department of Commerce, Bureau of the Census, *Persons of Hispanic Origin in the United States*, CP–3–3, August 1993; U.S. Department of Commerce, Bureau of the Census, *Asians and Pacific Islanders in the United States*, CP–3–5, August 1993; U.S. Department of Commerce, Bureau of the Census, *Characteristics of the Black Population*, CP–3–6, October 1994.

16. U.S. Department of Commerce, *Statistical Abstract 1995*, Table 748.

17. Ibid., Table 24.

18. U.S. Department of Commerce, *Statistical Abstract 1995*, Table 748; Butler et al., *Aging and Mental Health*, Chapter 1.

19. Hobbs and Damon, *65+ in the United States*, pp. 4–25.

20. Ibid., pp. 4–26.

21. Butler et al., *Aging and Mental Health,* Chapter 1.

22. Mae Thamer, Chrisitan Richard, Adrianne Waldman Casebeer, and Nancy Fox Ray, "Health Insurance Coverage among Foreign-Born Residents: The Impact of Race, Ethnicity, and Length of Residence," *American Journal of Public Health* 87, no. 1 (January 1997): 96–102.

23. D. M. Carlisle, B. D. Leake, and M. F. Shapiro, "Racial and Ethnic Disparities in the Use of Cardiovascular Procedures: Association with Type of Health Insurance," *American Journal of Public Health* 87, no. 2 (February 1997): 263–67.

24. Robin A. Cohen and Joan F. Van Nostrand, "Trends in the Health of Older Americans: United States, 1994," National Center for Health Statistics, *Vital and Health Statistics* 3, no. 30 (April 1995): 307, Table 4.

25. National Center for Health Statistics, *Vital and Health Statistics* 45, no. 11, Supplement 2 (June 12, 1997).

26. U.S. Department of Health and Human Services, Agency for Health Care Policy and Research, *Research Activities* 200 (January 1997): 13.

27. Diane Makuc, Virginia M. Freid, and P. Ellen Parsons, "Health Insurance and Cancer Screening among Women," *Advance Data from Vital and Health Statistics of the Centers for Disease Control and Prevention, National Center for Health Statistics* 254 (August 3, 1994).

28. Judith Fields and Edward N. Wolff, "Gender Wage Differential, Affirmative Action, and Employment Growth on the Industry Level," Working Paper no. 186, Jerome Levy Economics Institute, Annandale-on-Hudson, N.Y., March 1997.

29. Patrick A. Simmons, *Housing Statistics of the United States* (Lanham, Md.: Bernan Press, 1997), Preface; John Yinger, "Evidence on Discrimination in Consumer Markets," *Journal of Economic Perspectives* 12, no. 2 (Spring 1998): 23–40; Helen F. Ladd, "Evidence on Discrimination in Mortgage Lending," *Journal of Economic Perspectives* 12, no. 2 (Spring 1988): 41–62.

30. Tracy L. Skaer et al., "Breast Cancer Mortality Declining but Screening among Subpopulations Lags" (letter), *American Journal of Public Health* 88, no. 2 (February 1998): 307–8.

31. Marilyn Moon, Barbara Gage, and Allison Evans, "An Examination of Key Medicare Provisions in the Balanced Budget Act of 1997," Commonwealth Fund, New York, September 1997.

32. "Survey Finds More Rapid Health Care Cost Growth in 1999," AOL News @aol.com, January 6, 1999, citing the Towers Perrin 1999 Health Cost Survey.

33. Personal communication with Stanford Roman, dean, Sophie M. Davis School of Biomedical Education, City University of New York, February 9, 1999.

34. U.S. Department of Commerce, Bureau of the Census, *Statistical Abstract of the United States 1997*, Tables 243 and 245.

35. "Medicare and Medicaid: Many Eligible People Not Enrolled in Qualified Medicare Beneficiary Program," GAO/HEHS–94–52, U.S. General Accounting Office, January 1994.

CHAPTER 6

1. Eric R. Kingson, B. A. Hirshorn, and John M. Cornman, *Ties that Bind: The Interdependence of Generations* (Cabin John, Md.: Seven Locks Press, 1986); Fay Lomax Cook and Edith J. Barrett, *Support for the American Welfare State: The Views of Congress and the Public* (New York: Columbia University Press, 1992); Fay Lomax Cook et al., "The Salience of Intergenerational Equity in Canada and the United States," in Theodore R. Marmor, Timothy M. Smeeding, and Vernon L. Greene, eds., *Economic Security and Intergenerational Justice* (Washington, D.C.: Urban Institute Press, 1994), pp. 91–129; Fay Lomax Cook, "Public Support for Programs for Older Americans: Continuities amidst Threats of Discontinuities," in Vern Bengtson, ed., *Continuities and Discontinuities in Adulthood and Aging* (New York: Springer, 1996), pp. 327–46; Alan Walker, ed. *The New Generational Contract* (London: VCL Press, 1996); Virginia P. Reno and Robert B. Friedland, "Strong Support but Low Confidence: What Explains the Contradiction?" in Eric R. Kingson and James H. Schulz, eds. *Social Security in the 21st Century* (New York: Oxford University Press, 1996), pp. 178–94.

2. An example of this type of reasoning can be found in Vern L. Bengtson, "Is the 'Contract Across Generations' Changing? Effect of Population Aging on Obligations and Expectations Across Age Groups," in Vern L. Bengtson and W.

Andrew Achenbaum, eds., *The Changing Contract across Generations* (New York: Aldine de Gruyter, 1993), pp. 3–23.

3. Robert H. Binstock, "Transcending Intergenerational Equity," in Marmor, Smeeding, and Greene, *Economic Security and Intergenerational Justice*, pp. 155–68.

4. Subrata N. Chakravaty and Katherine Weisman, "Consuming Our Children?" *Forbes*, November 14, 1988, pp. 222–32.

5. Samuel H. Preston, "Children and the Elderly in the U.S.," *Scientific American*, December 1984, pp. 44–49. Preston argued that since the socioeconomic situation was improving for the elderly at the same time that it was becoming worse for children, it followed that the former was the cause of the latter.

6. Robert J. Samuelson, "The Withering Freedom to Govern: Soaring Costs for Elderly Curb President's Choices," *Washington Post*, March 5, 1978, pp. C1, C5.

7. Lester C. Thurow, "The Birth of a Revolutionary Class," *New York Times Magazine*, May 19, 1996, pp. 46–47.

8. The ratios vary, depending on the projection assumptions chosen and the start/end years used. The numbers in the text are from a Social Security Trustees' annual report and were published in Joseph F. Quinn, *Entitlements and the Federal Budget: Securing Our Future* (Washington, D.C.: National Academy on Aging, 1996).

9. For a good explanation of this basic fact, see Donald O. Cowgill, *Aging around the World* (Belmont, Calif.: Wadsworth Publishing, 1986).

10. See, for example, Ben J. Wattenberg, *The Birth Dearth* (New York: Pharos Books, 1987).

11. Estimates of economist Robert Eisner, reported in Richard C. Leone, "Why Boomers Don't Spell Bust," *American Prospect*, January-February 1997, pp. 68–71.

12. James H. Schulz, Allan Borowski, and William H. Crown, *Economics of Population Aging: The "Graying" of Australia, Japan, and the United States* (New York: Auburn House, 1991). See also Donald J. Adamchak, "Demographic Aging in the Industrialized World: A Rising Burden?" *Generations* (Winter 1993), pp. 6–9.

13. The basic projections were carried out using a real growth rate of 3.0 percent. Sensitivity testing was then carried out using lower and higher rates, demonstrating that burdens are very sensitive to economic growth rates but not to assumptions regarding population growth rates or labor force participation rates.

14. Most of Easterlin's many research studies on this topic are summarized in Richard A. Easterlin, "Implications of Demographic Patterns," in Robert H. Binstock and Linda K. George, eds., *Handbook of Aging and the Social Sciences*, 4th ed. (San Diego: Academic Press, 1995), pp. 73–93.

15. Population growth was a part of the first neoclassical growth models (e.g., Harrod-Domar) and the discussions of "optimal growth rates." But the main focus of these discussion was about saving/capital formation. A good survey of the literature can be found in Jack Habib, "Population Aging and the Economy," in Robert H. Binstock and Linda K. George, *Handbook of Aging and the Social Sciences*, 3d ed. (San Diego: Academic Press, 1990), pp. 328–45.

16. Lawrence H. Thompson, "Private and Public Aspects of Pension Management," *Asia and Pacific News Sheet* 36, no. 3 (September 1996): 18–25.

17. Martin S. Feldstein, "Social Security, Induced Retirement, and Aggregate Capital Accumulation," *Journal of Political Economy* 82, no. 5 (September-October 1974): 905–26. The errors were reported by Dean R. Leimer and Selig D. Lesnoy in "Social Security and Private Saving: New Time Series Evidence," *Journal of Political Economy* 90, no. 3 (June 1982): 606–29. An excellent summary of the literature on this controversy is in Congressional Budget Office, *Assessing the Decline in the National Saving Rate* (Washington, D.C.: U.S. Government Printing Office, 1993).

18. See, for example, pp. 93–97 in *Ageing in OECD Countries*, Social Policy Studies no. 20 (Paris: Organization for Economic Cooperation and Development, 1996).

19. See the discussion of the literature in Richard Disney, *Can We Afford to Grow Older?* (Cambridge, Mass.: MIT Press, 1996).

20. Speech given at conference titled, "Coming of Age: The Economic and Political Impact of an Aging Society," sponsored by the World Affairs Council of Philadelphia, April 3, 1997. In his speech Volcker did make a passing reference to other factors affecting growth, but his main concern was increasing saving.

21. Bipartisan Commission on Entitlement and Tax Reform, *Interim Report to the President*, Washington, D.C., August 1994. Kerrey and Danforth focus their remarks in both the interim and final report on saving and investment. No other growth factors are seriously considered.

22. *Economic Report of the President, 1997* (Washington, D.C.: U.S. Government Printing Office, 1997).

23. James M. Buchanan, "We Should Save More In Our Own Economic Interest," in Lee M. Cohen, ed., *Justice across Generations: What Does It Mean?* (Washington, D.C.: American Association of Retired Persons, 1993), pp. 269–82.

24. Robert A. Blecker, review of *Macroeconomic Policy after the Conservative Era: Studies in Investment, Saving and Finance* by Gerald A. Epstein and Herbert M. Gintis (Cambridge: Cambridge University Press, 1996), *Journal of Economic Literature* 35 (March 1997): 131–32.

25. Edward M. Gramlich, "How Does Social Security Affect the Economy?" in Kingson and Schulz, *Social Security in the 21st Century*, pp. 147–55. The neoclassical model Gramlich refers to is stated in Robert M. Solow, "A Contribution to the Theory of Economic Growth," *Quarterly Journal of Economics* (February 1956): 65–94.

26. Martin Feldstein, "Transition to a Fully Funded Pension System: Five Economic Issues," NBER Working Paper no. 6149, National Bureau of Economic Research, Cambridge, Mass., 1997.

27. Solow's modeling was much more "general" than is sometimes thought. For example, some attempt is made to take account not just of physical capital and the amount of labor but also of changes in the quality of labor (due to better

education, health, etc.). The literature on technological change is large. See, for example, the review article by Wesley Cohen and Richard Levin, "Empirical Studies of Innovation and Market Structure," in R. Schmalensee and Robert D. Willig, eds., *Handbook of Industrial Organization* (New York: North Holland, 1989), pp. 1059–1107.

28. David M. Gordon, "Putting the Horse (Back) before the Cart: Disentangling the Macro Relationship between Investment and Saving," in Epstein and Gintis, *Macroeconomic Policy after the Conservative Era*, pp. 57–108.

Some prominent economists argue, in fact, that it is sometimes not so much a shortage of saving in the United States that has limited investment but a shortage of investment opportunities in the face of economic uncertainty, low profits, or reduced market expectations. Nobel laureate Franco Modigliani, for example, asserts that "when a country needs capital to drive rapid growth, capital will be forthcoming." Franco Modigliani, "The Key to Saving Is Growth, not Thrift," *Challenge* 30 (May-June 1987): 24–29.

29. Bryn Davies, *Better Pensions for All* (London: Institute for Public Policy Research, 1993).

30. "Introduction," in Epstein and Gintis, eds., *Macroeconomic Policy after the Conservative Era*.

31. See, for example, the findings of V. Bhaskar and Andrew Glyn, "Investment and Profitability: The Evidence from the Advanced Capitalist Countries," in Epstein and Gintis, *Macroeconomic Policy after the Conservative Era*, pp. 175–96.

32. Richard Nelson, "How New Is New Growth Theory?" *Challenge* 40, no. 5 (September-October 1997): 29–58.

33. Jane Katz, "The Joy of Consumption," *Federal Bank of Boston Regional Review* 7, no. 1 (Winter 1997): 12–17.

34. W. C. Dunkelberg, "Analyzing Consumer Spending and Debt," *Business Economics* 24, no. 3 (July 1989): 17–22.

35. "Give Card Companies Some Credit for Delinquency," *USA Today*, September 24, 1997.

36. Dagobert L. Brito and Peter R. Hartley, "Consumer Rationality and Credit Cards," *Journal of Political Economy* 103, no. 2 (April 1995): 400–433.

37. Credit is not necessarily used for consumption expenditures. Household appliances, cars, and housing are often viewed as investment (depending on how they are used).

38. A book on saving by a prominent economist working in the area has only this to say about credit: "Economic [tax] incentives combined with appealing market strategies to create a booming demand for credit. In the absence of tax breaks [that were repealed by Congress], marketing will become more problematic, and the credit industry will probably decline." B. Douglas Bernheim, *The Vanishing Nest Egg: Reflections on Saving in America* (New York: Priority Press Publications, 1991), p. 116. Given contemporary events, it is difficult to agree with Bernheim's

prediction. More important, there is absolutely no discussion in the Bernheim book about how the accessibility of credit cards may have negatively influenced household saving in the United States. In his chapter "Why Do Americans Save So Little?" there is only one sentence that mentions credit: "For example, the development of a consumer credit industry may tempt individuals to invade certain mentally 'reserved' accounts in order to spend" (p. 71).

39. "Credit Card Debt May Present Growing Problem," *USA Today*, December 17, 1997, p. B–1. In 1996, the average amount of credit card debt for *all* households (i.e., those with revolving debt and those without) was $2,500. David R. Francis, "Easy Credit Fuels Rise in Bankruptcy," *Christian Science Monitor*, April 11, 1997, pp. 1, 8.

40. Ibid.

41. James Medoff and Andrew Harless, "Missing the Turn," *Challenge* 40, no.2 (March-April 1997): 6–12.

42. The implications of the rising rate of bankruptcies are not entirely clear. As pointed out by Edgar Fiedler, "the rising rate of bankruptcies, which has been going on not just in recent years but for decades, is, I strongly believe, due almost entirely to changes in bankruptcy law (making it an easier process), rather than to rising incidence of consumers taking on an excessive debt burden." Edgar Fiedler, personal correspondence with author, January 1998.

43. See, for example, the discussion of this point by Lester Thurow, "Tax Wealth, Not Income," *New York Times Magazine*, April 11, 1976, p. 32.

44. World Bank, *Averting the Old Age Crisis* (Oxford: Oxford University Press, 1994).

45. Arthur Okun, *Equality and Efficiency: The Big Trade-off* (Washington, D.C.: Brookings Institution, 1975).

46. Alfred Marshall, *Principles of Economics: An Introductory Volume* (New York: Macmillian, 1948).

47. An increasing number of economists argue that investment should be defined explicitly to include expenditures on research and "human capital."

48. "Silicon Valley," survey, *Economist*, March 29, 1997.

49. Ibid.

50. Richard R. Nelson, *The Sources of Economic Growth* (Cambridge, Mass.: Harvard University Press, 1996). With regard to the development of new technology, Nelson points out that there are four aspects of the process that are suppressed or ignored in most economic models: (1) the uncertainty involved; (2) the fact that there are many different firms in various industries exploring opportunities for research and development; (3) the fact that "when R & D is done competitively, the regime of property rights in technology significantly influences, and warps R & D incentives" (p. 32); and (4) the documented fact that in many technologies, learning by doing is an important complement to R & D.

51. Theodore W. Schultz, *Investing in People: The Economics of Population Quality* (Los Angeles: UCLA Press, 1981). See also Schultz's *Restoring Economic*

Equilibrium: Human Capital in the Modernizing Economy (Oxford: Basil Blackwell, 1990).

52. "Education and the Wealth of Nations," *Economist*, March 29, 1997, pp. 15–16.

53. Robert Eisner, "U.S. National Saving and Budget Deficits," in Epstein and Gintis, *Macroeconomic Policy after the Conservative Era*, pp. 109–42.

54. Schultz, *Restoring Economic Equalibriums*.

55. Israel M. Kirzner, "Entrepreneurial Discovery and the Competitive Market Process: An Austrian Approach," *Journal of Economic Literature* 35 (March 1997): 60–85.

56. Thus, a recent study of growth determinants states: "We conclude that differences in levels of economic success across countries are driven primarily by the institutions and government policies (or infrastructure) that frame the economic environment in which people produce and transact." Robert E. Hall and Charles I. Jones, "Levels of Economic Activity across Countries," *American Economic Review, Proceedings* 87, no. 2 (May 1997): 173–80.

57. Disney, *Can We Afford to Grow Older?*

58. Michael Cichon, "The Ageing Debate in Social Security: Barking up the Wrong Tree?" in *Protecting Retirement Incomes: Options for Reform*, ISSA Studies and Research no. 37 (Geneva: International Social Security Association, 1996), pp. 83–99.

59. Peter G. Peterson, *On Borrowed Time: How the Growth of Entitlement Spending Threatens America's Future* (San Francisco: Institute for Contemporary Studies Press, 1988).

60. Bipartisan Commission on Entitlement and Tax Reform, *Interim Report to the President*.

61. For a more extensive discussion of this point, see Robert J. Myers, "Social Security and the Federal Budget: Some Mirages, Myths, and Solutions," *Journal of the American Society of CLU & ChFC* (March 1989): 58–63.

62. Prior to the Tax Reform Act of 1983, federal income tax brackets were not indexed. As inflation in the economy occurred, it tended to increase money incomes of individuals. Thus, a portion of rising taxable income did not represent *real* income. Workers, however, were pushed by rising wages (granted in part to compensate for inflation) gradually into higher tax brackets, with more of their income being taxed at higher marginal rates. This was a relatively invisible way of augmenting tax revenues over time—minimizing the political issues that inevitably arise around increasing taxes. The indexing of the brackets was enacted to stop this practice, making it more difficult to generate the revenues necessary to pay for federal expenditure increases in future years arising, in part, out of the same inflationary pressures.

63. See the extensive discussion of this point in Kingson and Schulz, *Social Security in the 21st Century*.

64. Another argument made for privatization of pensions is to promote greater equity and to deal with an alleged problem of giving future retirees their "money's

worth." Discussion of this topic is beyond the scope of the chapter. For an extensive overview of the topic, see "Are Returns on Payroll Taxes Fair?" in ibid.

65. Andrew Glyn, "Stability, Inequalitarianism, and Stagnation: An Overview of the Advanced Capitalist Countries in the 1980s," in Epstein and Gintis, *Macroeconomic Policy after the Conservative Era*, pp. 18–56.

66. The discussion that follows is treated more extensively in James H. Schulz, "To Old Folks with Love: Aged Income Maintenance in America," *Gerontologist* 25, no. 5 (October 1985): 464–71; James H. Schulz and John Myles, "Old Age Pensions: A Comparative Perspective," in Binstock and George, *Handbook of Aging and the Social Sciences*, 3d ed., pp. 398–414.

67. The traditional reasons given for government pensions are information inefficiencies, adverse selection, and the "free rider" problem. See, for example, Zvi Bodie and Olivia S. Mitchell, "Pension Security in an Aging World," in Zvi Bodie, Olivia S. Mitchell, and J. A. Turner, eds., *Securing Employer-based Pensions: An International Perspective* (Philadelphia: University of Pennsylvania Press, 1996), pp. 1–30. Our emphasis here is on the influence of chronic unemployment on policies to encourage retirement through pensions.

68. James H. Schulz, "Epilogue: The 'Buffer Years': Market Incentives and Evolving Retirement Policies," in John Myles and Jill Quadagno, eds., *States, Labor Markets, and the Future of Old-Age Policy* (Philadelphia: Temple University Press, 1991), pp. 295–308.

69. Dan Jacobson, "Optional Early Retirement: Is It a Painless Alternative to Involuntary Layoffs?" in S. Bergman, G. Naegele, and W. Tokarski, eds., *Early Retirement: Approaches and Variations* (Israel: Brookdale Institute of Gerontology and Human Development, 1988), pp. 11–24.

CHAPTER 7

1. Robert Myers, "Dispelling Myths about Social Security," pp. 9–23 of this volume; Eric M. Engen and William G. Gale, "Social Security Reform and Saving," in Robert Triest, ed., *Social Security Reform: Links to Saving, Investment, and Growth* (Boston: Federal Reserve Bank of Boston, 1998), pp. 103–42.

2. The shift in the composition of pensions toward defined contribution plans has tended to blur the distinction between the second and third legs of the retirement income stool.

3. James M. Poterba, Steven F. Venti, and David A. Wise, "Targeted Retirement Saving and the Net Worth of Elderly Americans," *American Economic Review* 84, no. 2 (May 1994): 180–85.

4. B. Douglas Bernheim and John Karl Scholz, "Private Saving and Public Policy," in James M. Poterba, ed., *Tax Policy and the Economy*, vol. 7 (Cambridge, Mass.: MIT Press, 1993).

5. However, the appropriate figure will vary depending on a household's specific situation.

6. Poterba, Venti, and Wise, "Targeted Retirement Saving."

7. B. Douglas Bernheim, "Is the Baby Boom Preparing Adequately for Retirement?" Technical Report, Merrill Lynch & Co., Inc., New York, September 1992; B. Douglas Bernheim, "The Merrill Lynch Baby Boom Retirement Index: Update '95," Merrill Lynch & Co., Inc., New York, February 1995.

8. These are not unreasonable estimates of Social Security and pension benefits. According to TIAA-CREF, a worker with thirty-five years of covered service in Social Security, a spouse, and a final salary of $40,000 would have initial Social Security benefits equal to 47 percent of final earnings ("Making Sense of Social Security," Teachers Insurance and Annuity Association/College Retirement Equities Fund, New York, 1994). If retirement income needs are, by rule of thumb, 75 percent of final earnings, Social Security benefits constitute 63 percent (47/75) of retirement income needs. The replacement rate would be even higher for workers with lower earnings. Andrew A. Samwick, "Retirement Incentives in the 1983 Pensions Provider Survey" (mimeo, Massachusetts Institute of Technology, April 1993), estimates that expected private pension benefits in the 1983 Survey of Consumer Finances average 20–30 percent of final earnings. Using the rule of thumb above, private pension benefits would constitute 27–40 percent of retirement income needs for workers who have such benefits.

9. "Pension and Health Benefits of American Workers: New Findings from the April 1993 Current Population Survey," U.S. Department of Labor, 1994.

10. Samwick, "Retirement Incentives in the 1983 Pensions Provider Survey."

11. B. Douglas Bernheim, "The Adequacy of Personal Retirement Saving: Issues and Options," in David A. Wise, ed., Facing the Age Wave (Stanford, Calif.: Hoover Institution Press, 1997).

12. David M. Cutler, "Re-examining the Three-Legged Stool," in Peter A. Diamond, David C. Lindeman, and Howard Young, eds., Social Security: What Role for the Future? (Washington, D.C.: National Academy of Social Insurance, 1996).

13. Bernheim and Scholz, "Private Saving and Public Policy."

14. Christopher Ruhm, "Bridge Jobs and Partial Retirement," Journal of Labor Economics 8, no. 4 (October 1990): 482–501.

15. N. Gregory Mankiw and David N. Weil, "The Baby Boom, the Baby Bust, and the Housing Market," Regional Science and Urban Economics 19, no. 2 (May 1989): 143–203; James Poterba, "House Price Dynamics: The Role of Tax Policy and Demography," Brookings Papers on Economic Activity 2 (1991): 143–203.

16. This issue is distinct from the point that models that do not include the reduction in mortgage payments as households pay off their homes will overstate retirement needs.

17. Sylvester J. Schieber and John B. Shoven, "The Consequences of Population Aging on Pension Fund Saving and Asset Markets," NBER Working Paper no. 4665, National Bureau of Economic Research, Cambridge, Mass., March 1994.

18. Employee Benefit Research Institute, "Employment-Based Retirement Income Benefits: Analysis of the April 1993 Current Population Survey," *EBRI Special Report SR-25*, Washington, D.C., September 1994, Table 2. This participation rate includes salary reduction plans as well as more traditional defined benefit and defined contribution plans.

19. Poterba, Venti, and Wise, "Targeted Retirement Saving," Table 1. At the aggregate level, reserves in private pension funds have accounted for more than 20 percent of net worth in the household sector in recent years ("Balance Sheets for the U.S. Economy," Board of Governors of the Federal Reserve System, 1995). Private pensions and other tax-deferred accounts, such as IRAs, Keoghs, and 401(k) plans, have accounted for more than 90 percent of net personal saving since 1987. Refer to John Sabelhaus, "Public Policy and Saving Behavior in the U.S. and Canada," mimeo, Congressional Budget Office, February 1996; John B. Shoven, *Return on Investment: Pensions Are How America Saves* (Washington, D.C.: Association of Private Pension and Welfare Plans, September 1991).

20. Alfred M. Skolnik, "Private Pension(s) no Plans, 1950–74," *Social Security Bulletin*, Social Security Administration, June 1976, pp. 3–7.

21. Daniel J. Beller and Helen H. Lawrence, "Trends in Private Pension Plan Coverage," in John A. Turner and David J. Beller, eds., *Trends in Pensions 1992* (Washington, D.C.: U.S. Department of Labor, 1992), pp. 59–96.

22. For further discussion, see Robert L. Clark and Ann A. McDermed, *The Choice of Pension Plans in a Changing Regulatory Environment* (Washington, D.C.: American Enterprise Institute Press, 1990); William G. Gale, "Public Policies and Private Pension Contributions," *Journal of Money, Credit, and Banking* 26, no. 3, part 2 (August 1994): 710–32; Richard A. Ippolito, "Selecting and Retraining High-Quality Workers: A Theory of 401(k) Pensions," unpublished paper, Pension Benefit Guaranty Corporation, Washington, D.C., April 1993; Douglas S. Kruse, "Pension Substitution in the 1980s: Why the Shift toward Defined Contribution Pension Plans?" NBER Working Paper no. 2882, National Bureau of Economic Research, Cambridge, Mass., October 1991.

23. Ippolito, "Selecting and Retraining High-Quality Workers."

24. Richard Thaler, "Anomalies: Saving, Fungibility, and Mental Accounts," *Journal of Economic Perspectives* 4, no. 1 (Winter 1990): 193–205; B. Douglas Bernheim, "Rethinking Savings Incentives," in Alan Auerbach, ed., *Fiscal Policy: Lessons from Economic Research* (Cambridge, Mass.: MIT Press, 1996), p. 25.

25. B. Douglas Bernheim, "Personal Saving, Information, and Economic Literacy: New Directions for Public Policy," in *Tax Policy and Economic Growth in the 1990s* (Washington, D.C.: American Council for Capital Formation, 1994): 53–78.

26. William G. Gale, "The Effect of Pensions on Wealth: A Re-Evaluation of Theory and Evidence," mimeo, Brookings Institution, Washington, D.C., June 1995. In some cases, the biases can generate an estimated positive effect of pensions on nonpension wealth, even when the true relation is that a dollar increase in the pension wealth causes a one-dollar reduction in other wealth.

27. Bernheim and Scholz, "Private Saving and Public Policy"; Gale, "Effect of Pensions on Wealth."

28. The literature is reviewed in Bernheim, "Rethinking Savings Incentives"; Eric M. Engen, William G. Gale, and John Karl Scholz, "The Illusory Effects of Saving Incentives on Saving," *Journal of Economic Perspectives* 10, no. 4 (Fall 1996): 113–38; James M. Poterba, Steven F. Venti, and David A. Wise, "How Retirement Savings Programs Increase Saving," *Journal of Economic Perspectives* 10, no. 4 (Fall 1996): 91–112.

29. For further discussion, see Zvi Bodie, Alan J. Marcus, and Robert C. Merton, "Defined Benefit versus Defined Contribution Pension Plans: What Are the Real Tradeoffs?" in Zvi Bodie, John B. Shoven, and David A. Wise, eds., *Pensions in the U.S. Economy* (Chicago: University of Chicago Press, 1988), pp. 139–60; Andrew A. Samwick and Jonathan Skinner, "How Will Defined Contribution Pension Plans Affect Retirement Income?" mimeo, Dartmouth College, June 1995.

30. James M. Poterba, Steven F. Venti, and David A. Wise, "Lump-sum Distributions from Retirement Saving Plans: Receipt and Utilization," NBER Working Paper no. 5298, National Bureau of Economic Research, Cambridge, Mass., October 1995.

31. Samwick and Skinner, "How Will Defined Contribution Pension Plans Affect Retirement Income?"

32. These tabulations were carried out by Joel Dickson at the Federal Reserve Board. A number of studies reach similar conclusions. See Emily S. Andrews, "The Growth and Distribution of 401(k) Plans," in Turner and Beller, *Trends in Pensions 1992*; Leslie E. Papke, Mitchell Petersen, and James M. Poterba, "Did 401(k) Plans Replace Other Pensions?" NBER Working Paper no. 4501, National Bureau of Economic Research, Cambridge, Mass., October 1993; "Current 401(k) Plan Practices: A Survey Report," Buck Consultants, Secaucus, N.J., 1989.

33. Leslie E. Papke, "Are 401(k) Plans Replacing Other Employer-Provided Pensions? Evidence from Panel Data," mimeo, Michigan State University, August 1996.

34. Similar effects of 401(k)s on outright plan termination appear to have been a relatively rare response in the early 1980s (see Kruse, "Pension Substitution in the 1980s"), perhaps because converting already existing thrift plans would be a much less disruptive way to add a 401(k).

35. The following congressional testimony, by an executive of a major corporation, is not atypical: "A recent major change occurred in 1995. We generally reduced the value of our defined benefit plan. . . . Correspondingly, we increased the match in our 401(k) plan." Donald H. Sauvigne, "Statement of the American Savings Education Council before the House Education and Workforce Subcommittee on Employee-Employer Relations," U.S. Congress, House, 105th Cong., 1st sess., February 12, 1997.

36. Daniel I. Halperin, "Tax Policy and Retirement Income: A Rational Model For the 21st Century," in Jack L. Vanderhei, ed., *Search for a National Retirement Income Policy* (Homewood, Ill.: Richard D. Irwin, Inc., 1987), pp. 159–95.

CHAPTER 8

1. S. Crystal, "Economic Status of the Elderly," in Robert H. Binstock and Linda K. George, eds., *Handbook of Aging and the Social Sciences* (San Diego: Academic Press, 1996), pp. 389–409; D. B. Radner, *Changes in the Money Income of the Aged and Nonaged, 1976–1983* (Washington, D.C.: U.S. Department of Health and Human Services, 1986).

2. S. Crystal and K. Waehrer, "Later-life Economic Inequality in Longitudinal Perspective," *Journal of Gerontology: Social Sciences* 51B, no. 4 (July 1996): S307–18.

3. T. M. Calasanti, "Gender and Life Satisfaction in Retirement: An Assessment of the Male Model," *Journal of Gerontology: Social Sciences* 51B, no. 1 (January 1996): S18–23; J. Liang and T. Fairchild, "Relative Deprivation and Perception of Financial Adequacy among the Aged," *Journal of Gerontology* 34, no. 6 (November 1979): 746–59; K. Seccombe and G. R. Lee, "Gender Differences in Retirement Satisfaction and Its Antecedents," *Research on Aging* 8, no. 4 (December 1986): 426–40.

4. E. B. Palmore et al., *Retirement: Causes and Consequences* (New York: Springer Publishing, 1985).

5. Angus Campbell, *The Sense of Well Being in America: Recent Patterns and Trends* (New York: McGraw-Hill, 1980); Calasanti, "Gender and Life Satisfaction in Retirement," S18–29; Linda K. George and L. R. Landerman, "Health and Subjective Well-being: A Replicated Secondary Analysis," *International Journal of Aging and Human Development* 19, no. 2 (April 1984): 133–56; J. Liang, E. Kahana, and E. Doherty, "Financial Well-being among the Aged: A Further Elaboration," *Journal of Gerontology* 35, no. 4 (July 1980): 409–20.

6. Campbell, *Sense of Well Being in America*; Linda K. George, L. R. Landerman, and G. G. Fillenbaum, *Developing Measures of Functional Status and Service Utilization: Refining and Extending the OARS Methodology* (Durham, N.C.: Duke University Center for the Study of Aging and Human Development, 1982).

7. George and Landerman, "Health and Subjective Well-being"; George, Landerman, and Fillenbaum, *Developing Measures of Functional Status and Service Utilization*.

8. D. R. Vaughan, *Using Subjective Assessments of Income to Estimate Family Equivalence Scales: A Report of Work in Progress* (Washington, D.C.: Social Security Administration, 1980).; D. R. Vaughan and C. G. Lancaster, "Income Levels and

Their Impact on Two Subjective Measures of Well-being: Some Early Speculations from Work in Progress," *1979 Proceedings of the American Statistical Association*, American Statistical Association, Washington, D.C., 1980; D. R. Vaughan and C. G. Lancaster, "Applying a Cardinal Measurement Model to Normative Assessments of Income: Synopsis of a Preliminary Look," *1980 Proceedings of the American Statistical Association*, American Statistical Association, Washington, D.C., 1981.

9. D. M. Bass and L. S. Noelker, "The Influence of Family Caregivers on Elders' Use of In-Home Services," *Journal of Health and Social Behavior* 28, no. 2 (June 1987): 184–96.; L. S. Noelker and D. M. Bass, "Home Care for Elderly Persons: Linkages between Formal and Informal Caregivers," *Journal of Gerontology: Social Sciences* 44, no. 1 (January 1989): S63–70.; W. G. Weissert, C. M. Cready, and J. E. Pawelak, "The Past and Future of Home- and Community-based Long-term Care," *Millbank Quarterly* 66, no. 2 (June 1988): 309–88.

10. See D. Cox and M. R. Rank, "Inter-Vivos Transfers and Intergenerational Exchange," *Review of Economics and Statistics* 74, no. 3 (May 1992): 305–14; K. McGarry and R. F. Schoeni, "Transfer Behavior: Measurement and the Redistribution of Resources within the Family," *Journal of Human Resources* 30, no. 2 (June 1995): 194–226; Franco Modigliani, "The Role of Intergenerational Transfers and Life Cycle Savings in the Accumulation of Wealth," *Journal of Economic Perspectives* 2, no. 1 (January 1988): 15–40.

11. D. Cox, "Motives for Private Income Transfers," *Journal of Political Economy* 95, no. 6 (December 1987): 509–46.

12. McGarry and Schoeni, "Transfer Behavior," pp. 194–226.

13. D. J. Eggebeen, "Family Structure and Intergenerational Exchange," *Research on Aging* 14, no. 4 (December 1992): 427–47; D. J. Eggebeen and D. P. Hogan, "Giving between the Generations in American Families," *Human Nature* 1, no. 2 (February 1990): 211–32; D. P. Hogan, D. J. Eggebeen, and C. C. Clogg, "The Structure of Intergeneration Exchanges in American Families," *American Journal of Sociology* 98, no. 12 (December 1993): 1428–58; McGarry and Schoeni, "Transfer Behavior," pp. 194–226.

14. McGarry and Schoeni, "Transfer Behavior," pp. 194–226; G. S. O'Neill, "Beyond Dyads: The Effect of Extended Family Resources and Demands upon Time and Money Transfers from Adult Children to Parents," Ph.D. diss., Duke University, 1997.

15. Eggebeen, "Family Structure and Intergenerational Exchange"; Eggebeen and Hogan, "Giving between the Generations in American Families"; McGarry and Schoeni, "Transfer Behavior," pp. 194–226.

16. Eggebeen, "Family Structure and Intergenerational Exchange"; Eggebeen and Hogan, "Giving between the Generations in American Families."

17. Eggebeen, "Family Structure and Intergenerational Exchange"; McGarry and Schoeni, "Transfer Behavior," pp. 194–226; O'Neill, "Beyond Dyads."

18. McGarry and Schoeni, "Transfer Behavior," pp. 194–226.

19. Ibid.; O'Neill, "Beyond Dyads."

20. Eggebeen, "Family Structure and Intergenerational Exchange."

21. McGarry and Schoeni, "Transfer Behavior," pp. 194–226.

22. O'Neill, "Beyond Dyads."

23. See McGarry and Schoeni, "Transfer Behavior," pp. 194–226.

24. Eggebeen, "Family Structure and Intergenerational Exchange"; Eggebeen and Hogan, "Giving between the Generations in American Families."

25. J. P. Smith, "Racial and Ethnic Differences in Wealth," *Journal of Human Resources* 30, no. 2 (June 1995): 158–83.

26. P. Kemper, "The Use of Formal and Informal Home Care by the Disabled Elderly," *Health Services Research* 27, no. 4 (December 1992): 421–51; J. R. Logan and G. Spitze, "Informal Support and the Use of Formal Services by Older Americans," *Journal of Gerontology: Social Sciences* 49, no. 1 (January 1994): S25–34; McGarry and Schoeni, "Transfer Behavior," pp. 194–226; R. Stone, G. L. Cafferata, and J. Sangl, "Caregivers of the Frail Elderly: A National Profile," *Gerontologist* 27, no. 6 (December 1987): 616–26.

27. See L. G. Branch and A. M. Jette, "Elders' Use of Informal Long-term Care Assistance," *Gerontologist* 23, no. 1 (Febuary 1983): 51–56; McGarry and Schoeni, "Transfer Behavior," pp. 194–226; O'Neill, "Beyond Dyads"; G. Spitze and J. R. Logan, "Helping as a Component of Parent-Adult Child Relations," *Research on Aging* 14, no. 2 (June 1992): 291–312; Stone, Cafferata, and Sangl, "Caregivers of the Frail Elderly."

28. See Stone, Cafferata, and Sangl, "Caregivers of the Frail Elderly"; U.S. Congress, Senate, Select Committee on Aging, *Aging in America* (Washington, D.C.: U.S. Government Printing Office, 1988).

29. McGarry and Schoeni, "Transfer Behavior," pp. 194–226; Stone, Cafferata, and Sangl, "Caregivers of the Frail Elderly."

30. Logan and Spitze, "Informal Support and the Use of Formal Services by Older Americans"; McGarry and Schoeni, "Transfer Behavior," pp.194–226; O'Neill, "Beyond Dyads."

31. McGarry and Schoeni, "Transfer Behavior," pp. 194–226.

32. Branch and Jette, "Elders' Use of Informal Long-term Care Assistance"; O'Neill, "Beyond Dyads."

33. See M. H. Cantor, "Strain among Caregivers: A Study of Experience in the United States," *Gerontologist* 23, no. 6 (December 1983): 597–604; A. Horowitz, "Family Caregiving to the Frail Elderly," *Annual Review of Gerontology and Geriatrics* 5 (1985): 194–246; McGarry and Schoeni, "Transfer Behavior," pp. 194–226; O'Neill, "Beyond Dyads"; Stone, Cafferata, and Sangl, "Caregivers of the Frail Elderly."

34. See Stone, Cafferata, and Sangl, "Caregivers of the Frail Elderly"; U.S. Congress, *Aging in America*.

35. Cantor, "Strain among Caregivers"; Horowitz, "Family Caregiving to the Frail Elderly"; Stone, Cafferata, and Sangl, "Caregivers of the Frail Elderly."

36. O'Neill, "Beyond Dyads."

37. See Logan and Spitze, "Informal Support and the Use of Formal Services by Older Americans"; McGarry and Schoeni, "Transfer Behavior," pp. 194–226.

38. See E. Mutran, "Intergenerational Support among Blacks and Whites: Response to Culture or to Socioeconomic Differences?" *Journal of Gerontology* 40, no. 4 (July 1985): 382–89; R. J. Taylor, "Receipt of Support from Family among Black Americans: Demographic and Familial Differences," *Journal of Marriage and the Family* 48, no. 1 (January 1986): 67–77.

39. Eggebeen, "Family Structure and Intergenerational Exchange"; Eggebeen and Hogan, "Giving between the Generations in American Families."

40. Eggebeen and Hogan, "Giving between the Generations in American Families"; Spitze and Logan, "Helping as a Component of Parent-Adult Child Relations."

41. Eggebeen and Hogan, "Giving between the Generations in American Families"; O'Neill, "Beyond Dyads"; Spitze and Logan, "Helping as a Component of Parent-Adult Child Relations."

42. Eggebeen and Hogan, "Giving between the Generations in American Families."

43. D. L. Hoyert, "Financial and Household Exchanges between Generations," *Research on Aging* 13, no. 2 (June 1991): 205–25.

44. Eggebeen and Hogan, "Giving between the Generations in American Families."

45. Eggebeen and Hogan, "Giving between the Generations in American Families"; O'Neill, "Beyond Dyads."

46. O'Neill, "Beyond Dyads."

47. Eggebeen, "Family Structure and Intergenerational Exchange"; Eggebeen and Hogan, "Giving between the Generations in American Families."

48. See Eggebeen, "Family Structure and Intergenerational Exchange"; Spitze and Logan, "Helping as a Component of Parent-Adult Child Relations."

49. J. C. Henretta et al., "Selection of Children to Provide Care: The Effect of Earlier Parental Transfers," *Journal of Gerontology: Social Sciences* 52B, no. 1 (January 1997): S110–19.

50. Cox and Rank, "Inter-Vivos Transfers and Intergenerational Exchange"; McGarry and Schoeni, "Transfer Behavior," pp. 194–226.

51. V. L. Bengston and R. E. L. Roberts, "Intergenerational Solidarity in Aging Families: An Example of Formal Theory Construction," *Journal of Marriage and the Family* 53, no. 6 (November 1991): 856–70; Linda K. George, "Caregiver Burden: Conflict between Norms of Reciprocity and Solidarity," in Karl A. Pillemer and Rosalie S. Wolf, eds., *Elder Abuse: Conflict in the Family* (Dover, Mass.: Auburn House, 1986), pp. 67–92.

CHAPTER 9

1. Murray Gendell and Jacob S. Siegel, "Trends in Retirement Age by Sex, 1950–2005," *Monthly Labor Review* 115, no. 7 (July 1992): 22–29; Bureau of Labor Statistics, *Employment and Earnings* 46, no. 1 (January 1998): 168; see also David A. Wise, "Retirement against the Demographic Trend: More Older People Living Longer, Working Less, and Saving Less," *Demography* 34, no. 1 (February 1997): 83–95.

2. Statistics for the 1940s are from U.S. Department of Commerce, Bureau of the Census, *Historical Statistics of the United States: Colonial Times to 1970*, Part 1 (Washington, D.C.: U.S. Government Printing Office, 1975), p.132.

3. David A. Weaver, "The Work and Retirement Decisions of Older Women: A Literature Review," *Social Security Bulletin* 57, no. 1 (1994), p. 3.

4. Nestor E. Terleckyj and Charles D. Coleman, *Growth of the U.S. Economy, 1996–2025*, Vol. 2 (Washington, D.C.: National Planning Association Data Services, Inc., 1995).

5. Howard N Fullerton, Jr., "The 2005 Labor Force: Growing, But Slowly," *Monthly Labor Review* 18, no. 11 (November 1995): 29–44; Howard N Fullerton, "Labor Force 2006: Slowing Down and Changing Composition," *Monthly Labor Review* 120, no. 11 (November 1997): 6–38.

6. James H. Schulz, *The Economics of Aging*, 6th ed. (Westport, Conn.: Auburn House, 1995), pp. 82–84.

7. Michael D. Packard and Virginia P. Reno, "A Look at Very Early Retirees," *Social Security Bulletin* 52, no. 3 (March 1989): 16–29.

8. Laurence J. Kotlikoff and David A. Wise, "The Incentive Effects of Private Pension Plans," in Zvi Bodie, John B. Shoven, and David A. Wise, eds., *Issues in Pension Economics* (Chicago: University of Chicago Press, 1987), pp. 283–339.

9. Robert L. Clark, "Employment Costs and the Older Worker," in Sara E. Rix, ed., *Older Workers: How Do They Measure Up?* (Washington, D.C.: American Association of Retired Persons, 1994), pp. 1–26; Brigitte C. Madrian, "The Effect of Health Insurance on Retirement," *Brookings Papers on Economic Activity*, no. 1 (1994): 181–232; Wise, "Retirement against the Demographic Trend."

10. Murray Gendell and Jacob S. Siegel, "Trends in Retirement Age in the United States, 1955–1993, by Sex and Race," *Journals of Gerontology: Social Sciences* 51B, no. 3 (May 1996): S138.

11. John R. Besl and Balkrishna D. Kale, "Older Workers in the 21st Century: Active and Educated—A Case Study," *Monthly Labor Review* 119, no. 6 (June 1996): 18–28.

12. William R. Grady, "Labor Force Withdrawal Patterns among Older Men in the United States," *Social Science Quarterly* 70, no. 2 (June 1989): 425–48.

13. Mark D. Hayward, *Career Mobility and Labor Force Withdrawal among Older Men in the United States: Final Report to the AARP Andrus Foundation*, (Los

Angeles: University of Southern California, Andrus Gerontology Center, 1991), pp. 46–59.

14. Olivia S. Mitchell, Phillip B. Levin, and Silvana Pozzebon, "Retirement Differences by Industry and Occupation," *Gerontologist* 28, no. 4 (August 1988): 545–51.

15. Diane E. Herz, "Work after Early Retirement: An Increasing Trend among Men," *Monthly Labor Review* 118, no. 4 (April 1995): 13–20.

16. Social Security Administration, *Income of the Population 55 or Older, 1996* (Washington, D.C.: U.S. Government Printing Office, 1998), Table VII.3.

17. Gendell and Siegel, "Trends in Retirement Age by Sex."

18. Richard V. Burkhauser and Joseph F. Quinn, "Implementing Pro-Work Policies for Older Americans in the Twenty-first Century," paper delivered before U.S. Congress, Senate, Special Committee on Aging, Workshop on Preparing for the Baby Boomers' Retirement: The Role of Employment, 105th Cong., 1st sess., July 25, 1997.

19. Jan E. Mutchler et al., "Pathways to Labor Force Exit: Work Transitions and Work Instability," *Journals of Gerontology: Social Sciences* 52B, no. 1 (January 1997): S4–12.

20. Ibid.; Joseph F. Quinn and Michael Kozy, "The Role of Bridge Jobs in the Retirement Transition: Gender, Race, and Ethnicity," *Gerontologist* 36, no. 3 (June 1996): 363–72; Christopher J. Ruhm, "Secular Changes in the Work and Retirement Patterns of Older Men," *Journal of Human Resources* 30, no. 2 (Spring 1995): 362–85.

21. Christopher J. Ruhm, "Bridge Employment and Job Stopping: Evidence from the Harris/Commonwealth Fund Survey," *Journal of Aging and Social Policy* 6, no. 4 (1994): 73–99; Kathryn Anderson, Richard Burkhauser, and George Slotsve, "A Two Decade Comparison of Work after Retirement in the United States," *Geneva Papers on Risk and Insurance* 17, no. 62 (January 1992): 26–39.

22. Ruhm, "Bridge Employment and Job Stopping."

23. *Displaced Workers: Trends in the 1980s and Implications for the Future* (Washington, D.C.: Congressional Budget Office, 1993), pp. 11–25.

24. "Phased Retirement Gradually Makes Its Way into the Workplace," *Watson Wyatt Insider* (Bethesda, Md.), April 1997, pp. 6–12.

25. Barbara A. Hirshorn and Denise Tanguay Hoyer, *Private Sector Employment of Retirees: The Organizational Experience* (Detroit: Wayne State University, 1992).

26. Ruhm, "Bridge Employment and Job Stopping," p. 95.

27. Mutchler et al., "Pathways to Labor Force Exit," p. S10.

28. *American Business and Older Workers: A Road Map to the 21st Century* (Washington, D.C.: AARP, 1995), p. 9.

29. Anne E. Polivka, "A Profile of Contingent Workers," *Monthly Labor Review* 119, no. 10 (October 1996): 10–21; "Contingent and Alternative Employment Arrangements, February 1997," *News*, USDL 97–422, U.S. Department of Labor, Bureau of Labor Statistics, December 1997.

30. Peter Cappelli et al., *Change at Work: Trends that Are Transforming the Business of Business* (Washington, D.C.: National Policy Association, 1997), pp. 17–18.

31. Quinn and Kozy, "Role of Bridge Jobs in the Retirement Transition."

32. David S. Evans and Linda S. Leighton, "Small-Business Formation by Unemployed Workers," paper prepared for the Office of Advocacy, U.S. Small Business Administration, 1989 (mimeo).

33. U.S. Department of Labor, Bureau of Labor Statistics, *Employment and Earnings* 46, no. 1 (January 1999) p. 187.

34. Louis Harris and Associates, *1979 Study of American Attitudes toward Pensions and Retirement* (New York: Johnson and Higgins, 1979).

35. "Health and Retirement Study," press release, National Institute on Aging, Washington, D.C., June 17, 1993.

36. *The First Baby Boomers Turn Fifty: A Survey of the Attitudes and Opinions of People Born in 1946* (Phoenix: Del Webb Corporation, 1996).

37. Paul Yakoboski and Allen Schiffenbauer, "The Reality of Retirement Today: Lessons in Planning for Tomorrow," *EBRI Issue Brief* no. 181, Employee Benefit Research Institute, Washington, D.C., January 1997.

38. U.S. Department of Labor, *Employment and Earnings*, p. 210.

39. *Americans Over 55 at Work Program: Research Reports 1 and 2* (New York: Commonwealth Fund, 1990); *The Untapped Resource* (New York: Commonwealth Fund, 1993).

40. Herbert S. Parnes and David G. Sommers, "Shunning Retirement: Work Experience of Men in Their Seventies and Early Eighties," *Journal of Gerontology: Social Sciences* 49, no. 3 (May 1994): S117–24.

41. Michael D. Hurd, "Research on the Elderly: Economic Status, Retirement, and Consumption and Saving," *Journal of Economic Literature* 28, no. 2 (June 1990): 565–637.

42. Mark D. Hayward, Eileen M. Crimmins, and Linda A. Wray, "The Relationship between Retirement Life Cycle Changes and Older Men's Labor Force Participation Rates," *Journals of Gerontology: Social Sciences* 49 no. 5 (September 1994): S219–30.

43. Terleckyj and Coleman, *Growth of the U.S. Economy*, pp. 43–44; Fullerton, "The 2005 Labor Force," p. 28.

44. *American Business and Older Workers*, p. 9.

45. Michael C. Barth, William McNaught, and Philip Rizzi, "Corporations and the Aging Workforce," in Philip H. Mirvis, ed., *Building the Competitive Workforce: Investing in Human Capital for Corporate Success* (New York: John Wiley and Sons, 1993), p. 163.

46. *Valuing Older Workers: A Study of Costs and Productivity* (Washington, D.C.: AARP, n.d.).

47. Quoted in Rajiv Chandrasekaran, "Netscape's Boy Wonder Looks beyond the Browser," *Washington Post*, March 25, 1997, p. C1.

48. *American Business and Older Workers*, p. 11.

49. Barth, McNaught, and Rizzi, "Corporations and the Aging Workforce," p. 167.

50. *How Workers Get Their Training: A 1991 Update*, U.S. Department of Labor, Bureau of Labor Statistics, August 1992, p. 30.

51. "BLS Reports on the Amount of Formal and Informal Training Received by Employees," *News*, USDL 96–515, U.S. Department of Labor, Bureau of Labor Statistics, December 1996.

52. Mildred Doering, Susan R. Rhodes, and Michael Schuster, *The Aging Worker: Research and Recommendations* (Beverly Hills, Calif.: Sage Publications, 1983), p. 113.

53. Harvey L. Sterns and Michael A. McDaniel, "Job Performance and the Older Worker," in Rix, *Older Workers*, p. 34.

54. Ibid.

55. *Case Studies at Major Corporations Show Why Employing Workers over 50 Makes Good Business Sense* (New York: Commonwealth Fund, 1991).

56. Michael C. Barth, William McNaught, and Philip Rizzi, "The Costs and Benefits of Older Workers," in William H. Crown, ed., *Handboook on Employment and the Elderly* (Westport, Conn.: Greenwood Press, 1996), p. 329.

57. Ibid., p. 335.

58. Sterns and McDaniel, "Job Performance and the Older Worker," pp. 27–51; Sara J. Czaja, "Aging and Work Performance," *Review of Public Personnel Administration* 15, no. 2 (Spring 1995): 46–61.

59. *Valuing Older Workers*, p. iii.

60. *Employer Attitudes: Implications of an Aging Workforce* (New York: William M. Mercer, 1981), p. 5.

61. "Getting the Job Done: Alternative Work Arrangements," *Watson Wyatt Insider* (Bethesda, Md.), June 1997, pp. 14–21.

62. Hirshorn and Hoyer, *Private Sector Employment of Retirees*, pp. 108–111.

63. Besl and Kale, "Older Workers in the 21st Century."

64. "If Aging Boomers Work Smart," *Forecast*, Faulkner and Gray, New York, June 1997, p. 9.

65. James H. Schulz, "Job Matching in an Aging Society: Barriers to the Utilization of Older Workers," paper delivered at the annual meeting of the Gerontological Society of America, San Francisco, November 1988.

66. Michael C. Barth, "Older Workers: Perception and Reality," paper delivered before U.S. Congress, Senate, Special Committee on Aging, Workshop on Preparing for the Baby Boomers' Retirement: The Role of Employment, 105th Cong., 1st sess., July 25, 1997, p. 9.

67. See, e.g., Scott, Bass, "Creating Pro-Work Policies and Programs for a Graying America," paper delivered before U.S. Congress, Senate, Special Committee on Aging, Workshop on Preparing for the Baby Boomers' Retirement: The Role of Employment, 105th Cong., 1st sess., July 25, 1997; Burkhauser and Quinn, "Implementing Pro-Work Policies for Older Americans"; Alan Reynolds,

"Restoring Work Incentives for Older Americans," paper delivered before U.S. Congress, Senate, Special Committee on Aging, Workshop on Preparing for the Baby Boomers' Retirement: The Role of Employment, 105th Cong., 1st sess., July 25, 1997.

68. Marcus Rebick, "The Japanese Approach to Finding Jobs for Older People," in Olivia S. Mitchell, ed., *As the Workforce Ages: Costs, Benefits, and Policy Challenges* (Ithaca, N.Y.: ILR Press, 1993), pp. 103–124.

69. Richard W. Judy and Carol D'Amico, *Workforce 2020: Work and Workers in the 21st Century* (Indianapolis: Hudson Institute, 1997), p. 105.

70. Manuel London, "When Older Workers Are Not Expendable: Organizational Conditions Associated with Hiring and Developing People over Age 55," *International Journal of Career Management* 4, no. 2 (1992): 15–25.

INDEX

About the Contributors

ROBERT H. BINSTOCK is professor of aging, health, and society at Case Western Reserve University. A former president of the Gerontological Society of America, he has served as director of a White House Task Force on Older Americans for President Lyndon B. Johnson, and as chairman and member of a number of advisory panels to the United States government, state and local governments, and foundations. He is presently chair of the Gerontological Health Section of the American Public Health Association. He is the author of more than 150 articles on the politics and policies affecting aging. His nineteen books include *The Future of Long-Term Care: Social and Policy Issues* and *Dementia and Aging: Ethics, Values, and Policy Choices,* and he is coeditor (with Linda K. George) of four editions of the *Handbook of Aging and the Social Sciences.*

ROBERT N. BUTLER, M.D., is the director of the International Longevity Center (ILC-USA) and professor of geriatrics at the Henry L. Schwartz Department of Geriatrics and Adult Development at the Mount Sinai School of Medicine. From 1975 to 1982, he was the first and founding director of the National Institute on Aging of the National Institutes of Health. In 1982, he founded the first department of geriatrics in a U.S. medical school and there held the Brookdale Professorship of Geriatrics for more than a dozen years. In 1990, with Shigeo Morioka, he cofounded the International Longevity Center (ILC) (Japan-U.S.A.), which studies the impact of longevity upon society and its institutions. In 1995, he was chair of the advisory committee of the White House Conference on Aging. In 1976, Dr. Butler won the Pulitzer Prize for his book *Why Survive? Being Old in America,* which has been translated into Japanese and was published in Japan in 1992. He is coauthor (with Myrna I. Lewis) of the books *Aging and Mental Health* and *Love and Sex after 60.* He is presently working on a book, *The Longevity Revolution.*

WILLIAM G. GALE is the Joseph A. Pechman Fellow in the economic studies program at the Brookings Institution. His areas of expertise include saving behavior, public and private pensions, and tax policy. Before joining Brookings, he was an assistant professor in the Department of Economics at the University of California at Los Angeles, and a former senior staff economist for the Council of Economic Advisers. He has written widely in both academic journals and popular outlets. He coedited *Economic Effects of Fundamental Tax Reform* with Henry J. Aaron and is currently working on a book with Aaron entitled *Building a Better Tax System*.

LINDA K. GEORGE is a professor of sociology at Duke University, where she also serves as associate director of the Center for the Study of Aging and Human Development. A former president of the Gerontological Society of America, her major research interests are health and well-being, including financial well-being, across the life course. She is the author of over two hundred journal articles and six books, including *Quality of Life in Older Persons: Meaning and Measurement* and *Role Transitions in Later Life*, and is coeditor (with Robert H. Binstock) of the *The Handbook of Aging and the Social Sciences*.

LAWRENCE K. GROSSMAN's career in print and electronic communications spans almost five decades. From 1984 to 1988 Grossman was president of NBC News. Prior to that he was president of PBS (the Public Broadcasting Service). He has also held positions in charge of advertising and promotion at NBC, and in advertising and promotion at CBS and *Look* magazine. For ten years Grossman headed his own media and advertising agency. A prolific writer on media and political issues, he is author of the widely praised book *The Electronic Republic: Reshaping Democracy in the Information Age*. He writes a regular column, "In the Public Interest," for the *Columbia Journalism Review* and has contributed numerous articles on media and politics to newspapers, magazines, and journals. He held the Frank Stanton Chair on the First Amendment at the Kennedy School of Government at Harvard and was a senior fellow at the Gannett Center for Media Studies at Columbia University's Graduate School of Journalism.

MARILYN MOON is a senior fellow with the Health Policy Center of the Urban Institute. She also serves as a public trustee for the Social Security and Medicare trust funds. She has written extensively on health policy,

policy for the elderly, and income distribution. Her two most recent books, published by the Urban Institute Press, are *Entitlements and the Elderly: Protecting Promises, Recognizing Realities* and *Medicare Now and in the Future*. Since October 1993, she has been writing a periodic column for the Health section of the *Washington Post* on health reform and health coverage issues.

CHARLOTTE MULLER has an extensive research record in health economics. Her book *Health Care and Gender* was published by the Russell Sage Foundation. She is professor emerita in the economics doctoral program of City University of New York and senior economist at the International Longevity Center-USA. She has conducted international comparisons of the socioeconomic conditions, work, and housing of the elderly and served on the UN's expert working group to plan the 2000 census.

ROBERT J. MYERS is an actuarial consultant to several foreign countries. He was chief actuary for the Social Security Administration (1947–70), deputy commissioner of Social Security (1981–82), executive director of the national commission on social security reform (1982–83), chairman of the Commission on Railroad Retirement Reform (1988–90), and a member of the Commission on the Social Security "Notch" Issue (1993–94). He is the president of the International Fisheries Commissions Pension Society and a consultant on Social Security to William M. Mercer, Inc. Myers has written five books and nearly one thousand articles. He was the secretary and a member of the board of directors of the National Academy of Social Insurance.

MIA R. OBERLINK is a writer and editor specializing in health care and aging issues. She has coauthored and edited numerous books and articles for professional and lay audiences on a variety of subjects including women's health, mental health, health care policy, social entitlements, and biomedical research.

SARA E. RIX is a senior policy adviser with the Economics Team of the Public Policy Institute of AARP, where she focuses on the economics of aging, labor force and demographic trends, employment and retirement policy, and older worker employment issues. She has written and spoken extensively on the aged, an aging society, and aging issues for over twenty years. She is the coauthor of *The Graying of Working America* (with

Harold L. Sheppard) and *Retirement-Age Policy: An International Perspective* (with Paul Fisher). She is also the author of *Older Workers: Choices and Challenges*. She has been involved in numerous international activities that focus on the problems of, and prospects for, an aging world, including serving for many years as a lecturer on income security in developing countries at the International Institute on Aging in Malta. Before coming to AARP, she was director of research for the Women's Research and Education Institute (WREI), a nonpartisan, policy-oriented research organization in Washington, D.C.

JAMES H. SCHULZ is professor of economics in the Florence Heller School at Brandeis University and holds the Meyer and Ida Kirstein Chair in Aging Policy. He is an associate of the National Policy and Resource Center on Women and Aging at Brandeis and editor of the Center's *Women and Aging Letter*. Past president of the Gerontological Society of America and a founding fellow of the National Academy on Social Insurance, he has testified before various congressional committees, the President's Commission on Pension Policy, and the National Commission on Social Security and has lectured widely throughout the United States. He is the author of more than one hundred books, reports, and articles in the general area of income distribution, pensions, and the economics of aging. He is especially well known for his computer simulation projections of the future economic status of the retired population and his analysis of the economic impact of private pension plans. His best-known book is *The Economics of Aging*.

ROBYN STONE is a researcher and expert in health care policy with a particular emphasis on health care for the elderly. She is currently working with the American Association of Homes and Services for the Aged to establish a new policy and research institute on the future of long-term care. She is also the director of the Center for Medicare Education, a resource center for professionals helping the elderly make health care decisions. She has held a number of key policy positions at the federal level, including acting assistant secretary for aging and deputy assistant secretary for disability, aging, and long term care policy, both at the U.S. Department of Health and Human Services. As the former executive director and chief operating officer of the International Longevity Center, she has established and executed a research agenda to study the impact of population aging on societies around the world. Her own research has focused on functional disability among the elderly and nonelderly, home health care and home and community-based care alternatives, caregiving, and managed care. She has published widely in the areas of long-term care, chronic care for the disabled, and family caregiving.

JOHN ZWEIG is chief executive of Specialist Communications within the WPP Group, one of the largest advertising and marketing services firms in the world. He is responsible for over thirty separate companies specializing in various communications disciplines, industry sectors, and audience segments—including corporate identity, direct marketing, healthcare, retail, ethnic, and kids and teen marketing, among others. Prior to joining the parent company of WPP, he was president of the CommonHealth, the largest healthcare marketing resource in the world; and previous to that he was a marketing and brand manager at Procter & Gamble. Earlier in his career, he was a partner at the Waymaker Institute, a management consulting firm specializing in corporate mission and organizational behavior and motivation.